Sir Larry

Other Nonfiction Books by Thomas Kiernan

The Road to Colossus

The Intricate Music: A Biography of John Steinbeck

The Arabs

The Roman Polanski Story

Jane: An Intimate Biography of Jane Fonda

Arafat: The Man and the Myth

The Miracle of Coogan's Bluff

The Secretariat Factor

How to Ask For More and Get It (CO-AUTHOR)

Shrinks, Etc.

Oh, My Aching Back (CO-AUTHOR)

The Miseries of the Weekend Athlete (CO-AUTHOR)

Cures Only Money Can Buy

Who's Who in the History of Philosophy

The Doctor's Fountain of Youth Book

Sir Larry

THE LIFE OF

Laurence Olivier

Thomas Kiernan

Times
BOOKS

FRONTISPIECE: Laurence Olivier as Oedipus in Sophocles' *Oedipus Rex*, at the Old Vic Theatre in 1946. *(Wide World Photos)*

Published by TIMES BOOKS, a division
of Quadrangle/The New York Times Book Co., Inc.
Three Park Avenue, New York, N.Y. 10016

Published simultaneously in Canada by
Fitzhenry & Whiteside, Ltd., Toronto

Library of Congress Cataloging in Publication Data
Kiernan, Thomas.
  Sir Larry: the life of Laurence Olivier.
  Includes bibliographical references and index.
  1. Olivier, Laurence, 1907–   2. Actors—
Great Britain—Biography. I. Title.
PN2598.O55K5 1981   792'.028'0924 [B] 81-50085
ISBN 0-8129-0989-5   AACR2

Manufactured in the United States of America

For "London Judy," the

one and only

ACKNOWLEDGMENTS

I first began the research for this book nearly fifteen years ago but was forced time and again to postpone the book's progress due to other writing commitments. Then, a little over two years ago, I learned that Kenneth Tynan, a longtime theatrical associate of Sir Laurence Olivier's, was at work on his own biography of the actor. With that I decided to put aside for good my work on Olivier's life—on the theory that Tynan, with his storehouse of personal knowledge, was in a much better position to write a definitive book about Olivier than I.

A few months later, through a mutual friend, I received a call from Tynan. He said that he had heard of the preliminary research I had done and asked whether I would be willing to let him see it. I agreed to meet with him at some future date to discuss the prospect. Before that meeting could take place, however, I discovered that Tynan, suffering from a debilitating illness, and possibly encouraged to do so by Olivier, had abandoned his biography of Sir Laurence. In light of that, I decided to revive mine, which was still, then, in the preliminary research stage. Thereafter I contacted Tynan and asked him if he would be willing to show me whatever material he had put together before terminating his project. He declined because of his commitment to another publisher, but he agreed to meet with me for the purpose of being interviewed about his association with Olivier. Subsequently we met twice, once in the Los Angeles area, where he lived, and once in New York shortly before his death. Because he was so forthcoming in providing me with his intimate impressions and knowledge of Laurence Olivier, I owe him a special debt of gratitude.

I am grateful as well to the scores of other people in England, America and elsewhere who, having known Olivier at various periods in his life, or having known members of Olivier's families, were willing to share their knowledge, recollections and impressions with me. Because this is an "unauthorized" biography—i.e., written without Sir Laurence Olivier's

Acknowledgments

cooperation or authorization—many of these sources requested anonymity. Those who had no objection to being identified I have named at the appropriate places in the chapter source notes at the end of the book.

For their unstinting support and help in bringing the book to its final published form, I wish also to thank Edward T. Chase, vice-president and editorial director of Times Books, and Jean Pohoryles, his intrepid editorial assistant.

—Thomas Kiernan

New York
1981

CONTENTS

Contents

Sir Larry

1

Something in a Name

SIR Ralph Richardson, close friend and longtime acting colleague of Sir Laurence Olivier, told me the following story in 1979. "Not long before the outbreak of the war, a group of us were at a gathering—Larry, Vivien, Johnny Gielgud, Peggy Ashcroft and, I believe, Katharine Cornell, Noel Coward and Doug Fairbanks, among others. We all got to playing a little game about our names. It started, of course, with Viv, who was very keen on thinking up such diversions. She was telling us how she had fallen on 'Leigh' as her stage name. Her maiden name had been Hartley and she had desperately wanted to use that as her stage name when she was discovered. But her agents wouldn't hear of it, saying that it had no romance, that it made her sound a bit of a schoolmistress. So 'Leigh' it became.

"From there we all got to wondering about what each of our careers would have been like if we had had different names, or not quite the names we had. For instance, what if my name had been Richards instead of Richardson? What kind of career would have suited a 'Ralph Richards'? They all decided that with a name like that, I could only have been a second-rate music-hall comedian. Noel—well, suppose he had been Noel 'Cow' instead of Coward? We all very boisterously agreed that a man called 'Noel Cow' would never have been accepted in the theatre, that he'd definitely have grown up to be a deputy accountant in the forwarding department at Harrod's, or something on that order.

"On we went through everyone's name, deciding how each one suited our careers as actors, much in the way the names of racing horses seem to suit the beauty, grace and function of those animals. Finally we came to Larry. What if he had been born 'Oliver' instead of Olivier? I mean, 'Laurence Oliver'—was that a name suited to a chap who by then was one of the leading lights of stage and films? 'Olivier' was a poetic name, it was mellifluous, lofty, with a quality of romance—in short, the sort of name that fitted the kind of performer Larry in fact was. But 'Oliver'! How could a man named 'Laurence Oliver' have ever turned out to be the actor Larry was?

"Thereupon Larry proceeded to do an absolutely brilliant improvised performance of himself in the guise of a man named Laurence Oliver. No, this man was not a grandiloquent actor. He was a painfully shy clergyman, greeting his flock outside the church at the end of the service, uttering inanities and spewing out the most trite drivel to each of us, his mock parishioners, as we greeted him. It was hilarious, and in the end we all had to agree that at least so far as actors go, there *is* something in a name. Had Larry been born Laurence Oliver, he'd never have grown up to be the actor he was. An actor, perhaps, but hardly one with his dash and sweep. 'Oliver' sort of stumbles off the tongue, whereas 'Olivier' flows and soars. The name is very much a reflection, even a function, of the man. In other words, Laurence Olivier was born to be the great, sweeping, soaring actor he turned out to be. Thank God his forebears maintained the name Olivier when they came to England, rather than changing it to Oliver."[1]

•

"Olivier" nevertheless is the French equivalent of Oliver, a name that like many denotes the craft or trade practiced by the ancient founders of a family. In this case the name refers to a clan whose distant ancestors once engaged in the olive trade—a staple industry in medieval southern Europe. And it is to medieval southern Europe that the modern Olivier family traces its roots—more specifically, to the olive-rich region of Gascony, in southern France, in the foothills of the Pyrenees.

The Oliviers of seventeenth-century France were rigorous Protestants in a country ruled by the iron hand of Catholic Rome. Fervently religious and no longer willing to suffer the dogmatic tyranny of King Louis XIV, several members of the family fled to Holland toward the end of the century and then moved on to England. One, a clergyman named Jourdain Olivier, arrived in England about 1688 as chaplain to William of Orange.

The Reverend Jourdain Olivier became the progenitor of the modern Olivier family in Britain. Over the next two hundred years the clan branched into dozens of subfamilies, but it retained its strong religious integrity and supplied the Church of England with an almost unending stream of clergymen-preachers. It might be said that by the time Sir Laurence Olivier was born, the Olivier blood ran thick with the genetic need to declaim and orate; from the pulpit, though, not the stage.

Indeed, up to the time of Laurence Olivier's birth, no one in the family had shown the slightest inclination toward the stage. The closest anyone had come was Olivier's father, himself the son of a churchman. Gerard Kerr Olivier had attended Oxford in the late 1880s and fallen in with a group of freethinkers and wealthy layabouts who dabbled in dramatics. Only fifty years before, actors had been classified by law as "rogues and vagabonds." Prejudices against people who engaged in acting still lingered among the "respectable" classes of England. When Gerard Olivier's parents learned of his activities at Oxford, they ordered him home and quashed any ideas he might have had about pursuing an acting career.

In 1907, when Laurence Olivier was born, his father was well embarked on a career as a clergyman. After being yanked from Oxford, Gerard Olivier had completed his education at Durham University and switched his extracurricular interests from dramatics to athletics, distinguishing himself as a cricket player. Thereafter he took a teaching job at Boxgrove, a private school for boys forty miles southwest of London at Guildford. At Boxgrove he met Agnes Crookenden, the headmaster's attractive young sister-in-law.

"I daresay that Gerard's original interest in my sister was mixed half of masculine attraction and half of concern for his career," Agnes's sister, the headmaster's wife, told a British journalist in 1939. "Gerard had settled down to being an educator and had great ambitions for himself. He was a slight but commanding chap, not terribly outgoing in private but very authoritative in a classroom of young boys. Although his interest in Agnes was most certainly sincere, I am sure that it did not fail to occur to him, when it came time for him to find a wife, that a girl from a family of educators could be a great asset. Originally, I think, he hoped to succeed my husband at Boxgrove. But when that failed to come to pass, because of Gerard's young age and certain youthful indiscretions he had not yet lived down, he rather abruptly decided to establish his own school. He and Agnes were married. Then, with some financial help from the family, the two of them leased a small building in Dorking and opened a school of their own. Of Gerard's, really, since it was his way of fulfilling his ambition to become a headmaster as soon as he could."[2]

Dorking was then a handsome provincial market town surrounded by lush farms and estates in the county of Surrey. Gerard and Agnes Olivier devoted the first few years of their marriage to building up their school and producing the first of their three children—Sybille, a daughter. According to Sybille Olivier, by 1900 the family had achieved a respectable and financially comfortable existence through the school. But her father had grown unsettled at the prospect of spending the rest of his life with children and dealing with their narrow-minded parents. Much to the surprise of his wife, he announced in 1902 that he intended to dispose of the school, abandon education and take up the priesthood —the vocation of his forebears and one more suited than teaching to what he perceived to be his power to influence people. The following year he secured an apprentice ministerial position at Dorking's St. Martin's Church. At about the same time, Agnes gave birth to their second child, Richard.

Gerard Olivier was in his mid-thirties, Agnes four years younger. The shift in careers meant an abrupt change in lifestyle, with the family moving from their spacious schoolhouse quarters in one of the better parts of Dorking to a modest Victorian parish house in the town's central working-class district. There, four years later, Laurence Olivier was born—at five in the morning of May 22, 1907. His father named him after Laurent Olivier, a sixteenth-century Frenchman who was his earliest known ancestor.

The house in which Laurence Olivier was born, then a rundown structure at 26 Wathen Road, still stands in Dorking—today practically a suburb of London. Unlike the birthplaces of many of England's celebrated citizens, the house bears no blue plaque attesting to its singularity. The lack of an historical marker is of no consequence to Olivier, he has said, since he has no recollection of having lived there.[3] Three years after his birth, his father accepted an assignment at a church in Notting Hill, just northwest of Hyde Park in London.

The Reverend Olivier had been respected and well liked in Dorking, where he managed to mix his newfound religious piety with amateur weekend cricket playing. He might have remained there for many years, forging a reputation as a social-minded and well-rounded provincial vicar, and eventually ascending to a higher executive level in the Church of England.

But such a cautious course was not in his character. "My father was a man who was never satisfied with the status quo," his son Richard told a newspaper in 1955. "As he gained confidence in his powers as a clerical orator, he envisioned greater and greater evangelical challenges for himself. He was not interested in aspiring to a high office within the Church. Rather, he was obsessed with delivering the Church's message to those most likely to be indifferent to it. Which is why, much to the consternation of my mother, he leapt at the chance to transfer to Notting Hill."[4]

The move to Notting Hill marked the beginning of a nomadic, journeyman clerical life for Gerard Olivier and his family. His increasing religious fervor and "creative" preaching offended the elders at the Notting Hill parish and he was soon on the move again. It was not until Christmas of 1912 that he finally found a parish that would accept his unique and intensely zealous—almost fire and brimstone—brand of priestliness. The church was St. Saviour's in working-class Pimlico, just below fashionable Belgravia and Buckingham Palace and hard by the north bank of the Thames. There the Olivier family settled into nondescript quarters at 22 Lupus Street. They would remain for six years. Pimlico, then, was where Laurence Olivier, five at the time of their move, grew up.

2

Agnes Olivier

IN an interview shortly before his death in 1980, Kenneth Tynan, a longtime friend and theatre associate of Laurence Olivier, told me this about the influence of Agnes Olivier on her son's life: "I don't put much credit in speculations about how enormously gifted people come by their talents—you know, who inherited what from which parent, that sort of thing. But from everything I've learned about Larry, from him and others, he is the product of a fortuitous, almost ideal melding of two distinct, powerful genetic inheritances. The one is what I would call his exterior gifts: his voice, his physical aspect, his athleticism, his daring, his self-absorption and his single-minded devotion to his work, all of which make for that compelling presence he has as an actor. These he clearly gets from his father. Yet had he possessed these alone, he would merely have been a competent actor. What served to ignite and transform all those traits into something unique were his interior gifts, which are what I believe he got from his mother. By these I mean his perception, his instinctive intelligence, his intuition for the absolutely right gesture and movement, his ability to plumb character, his powers of observation and mimicry, his clearly feminine sensitivity and emotional expanse. Evidently Larry's mother was a woman in whom all these traits powerfully reposed. I say 'reposed' because, as a woman raised in Victorian times and married to a man of Larry's father's rather tyrannical temperament, she never had a chance to really exercise her gifts. In the end, the only way she expressed them was by passing them on to her son.

"By herself she was probably not in any way a genius, nor was Larry's father. But the fortuitous combining of their two distinctive packages of traits produced in Larry a fertile ground in which a particular kind of genius could flourish when given the opportunity. This is where genetics are important. Parents don't directly produce geniuses. They merely create a field in whose soil a new human being grows. If they are lucky, the balance they impart to the soil through the combination of their own traits will produce the conditions for genius to flourish. That's what Larry's mother and father did when they conceived him. It was, of course, purely a matter of luck and fortunate coincidence."[1]

•

By all accounts, Agnes Crookenden Olivier embarked on marriage as a warmhearted, cultured, intelligent, humorous and high-spirited young woman. Raised in a family of relatively freethinking educators, she had vowed early in her life never to marry a clergyman because of what she felt to be the narrow-mindedness inherent in such a vocation. When she first met Gerard Olivier as a young teacher at the Boxgrove School, she had more than one reason to admire him. Although he came from a strict clerical family, he was in the process of carving out his own path independent of the Church and his family. Because of their mutual interest in education and matters of the intellect, the two seemed well suited to one another.

Shortly after their marriage, they embarked upon the pursuit of an ambition they had nurtured during their courtship by opening their own school in Dorking. Over the next few years, as the school became established, Agnes gave birth to her first child. But she began to sense a growing restlessness, bordering on dissatisfaction, in her husband. Finally he announced that he had made a mistake in choosing education as his profession. It was older souls to save, not young minds to develop, for which he was put on earth, he declared.

Had Gerard Olivier announced that he wanted to switch from education to a career in banking or industry, Agnes might have accepted the decision with more equanimity than she did. As it was, she felt betrayed and distressed. She had no choice but to go along with Gerard's decision, however; she was pregnant with their second child.

According to those familiar with the family history, Agnes went along but not as dutifully as she might have, given the times and what was expected of middle-class wives. She handled her first disappointment gracefully enough and adjusted without too much grudge to being the wife of a clergyman when Gerard took up his first clerical appointment at St. Martin's in Dorking. She even agreed to have a third child, once she was over her initial shock.

But Agnes, however well she handled the adjustment on the surface, was irrevocably damaged by it in spirit. The damage was compounded by Gerard's unilateral decision, three years after Laurence's birth, to abandon the familiar surroundings of Dorking for the harsh conditions of London's Notting Hill.

Agnes at first resisted the move. Mystified and disappointed earlier by Gerard's decision to go into the Church, now she was distressed by his increasing religious zealotry and intransigence. Although she tried to keep up appearances as his obedient and contented wife, she grew more and more discontented and began to withdraw from Gerard. The withdrawal was deepened by his demand that she share his religious fervor and instill it in their children. When she balked, he set out to do it himself. By the time they had settled in Pimlico, Gerard had all but taken over Sybille's and Richard's upbringing. He hectored them constantly about religious matters, punishing them severely whenever they transgressed his rules. He cast a pall of fear over the house that only Laurence, because he was still too young, was not immediately affected by.

But the five-year-old was affected in other, more indirect ways. Agnes, her rancor intensifying, decided that her mission was now to protect her children from being turned into religious fanatics by their father. Because Sybille and Richard were several years older than Laurence, she was unable to shield them completely from Gerard's influence. So she concentrated her energies on her youngest son, smothering him with almost neurotic attention and devotion.

In various public interviews over the years, Sybille Olivier has painted a graphic picture of what life was like in the Olivier household during that time. The impression is of a home easygoing and filled with laughter when her father was not there, tension-filled and uncomfortable when he was. Apparently Gerard Olivier, impeded by his wife from controlling his younger son, regularly extended his anger with Agnes to Laurence himself. In an interview with a London newspaper in 1973, Sybille said, "People were either devoted to [Father] or couldn't take him at all. And talk about temper—a storming, raging tornado which he'd turn on Larry in a way he never did on my brother Dick and me. Father didn't like Larry, and Larry was terrified of him." Whereas, "Mummy was just everything to Larry . . . she adored Larry. He was hers."[2]

According to Davina Rhodes, a family friend, "Larry grew up in an awful situation. There was a constant push-and-pull over him between his father and mother. He witnessed these horrible, violent arguments between the two, all of them over him. Gerard began to worry about what Agnes's overprotective treatment would turn Larry into. And rightly so, because she *was* overprotecting him. Not just to keep Larry from Gerard's wrath, but to retaliate against Gerard, to show her contempt for him. For example, when Larry was six or seven, Gerard insisted that he go out and play games, learn sports. Agnes wouldn't let him. She said there was too great a danger that Larry would injure himself. But that was only half the reason. The other half was her desire to deprive Gerard of seeing his son become proficient at sports. Sports were very important to Gerard, especially cricket. The result was that Larry grew up being terrible at sports, and this caused him no end of trouble with other boys his age. He was seen as a sissy and treated accordingly. So he would take further refuge in his mother, and she would comfort him and make it seem unimportant. Which would only serve to reinforce Larry's 'sissiness.' And this drove his father crazy. He would take his anger out on Larry, but he picked on him only to show his growing contempt for Agnes. Larry was caught in the middle of this constant, subtle but violent war between his father and mother. He was used as a pawn by both."[3]

Young Larry—or Kim, as his mother called him—had no confusion about where his loyalties lay. They were all with Agnes. The only thing his father represented was a source of tyrannical oppression that made his mother ever more indulgent of him. Indeed, suggests the family friend, as a six- and seven-year-old, Olivier learned deliberately to provoke his father's wrath in order to produce more love and attention from his mother.

This pattern of deep dependency on his mother carried over into Olivier's early schooling. Agonized over being separated from her, if only for a few hours a day when he first started primary school, he would feign illness and other afflictions in order to have Agnes summoned to his rescue. His first school was a neighborhood religious institution that insisted on sports instruction as a compulsory after-school activity. Agnes managed to get her son excused from these sessions. She replaced them at home by reading to him—her way, again, of counterbalancing any influence, however subliminal, his father's religious demands might have on him.

Laurence was not totally beyond Gerard's influence, however. Family attendance at Sunday services at St. Saviour's was a mandatory event that not even Agnes attempted to interfere with. Recalling them in a 1967 BBC television interview with Kenneth Tynan, Olivier said, "My father was an effective preacher, and as a boy, sitting in the choir watching him and others in the pulpit, I was fascinated by the way a sermon was delivered. Those preachers knew when to drop the voice, when to bellow about the perils of hellfire, when to slip in a gag, when suddenly to wax sentimental, when to turn solemn, when to pronounce the blessing. The quick changes in mood and manner absorbed me, and I have never forgotten them."[4]

So fascinated did young Olivier become by the pulpit orators that, according to his sister, he began to imitate them at home—out of his father's presence, of course. "In order to deflect him from any youthful ambition to become a clergyman himself, Mother encouraged Larry to turn his mock-sermonizing into recitations of monologues from well-known plays."[5] By the time Larry was eight he was a proficient reader, and Agnes gave him speeches from Shakespeare, Marlowe and other English classic playwrights to declaim in place of the manuscripts of his father's old sermons. Along with encouraging his recitations, much like a stage director preparing an actor for an audition she set the scenes and synopsized the actions within which the speeches took place. The boy's favorite recitation became Mark Antony's "Friends, Romans, countrymen" speech from Shakespeare's *Julius Caesar*.

At eight, Olivier's enthusiasm for "play-acting" became intensive enough for his older brother, at Agnes's insistence, to build him a small curtained stage in his bedroom. Thereafter he put on brief but increasingly complex family performances of scenes from plays—sometimes solo, other times with his brother and sister in a cast of three. Even Gerard Olivier found it hard to disapprove, for in his son's juvenile posturing he saw a pleasant reflection of himself; further, a sign that Laurence might have the talent to follow in his footsteps when he grew up.

It was the approval he got from his mother that was really the engine of Laurence's youthful performing drive. As he would say later to an interviewer: "Although the whole family would be present at my little theatricals, I played shamelessly to my mother. She would mouth the words with me, and whenever I stumbled she would urge me on, applauding deliriously when I got it right and suffocating me with hugs at the end. Soon she started to invite other people in to watch me perform—neighborhood ladies, relatives and the like. And it was always the same at the end—much applause, most of it polite, I'm sure, and a great deal of hugging and 'Isn't-he-darling' sort of praise. I suppose you could say that I decided at a very early age that acting was for me."[6]

3

An End to Childhood

ACTING would be a career that Laurence Olivier would pursue almost by default, however. As his brother Richard later told it: "By the time Larry was nine, he began to get a sense of himself as a male. For the first time he showed a need to break the bonds, if only tentatively, of Mother's attachment to him. To say that he was ready to emerge full speed ahead from the emotional cocoon she had wrapped him in would be to overstate it, of course. But he did begin to show signs—not of resentment, but of a young bird ready to test its wings. I was already at boarding school, and Larry was to follow me. I remember that I would come home for holidays and he would beat me about the ears with incessant questioning about what it was like. Mother would gaze upon us sadly, almost as if she knew she was losing her precious Larry. But she had too much sense to make a fuss about it. She was still number one in his eyes. But he had rather quickly come to realize that there was another world, a vastly more varied world beyond the one he knew, which was centered on Mother.

"The sorry thing was that Larry was so ill prepared for that new world.

It was a rough-house world of competitive, sports-minded boys sardined together in this little school in the middle of London. By that time, Larry was desperately interested in sports and confident that he'd be able to catch up. But in point of fact he was totally inept, and even at my tender age of twelve I had protective qualms about him coming to the school. Not only qualms on his behalf, but on my own, since I didn't fancy being embarrassed by a younger brother who failed to fit in."[1]

•

The school was All Saints, a Church of England choir school located near Oxford Circus in the heart of London. Admission was reserved for the sons of clergy who, it was thought, would be ripe for a later call to the cloth themselves. The school was monastic and rigid in its discipline, yet surprisingly varied and liberal in its curriculum. Aside from the usual religious training and compulsory choir singing, the school, which had room for only fourteen boys, offered courses in a wide range of nonclerical subjects. Moreover, it busied its students after hours in athletics and dramatics. The rationale for this was that the molding of effective priests demanded a proper grounding not only in theology but in the physical and oratorical skills that would better enable them to impart the Anglican creed to ordinary parishioners.

Olivier was a few months past his ninth birthday when his father enrolled him at All Saints in the fall of 1916. Although the school was only a few miles from the family home in Pimlico, it was a genuine boarding school and the boys were allowed to go home only one Saturday a month. If Agnes Olivier worried about how her favorite son would adjust to his sudden separation from her, her anxiety came to naught. As Richard Olivier later said, "Larry was most eager to get on with it once he knew he would be going to All Saints. Certainly he missed Mother at the beginning, and there were moments when he wished he could flee the school. But in all he adjusted well, probably more easily because I was there, a familiar face. It was as though he instinctively recognized that the time had come to stop being the protected little brat and make something of himself in the world of his peers. I daresay the adjustment was much more painful and difficult for Mother. She was left at home alone with Father, while the school kept Larry much too busy to dwell overlong on thoughts of home."[2]

Next to providing training in the rigors of orthodox theology, All Saints' principal function was to make its impeccably tuned fourteen-boy choir available to various churches in and around London for Sunday services. Laurence Naismith, another lad who grew up to be a celebrated actor, was a schoolmate of the Olivier brothers at All Saints. He once described the school as "a terribly tight community, a monastic life, really, with just two dormitories for fourteen boys and a day starting like that of a monk—up at 6:45 in the morning to serve in the church, then breakfast followed by choir practice and a full day of lessons, including plenty of Latin because we often had to sing in Latin, and then out on the playing fields in the afternoon for football or cricket."[3]

Olivier arrived at All Saints during the middle of World War I. England had suffered huge battlefield casualties in the trenches of Flanders, and London was for a time a target for German bombers. Yet life at the school went on almost as if the war didn't exist. Olivier devoted most of his early extracurricular energies to developing rudimentary skills in soccer and cricket. His efforts, however, went unrewarded. Naismith has said: "It was strange, because Larry was naturally athletic, had good coordination, that sort of thing. But when it came to games, he was as awkward as a cow trying to balance on a wire. I suppose this was because he had never been allowed to play sports before. By the time he started playing at All Saints, the other boys were way ahead of him in basic physical skills and they thoroughly rejected him, laughed him off the fields or only picked him to play if they were desperate for one last body to make up a side. Naturally he did not take to this treatment very well. In reaction he became quite a nasty young man, which only made him further disliked."[4]

With his hopes of becoming one of the boys on the athletic fields shattered, Olivier had only one other outlet through which he could impress himself upon his schoolmates: the after-school dramatics program. He threw himself into this with a vengeance. And having already had considerable practice at home in the basic routines of play-acting, he quickly made a mark as a performer of some competence when compared to many of the older boys. So impressive was he that, in his second year, the school's director assigned him the key role of Brutus in a Christmas production of Shakespeare's *Julius Caesar*.

The All Saints' Christmas productions were special affairs. Since the school's choir served numerous churches in London on a voluntary basis, it had become the custom for distinguished parishioners from those churches to attend the annual Christmas productions as a way of expressing their gratitude. On this occasion, no less a personage than Ellen Terry, the aging first lady of the English theatre, was in the audience. At the end of the performance she was expected to go backstage and say something politely praiseworthy to the company and its director. Dutifully, she did so. But in addition, she singled out the eleven-year-old Olivier for special praise. Apparently she was genuinely impressed by his playing of Brutus, for she returned to see the next evening's performance and then made note of it in her diary: "The small boy who played Brutus is already a great actor," she wrote.

The attention he received backstage from Miss Terry had the happy effect of establishing Olivier, finally, as one of the lads at All Saints. No longer would he be forced to struggle for acceptance on the school's athletic fields; the stage was his proper preadolescent milieu, and no one could ignore his natural excellence there.

Sybille Olivier has said that at the time of her brother's encounter with Ellen Terry, he didn't know who she was and was unaware of the significance of her praise; the old woman might just have been another doting grandparent. But it did not take Agnes Olivier very long to set her son straight. Olivier spent the Christmas holidays at home, and a day did not pass without Agnes pointing out proudly to family and friends that England's greatest actress had remarked favorably on Laurence's acting ability. Not only that, but another elderly, celebrated Shakespearean actor, Sir Johnston Forbes-Robertson, had seen a performance of the production. Afterward, upon being introduced to Reverend and Mrs. Olivier, he had exclaimed to Gerard: "My dear fellow, your son *is* Brutus."

When Laurence returned to All Saints after the Christmas recess, he was a changed boy. Until then he had been timid, tentative and, for the most part, introverted in the company of his schoolmates. Now, with a new sense of himself, he was no longer afraid to make his voice heard in classroom discussions. The change was sudden and striking, according to Naismith, and not a little insufferable: Olivier took to lording his newfound eminence over his schoolmates.

"Larry was not one of the better looking boys in All Saints," another contemporary recently told me. "He was thin and bony, with knobby matchsticks for arms and legs, and he had an awkward way of moving about. Nor was his visage all that attractive. He had a full head of hair, but it grew low out of his forehead. That, combined with his thick eyebrows, gave him a decidedly molelike appearance. This was heightened by his thin, rather pouty mouth and long, oblique nose. Passing him in the halls, one would be most unimpressed. Yet I must admit that when he was on stage, under lights, in costume and with his face made up to look like a Roman politician three or four times his own age, there was a startling transformation.

"On stage he had an eerie authority that immediately drew one's eyes to him. Most of the boys in *Julius Caesar* were clearly amateurs. I mean, when they didn't have lines to say they stood around like statues watching whoever else was speaking, or else they engaged in obviously stagey side business. But not Olivier. There was something in the way he handled himself, even when he was not engaged in the central action, that made you feel that here was no amateur. Of course, you knew that you were watching an eleven-year-old. But somehow he transported his character out of boyhood into a semblance of actual manhood. He did it with gestures, movement, even standing in repose. And with his eyes. For all Larry's physical imperfections, he possessed the most compelling eyes."[5]

Of that first appearance on stage as Brutus, Olivier himself has said: "I do remember there was quite a fuss made at the school over my performance. It has been cited often since as some sort of epiphany wherein I discovered my true calling as an actor. Perhaps, but I doubt it. I worked hard at it because I wanted so badly to be good and not seem an amateur—that much I'll say. I felt I was in a constant no-holds-barred competition with the other boys, and since I was such a bloody dud at sports and other things, I felt that if I mucked up there I would forever be a total outcast. So, yes, I did set out to distinguish myself, or at least save myself from embarrassment. And I suspect that I used a lot of tricks I had learned about realism from the play-acting I had done with my mother and sister at home.

"But no, it was not an epiphany for me in the sense of discovering that I was born to be on the stage. Indeed, even if I had experienced such feelings I would have had to deny them, since I had been brought up to believe that acting was not something that someone of our circumstances aspired to do with one's life. A diversion, perhaps, but not a vocation. Which is not to say that the experience wasn't an epiphany of another sort. What I mean is that it gave me a much more secure perception of myself than I had ever had before in a personal sense. Call it ego, self-esteem, self-confidence—whatever you wish. Having been made to feel rather worthless for so many years, it was a tremendous shot in the arm."[6]

If Olivier was unfetching in appearance as an eleven-year-old, what of his personality? His sister provided probably the best testimony when, in describing him to an interviewer in 1958, she said that her brother had something of a dual personality as a boy. On the one hand, he was often dour and guarded, self-absorbed and introspective, becoming lost in his thoughts for hours on end and communicating only perfunctorily with members of the family. He was particularly withdrawn in the presence of strangers, and he often provoked even his mother's displeasure when he glowered menacingly at visitors to the Olivier home.

On the other hand, he was just as often outgoing and cheerful, especially when his father wasn't around. "When he felt like it he could be very amusing," Sybille Olivier said. "He was very good at mimicking others and parodying their pompous traits. He could send all of us into gales of delighted laughter with his comic impressions of people we knew, although we would all afterward feel guilty for our pleasure because it was always at someone else's expense.

"Larry also had a very rapier tongue in those early years. Not quick, but sharp and facile. I mean, he was never very good in arguments, but after an argument or discussion he would go off and think for a while about what was said, then come back and make a kind of 'final' comment or pronouncement that sort of provided him with the last word. He hated to lose an argument, and in this way he managed to win most of them, although it took him a little while. He was very stubborn in this respect. Even if he had to spend days thinking up the right retort, he would come back after everyone else had forgotten the argument and make his winning comment."

Sybille added that she thought her brother's vacillating personality was due primarily to the ongoing conflict between their mother and father. "He tended always to be quiet and withdrawn when Father was in the house, and then burst out into his other much more ebullient self when he was gone, by way of compensation. Of course, Mother and Father themselves were a right opposite pair, and this may have had something to do with Larry's being first one way, then the other. Despite his attachment to Mother, he was in awe of Father. He wanted so for Father to like him. So he would often act like Father, whether intentionally or unconsciously—I suppose in the hope that he would gain Father's approval, or at least soften his disapproval. The pity of it was that Father simply had a blind spot when it came to Larry."[7]

The dual nature of Olivier's personality was expressed not only at home but in school as well. Laurence Naismith once recalled: "Larry was capable of alternating bouts of almost hysterical good cheer and despondence, mixed further with frequent expressions of rude behavior.

He went through a period while I was at All Saints when he was an inveterate show-off. At times he was an immature clod who conducted himself in the most boorish way. At other times he would disport himself in an elegant manner that was well beyond his years. He kept us all off balance in our attitude toward him. As I remember it, he had no close friends throughout his stay. No one could trust him to be constant. He would be your great pal one day, and then turn around and rather compulsively try to humiliate you the next. After that first business with *Julius Caesar,* one got the feeling that Larry was on stage all the time, that his whole life in school was devoted to testing out roles. It was impossible to tell the real Larry Olivier from some character he was temporarily playing."[8]

Richard Olivier, then still at All Saints, agreed. "But," he explained, "you must remember that in many ways my brother was a highly emotional boy by nature, which he got from our mother, and that his emotions were constantly stifled at home by Father. Once in school and away from Father, he was better able to let his emotions run free. The fact that he went overboard at times was simply akin to a wild animal being suddenly let out of a cage. . . . Larry *was* incorrigible for a while, but soon he got control of himself and learned to, as it were, 'edit' his behavior."[9]

Following his performance in *Julius Caesar,* Olivier was cast the following two Christmases in women's roles: that of Maria in *Twelfth Night* and then as the lead, Katherine, in *The Taming of the Shrew.* In the days of Shakespeare it was the convention in the theatre for male actors to play the women's parts, since females were not permitted to perform in public. Thus, young men dressing up and performing as women was a well-entrenched tradition followed in English boys' schools' theatrical productions during Olivier's youth; indeed, it was an elemental part of any young actor's training. (A similar tradition prevailed in all-girl schools, where female students played men's parts.)

Olivier was in his fourth year at All Saints when he appeared as Katherine in Shakespeare's familiar comedy. As earlier, Ellen Terry attended a performance, and again she rhapsodized about young Olivier. She had never seen the Shrew acted better "by any woman but Ada Rehan," a noted Shakespearean actress of her generation.

Also in attendance was Sybil Thorndike, then one of London's leading younger actresses and herself the offspring of a clergyman. She would later say: "I saw Larry in all those productions at All Saints and most of all I was impressed by his Kate. . . . His Shrew was really wonderful—the best Kate I ever saw. . . . Some people are born with technical ability. And Larry was. He didn't have to work hard enough at technical things because he knew it all from the start, instinctively."[10]

One might imagine that, playing a woman's role, Olivier would have spoken in falsetto and sought to make himself effeminate, which was the custom when boys acted female roles. Such was not the case. In fact, it was his ability to play the part using his own still-tenor voice and masculine mannerisms, yet appear a thoroughly natural female (with the help of gowns and dresses), that so impressed the Christmas audiences.

As another observer said, "He never once resorted to female mannerisms to convince us that the role he was playing was that of a woman. Yet after the first few moments of his appearance on stage we had no difficulty believing that he *was* this woman Kate. A hint of a gesture here, the taking of a stance there—everything he did spoke of a woman. It was all so natural and without any hesitancy or self-consciousness! We were so beguiled by Larry's physical performance that perhaps we paid too little attention to whether he said his lines as brilliantly as he could have, although I'm sure he was utterly competent in this respect too. But the creation this young boy made—the physical, attitudinal personification of this woman Kate—was a sight to behold."[11]

Olivier's success in *The Taming of the Shrew* portended a singular acting talent. Many wondered where he had found the inspiration for his performance. The answer was simple, although it would remain obscured for many years.

The spring before, Agnes Olivier had suddenly developed a brain tumor and, within a few weeks, died at the age of forty-eight. The last time her son saw her was the week before she passed away, when he was allowed to leave All Saints for a day to visit her bedside. As he prepared to return to school, she drew him feebly to her bed and kissed him good-bye. Before she let him go, she whispered, "Darling Larry, no matter what your father says, be an actor. Be a great actor. For me."[12]

Olivier did not realize at the time that his mother was dying. When he was informed a week later at school that she was gone, he collapsed in grief. But then he remembered her last words to him. He did not take them as her prescription for his future, however. He simply thought that she meant he should dedicate his next role to her memory. Which is what he set out to do when he was cast as Katherine in *The Taming of the Shrew*.

"I did not see him in it," his sister later told a reporter. "But I understand he modeled his character on Mother, and that it was this that enabled him to come across so well as a woman. Father was at one performance, I believe, and I understand he had to get up and leave, so shaken was he to see Larry recreating Mother down to the last detail. Father, of course, misunderstood. He castigated Larry for his 'sacrilege' in bringing mother back to life, so to speak, and for supposedly 'exploiting' her memory. He forbade Larry ever to act again, and I heard that he went so far as to register a protest with Reverend Heald, the director of the school."[13]

4

A Life in Limbo

K ENNETH TYNAN told me: "We
were preparing an interview program with Larry [for the BBC in 1967], and
I was sitting with him one afternoon going over the ground I wanted to
cover. We got onto the subject of his father and mother. He made it clear
that he didn't want to go into that business too deeply—it was long ago
and he was bored with people trying to make something more of his
relationship with his father than he thought was there. I wasn't willing to
yield so readily to his wishes. I had the very distinct feeling that it was a
case of he 'doth protest too much.'

"In the event, he got to talking about it in this pre-interview chat rather
a bit more than he intended to. He told me about the utter desolation he
experienced at his mother's death, and about how he had entertained
thoughts of going down to Chelsea Bridge, jumping off and drowning
himself in the Thames. He said that ever since then, whenever he crossed
Chelsea Bridge, or passed by it, he always thought of his mother and his
suicidal feelings.

"About his father he said—well, something to the effect that he grew

23

up terribly confused about the old boy, at once hating him and admiring him and wanting to be admired by him, and it all turning him into an emotional zombie. He spent the three or four years after his mother died with his emotions frozen, he told me, unable to resolve anything about himself. 'I was a sailing ship adrift, lying dead in the water, masts buckled and sails in tatters, at the mercy of the ocean's currents,' was the way he put it. Evidently he was waiting for his father to rescue him, to make an emotional attachment, guide him back to safe haven and set his life aright. But the old Reverend never did. Except for the schoolboy demands he put on Larry, he left him adrift.

"But it had all worked out for the best in the end, Larry insisted. Had it not been for his father's neglect, he would never have discovered the drive in himself to succeed in the theatre as he did. It was not just external drive he was talking about—an 'I'll-show-him' motivation. What he really meant was that in acting he discovered a way in which he could delve into and express emotions that he never dared do, never knew how to do, in real life.

"It was an extremely revealing moment. Larry was essentially not a man given to expressing himself with great emotional fervor when he was being himself offstage in normal conversation. Yet despite himself—and perhaps he was unaware of it—as he talked about his father he grew vastly more intense than I had ever seen him before. And a bit teary. I found myself wishing that we'd had a camera running. When I asked him if he would mind going over it once more for the actual interview, he of course declined. Oh, I did get him to talk a bit, but it had none of the passion and electricity of that moment."[1]

•

With Agnes Olivier no longer around to interfere, Gerard took over his younger son's upbringing with demonic intensity. After decreeing the end of any further dramatic activities in the wake of Laurence's performance in *The Taming of the Shrew,* Gerard took further measures to bring the fourteen-year-old under his full control by removing him from All Saints and enrolling him at St. Edward's School in Oxford, sixty miles from London. If All Saints was a preseminary school, St. Edward's—or Teddy's, as it was more commonly called—was practically the seminary itself. The boarding school had been founded in 1863 as a training ground for a more orthodox and zealous breed of clergymen than were then available in England, and it had maintained that tradition into the twentieth century. Gerard Olivier was now full bent on Laurence growing up to be an Anglican priest, his older son Richard having already disappointed him by declining to follow such a course. His orders to Laurence upon enrolling him at St. Edward's were to conform to his wishes or else.

It turned out to be "or else." In his first year at the school, in 1921, Olivier tried genuinely to follow his father's prescription. But he failed. A "new boy" still without any talent for the games that were a fundamental part of life at Teddy's, he quickly became a social and academic outcast. Although the school put on an annual Christmas play, he was still under his father's prohibition against acting and was thus unable to redeem himself in the one extracurricular activity for which he had a clear talent and growing affection. His only other obvious skill lay in choir singing, and his enthusiastic participation in that merely served to sharpen the image of him as an "aesthete" in the collective mind of a student body that measured a new boy largely by his enthusiasm for sports.

After Olivier's first few months at Teddy's, the headmaster showed concern for his plight and called him in for a talk. Grudgingly Laurence confessed his unhappiness and ascribed much of it to the fact that he was no good on the playing field, and that his father had forbidden him taking part in dramatics. The headmaster had heard about the boy's stage accomplishments at All Saints. He thereupon persuaded Gerard Olivier to lift his prohibition on the ground that continued experience in after-school stage work would not only stand Laurence in good stead as a minister later on, but might actually provoke him into pursuing the ministerial career he had so far displayed a strong hesitancy about.

With this reprieve, Olivier's career as a St. Edward's student brightened. Yet his first opportunity to distinguish himself did not come about through the school's dramatics society. As it happened, an anniversary festival was scheduled for the 1922 Easter holidays at the Shakespeare Memorial Theatre in Stratford-on-Avon, Shakespeare's birthplace. Theatrical troupes from all over England—professional and amateur—were invited, each to perform one of Shakespeare's plays. All Saints—Olivier's former school—had been asked to repeat its production of *The Taming of the Shrew*. The director, with Gerard Olivier's reluctant concurrence, arranged for Laurence to go to Stratford in order to repeat his role of Kate.

The week Olivier spent at Stratford established him at St. Edward's as a student to be reckoned with. But much more than that, it proved to be a turning point in his young life. Surrounded by theatre people —many of them well-known professionals from London's West End and the celebrated repertory theatres of Britain's outlying cities—he was fascinated by the pulsating energy, the alternately rigorous and easygoing pace and the earthy vitality of most of the performers' lives. If ever the smell of greasepaint got into a young man's blood, it did so that Easter. Olivier returned to St. Edward's after the holidays with a sheaf of laudatory newspaper notices about his performance as Kate. He returned also with, for the first time, an instinctive sense of where his future lay.

It was not something he could talk or even think about seriously. There was still no question in his mind that an acting career was beyond his wildest hopes. His father continued to insist on a life in the ministry for him. Since the theatre seemed beyond his reach, he sought out a compromise.

His eighteen-year-old brother, Richard, having rejected a life in the priesthood, was studying for a career in agriculture. He planned to journey to India in a year or two to apprentice himself on a tea plantation. Voyaging to India was an idea that engaged Laurence's fifteen-year-old imagination. He began to cultivate it, settling his mind on a life of adventure in the British merchant navy, steeling himself for the day when he would declare this as his chosen vocation to his father.

That day was still at least a year away. In the meantime, Laurence was obliged to complete his term at St. Edward's. His performance at Stratford had given him a new lease on life at the school, and on his return after the 1922 summer holidays he found himself grudgingly accepted, if not entirely popular. He devoted most of his spare time thereafter to dramatics. For the school's Christmas play of 1923 he was cast as Puck in Shakespeare's *A Midsummer Night's Dream*.

What had expressed itself as a pure, instinctive acting talent at All Saints bore the additional stamp of his Stratford experience when Olivier took to the stage in the role of Puck. Having witnessed actors playing for outrageous effect at the Stratford festival, having seen how professionals tried to upstage each other, having observed well-known performers indulge in numerous tricks and ham acting, Olivier went overboard in his portrayal of Puck. Rather than strive for a restrained, naturalistic characterization, he pranced and postured all over the stage, dominating the play and his fellow actors and drawing wild applause from the audience of parents, teachers and guests.

The critics on hand saw through his performance, however. As one wrote in a local newspaper, "The boy who played Puck, although he has a potent stage presence, emoted with frantic and altogether unnecessary effect, as though playing a joke on his fellow cast-members, indeed on the audience. Added to this defect was the fact that he indulged in some inexplicably modern costuming devices, which made the entire performance a cheap burlesque turn. One can only be surprised that the director, Mr. Cowell, let the young man—Master Lawrence [sic] Olivier is his name—get away with such tawdry insolence. Shakespeare has seldom been more ill-served."

Be that as it may, Laurence's performance remained a great hit with the audiences. And unbeknown to him, there was a woman in one audience who would play a brief but pivotal role in his destiny. The woman was the soon-to-be new Mrs. Gerard Olivier.

The Reverend Olivier had moved from Pimlico to the village of Letchworth, thirty miles north of London. After the death of his wife, he had embarked on a missionary journey to Jamaica. He had returned a few months later with a new woman in his life, and he brought her with him to watch his son perform as Puck at St. Edward's. More than once Gerard Olivier had described his younger son to her as sadly lacking in the vital qualities a growing boy should possess; for, after all, he was still without any skill or apparent interest in sports, his school grades were lackluster, and he had so far evinced no enthusiasm for a career in the ministry.

Laurence's future stepmother, after having first met him, had been inclined to sympathize with Gerard's pessimism. To her, Laurence had revealed himself as sullen, distant and without a shred of social grace or personal charm—attitudes he would later attribute to his bitter resentment over his father's decision to remarry. The woman was therefore agreeably surprised to see a completely different young man on the stage at St. Edward's.

"My goodness," she was reported to have said to his father, "he's a natural actor. That's what he should be—not a cricketer, not a preacher. Why, with a little training he could really become something in the theatre."[2]

Since Gerard's intended had had some experience in the theatre herself, and since he had learned to please her by showing interest in her opinions, he began to look at his son in a new light.

Laurence himself, although by now enamored of the idea of a career in the theatre, believed still that it was something he could only wish for but never realize. This was due to his father's previous insistence that he work toward the ministry and, failing that, toward a career in some respectable industry.

After the St. Edward's Christmas production, Olivier spent a few days at his father's home in Letchworth. Richard was getting set to leave for India the following month, and the talk in the rectory was almost exclusively of the adventures that awaited him there. Although most of the family's attention centered on Richard, Laurence frequently caught the ruminative, uncomfortable gaze of his father on himself.

As he would later say, "I had the feeling that my father was silently ruing the day I was born, so disgusted did I imagine him to be with me, compared to the pride he showed in Dicky. I felt terribly guilty, for I still harbored my secret of not wanting to study further for the church. I knew I would have to tell him soon, since I was due to start my final term at Teddy's in another month or so. I was desperately casting about for another line of study that I thought would blunt my father's anger. And since he was so supportive of Dicky's decision to go into agriculture, I naturally opted for this."[3]

Olivier's moment of confrontation with his father came in January, the day after the family returned to Letchworth from Tilbury, where they had gone to see Richard off for India. Laurence was taking a bath when his father burst into the bathroom and demanded to know what, now that his brother was gone, he intended to do with his life. Unprepared for the moment, Laurence timidly summoned up his barely rehearsed answer.

"I just don't think I have what it takes to enter the clergy," he said. "I think I should like to do what Dicky has done."

"And what is that?" the Reverend Olivier replied coldly.

"Study agriculture for a year or two. Then, when I'm old enough, go out to India."

"Is that a decision you have made because it is what *you* want to do, or because it is what your brother did?"

"I can't think of anything else."

"What about acting?"

"But I thought . . ."

"You thought what?"

"I thought you would be against that."

"What made you think that?"

"All the things you've said. And not said. And—I don't know. You've just made it very clear that you have little use for actors."

"Have I also not made it clear that I want my sons to be their own men?"

"Yes."

"Well, then, have you thought about acting?"

"Yes, sometimes."

"And why haven't you said anything about it?"

Laurence shrugged.

"Would you like to give it a try?" his father asked.

"Yes," Laurence submitted.

"More so than following Dicky?"

"Yes—but I don't understand. You have been so against my acting."

"Nonsense. I am told that you have it in you to become an actor. So an actor you'll be, if that's what you want. I don't know if you will ever amount to anything. But it is better to be a man doing what he feels he is cut out to do than a man doing what he thinks he ought to do to please others. It is a lesson I learned many years ago, before you were born. You are no more cut out to do agriculture than I am to ride in the Derby. So it is an actor you will be. Or until such time as you learn that you are not cut out for it."[4]

5

Rite of Passage

AN actor who first met Olivier
more than fifty years ago told me: "Larry was fresh out of acting school
and slinking around the West End looking for work. He was a curious
mixture of homely and handsome. One didn't know what to make of him.
He was on the withdrawn side, and it was difficult to tell how seriously
he took his prospects. Except for his eyes, his face was altogether unremarkable. He had a narrow brow that seemed wedged in between a wild
bush of hair and equally bushy eyebrows. His nose jutted from his face,
quite thick—almost coarse—around the nostrils, like an East End dock-
worker's. A thin-lipped mouth with gappy, irregular teeth, and a thick,
rounded, slightly clefted chin.

"Yet for all the disparateness of his features, there were times when,
if you caught a glimpse of him in a certain unconscious pose, from a certain
angle, he appeared very handsome indeed—well, if not exactly handsome
in the matinee-idol sense, most attractive. When I first got to know him
he was very self-conscious about his looks, very dissatisfied with his individual features. But people reassured him, I think, made him aware that

when he struck certain poses, held his head in a certain way, formed certain natural expressions, that he projected an aura that drew one's attention to him. Conscious of this power, he worked on it, refining the poses and so on.

"I thought it all a bit amusing, for despite the lavish attention he paid to his face there was the question of his body. It was as though the body didn't belong to the face. The body was thin, delicate, all bones and lumps and sunken chest, with legs as narrow and tubular as drinking straws. He had a mature man's face on a child's body, and for this reason I gave him small chance of ever becoming more than a knockabout actor. When I encountered him again, a few years later, I was astonished at the changes he had wrought in himself. He had turned from an awkward and somewhat homely eighteen-year-old into an almost ravishing physical specimen of twenty-one or -two."[1]

•

Later reports from members of the Olivier family hinted that Gerard Olivier's suggestion that Laurence pursue acting training derived not so much from paternal altruism as it did from the senior Olivier's desire to dispose of the problem his son represented. Gerard's allegiance and concern were directed to the woman he wanted to marry, particularly because Laurence had always been a problem and was now a relic of his troubled past with Agnes Olivier.

Gerard Olivier made it clear to his son that he was prepared to provide him with no help. If Laurence wished to pursue an acting career, he would be obliged to do it on his own. Not only would the senior Olivier not pay for his son's formal training, he would give him nothing more than a pittance on which to live.

So relieved was Laurence at what he took to be his father's sudden, permissive about-face that he made no objections. Instead, in the months that followed, he all but ignored his schoolwork at St. Edward's and investigated the opportunities that might be open to him in the form of dramatic training. Consulting with the Reverend Geoffrey Heald, his former director at All Saints, he learned that there were only two dramatic schools worth aiming for, both in London. One was the Royal Academy of Dramatic Arts, the other the less fashionable Central School of Speech Training and Dramatic Art. When Heald learned that Olivier would have to make his own financial way, he advised against applying to the RADA—the tuition was simply too steep. The Central

School, on the other hand, provided a limited number of scholarships to youngsters of exceptional talent, and an additional modest annual living subsidy for those without any financial resources. Heald, confident of young Laurence's talent for the stage and certain that no amount of persuasion could redirect him toward a career in the Church, had contacts at the Central School. He promised to recommend Laurence as a scholarship student.

The Reverend Heald carried through on his promise. In June 1924, upon leaving St. Edward's, Laurence was told to show up at the Central School for the requisite scholarship audition. For his test he chose the durable "Seven Ages of Man" speech, rehearsing it for several days beforehand under Heald's guidance. On the appointed day he arrived at the school, which was located in South Kensington alongside London's famous Royal Albert Hall. With an aplomb that was remarkable for a seventeen-year-old, he recited his speech before an audience of one—a redoubtable Irishwoman named Elsie Fogerty, the school's founder-director and one of the theatrical community's more colorful characters.

Elsie Fogerty, in her late fifties at the time, was a onetime actress whose lack of any physical attraction—many have described her as physically repulsive—had driven her from the stage into teaching. What she missed in comeliness, however, she more than made up for in linguistic ability and a fervor for correct stage speech. She had long served as a vocal coach for many leading English stage performers and was, when the young Olivier first encountered her, among the theatre's most celebrated "gurus."

She had established the Central School of Speech Training and Dramatic Art ten years before as a private enterprise in order to capitalize on her reputation as a voice teacher in the professional theatre. Much to her dismay, until 1924 the school had attracted few students of genuine theatrical talent. These had gravitated mostly to the RADA. The Central School had become, instead, a repository of students— mostly young girls—who were interested in flirting with a theatrical career or whose parents felt that a year of speech and dramatic training would round out their education.

When Elsie Fogerty watched Laurence Olivier give his audition speech, she sensed that she had caught a special talent—raw, to be sure, but a talent nevertheless. Olivier overacted shamefully, much as he had done in his role of Puck in *A Midsummer Night's Dream* the year before, punctuating the speech with wild gestures and sudden, illogical movements about the stage. But a basic, broad talent shone through all the posturing. Elsie Fogerty had inspected the boy before he mounted the stage and was amazed at the transformation that took place once he was under lights. Since he was wearing a baggy, hand-me-down suit, his frail body was well concealed. But his dull, placid face took on much more interesting angles and planes beneath the stage illumination than it possessed in normal light. Moreover, although his movements were naive and trite, they possessed a fluidity and grace that the boy lacked offstage. Finally there was his voice—clear as a bell, without any of the idiosyncratic regional strains and dialect peculiarities that marred the vocal effects of so many novice actors in England. It was a naturally musical voice, resonant and lyric, produced from the chest rather than the throat—a tribute, no doubt, to the years of choir training Fogerty had been told the boy received. It was a voice made for Shakespeare, for Shaw, for every playwright who had written for the effect of speech as well as for intricacy of plot and complexity of character.

Although she had letters of recommendation for a scholarship from Reverend Heald and family friend Sybil Thorndike, Elsie Fogerty later claimed that even without them she would have awarded Olivier free tuition, plus the fifty-pound yearly living stipend, solely on the basis of his audition.

In 1924, fifty pounds a year was roughly equivalent to two hundred and fifty dollars in American currency, less than seventy cents a day, although seventy cents a day then purchased much more than it does today. Nevertheless, Olivier, in accepting the offer, consigned himself to a penurious existence in order to study at the Central School. Starting in July of 1924, he rented a cheap, tiny room in Paddington, miles away from the school, and commuted by foot to his classes each day.

Classes consisted of a daily round of speech training, makeup, acting, movement, fencing, gymnastics, lighting, stage design, drama history, scenery painting and the like. Olivier plunged into them with an enthusiasm that apparently turned in short order into superior disdain, according to a student who knew him at the time.

"The school was made up mostly of girls," she says. "I don't believe there were more than four or five boys enrolled. Larry was by far the most prepossessing of the boys, and although he didn't show an excessive interest in us, he was certainly the object of our interest and fascination. He changed very rapidly during the first few months. When we first saw him he was nervous, shy, withdrawn. But he got hold of the place very fast, and in no time he was king of the roost. He became very

33

affected with himself and spent much of his time demonstrating how bored he was by all the rather routine classes. Among the male students and teachers, many were flaming homosexuals. Larry was generally absorbed in changing his appearance and making cutting remarks about the school. There may be no particular significance in his relating, it seemed, much more happily to the males than the females."[2]

The question of Olivier's youthful, sexual preferences has long been the subject of speculation in and out of the theatre. In November 1924 he was given a walk-on part—his first paying role—in a London play produced by and starring one of his Central School teachers, an actor named Henry Oscar. In the memory of some, Oscar was a homosexual—not at all an unusual status among English actors—who took more than a professional shine to Olivier. There is no evidence that Olivier reciprocated Oscar's apparent feelings.

Olivier dropped out of Miss Fogerty's school in the spring of 1925, not long after his eighteenth birthday, to take a small part for the summer in a one-act play in the seaside resort of Brighton. It was there that he began his physical transformation, exercising vigorously on the beach every day in the company of several friends and appearing on stage at night. At the end of the summer he returned to his sparse room in London's Paddington district and set out in quest of further stage work.

One of the friends he had made was actor Alan Webb, a few years older. According to Webb, it was as a result of their friendship that Olivier obtained his next acting job. "I had signed on with a little traveling repertory troupe for the 1925 winter season. It was directed by a lady named Lena Ashwell, and though stationed in London, our principal work was to travel about the outlying towns giving performances of the classics in schools and church halls. The pay was miserable and the conditions worse, but what was one to do?—we took work where we could find it. As we were about to start the season, several of the players dropped out for better opportunities, and I got Larry in as a last-minute substitute.

"He didn't last, though. Much to my embarrassment he was sacked for fooling about on stage during a performance of *Julius Caesar*. In those days he took rather an amateurish approach to stage work. He was a cut-up, ever seeking attention and making trouble for himself—what you hear people in Hollywood call a 'wiseacre.' Of course, we were all cut-ups after a fashion. None of us took what we were doing very seriously, since we were all aiming for the West End and this was as far from the West End as we could be without being in South Africa or Australia. However, most of us tried to be diligent during actual performances.

"Not Larry, though. He was in his mischievous period. For instance, if I was giving an important speech and he was downstage with his back to the audience, facing me, he would silently mug and roll his eyes about, or do something else outrageous with his face or hands to distract my attention and try to send me up in my lines. I finally had to remonstrate with him, but it did little good. He was hell-bent on causing trouble, and more often than not he succeeded. I loved the boy dearly, but I can say in all honesty that I was relieved when he was given the sack."[3]

Word of Olivier's firing, along with stories, apparently, of other misadventures during his year in London, got back to his father, who was still living in Letchworth. According to Sybil Thorndike, by then one of the West End's leading actresses, she and her husband, actor-producer Lewis Casson, received an urgent visit from the elder Olivier. Wasn't there anything they could do to divert his son from the dubious road he had embarked on? Had Gerard known the evils to which Laurence would be exposed, he would never have permitted him to pursue an acting career. Now, it seemed, Laurence was less interested in serious acting than in making a fool of himself and casting shame on the Olivier name.

Something had to be done. Would the Cassons help? Gerard appealed to Sybil Thorndike's friendship with the late Agnes Olivier. "It was you, after all," he added, "who spoke so highly of Laurence as a potential actor when he was back at All Saints."

Sybil Thorndike, then forty-two, agreed to talk to Olivier. She summoned him a few days later and said, "What are you up to, young man? I hear the most dreadful things."

Olivier, embarrassed, ill at ease, mumbled something about seeking an audition with Gerald du Maurier, London's leading matinee idol and prime advocate of the new naturalistic style of acting.

"Don't be an utter fool," said Thorndike. "Gerald's all right, but he's not someone whose shadow you want to grow up in."

Thorndike was struck by how much Olivier resembled his mother, with, as she would say later, "that very gypsy face, its darkly sullen but marvelously expressive eyes."

"You have it in you to become a fine actor," she went on. "But you are wasting your time if all your ambition amounts to is to emulate du

Maurier. You must decide what it is you want to be. A dilettante, such as I understand you are busy being now with all your friends? Or a true man of the theatre? If you choose the former, then be gone with you. If the latter, then we can help you."

Help him how? Olivier inquired.

Lewis Casson, Thorndike's husband, had been listening. Now he stepped in, explaining that he was putting together a major London production of Shakespeare's *Henry VIII* for the 1925–26 winter season, to be followed by a revival of the verse play *The Cenci* by Shelley. "I will give you some understudy work and an assistant stage manager's job for the season—three pounds a week. If you behave yourself and do your work well, I might even give you a small part in each play."

Three pounds (fifteen dollars) a week was more than Olivier had ever earned. He gratefully, modestly assented. "There's one other thing," Casson said. "I want you to give up the crowd you've been hanging about with. They are not my kind of people and I'll not have anyone working for me who associates with them. I would not hire a one of them—insincere fops and dandies—and I will not hire anyone who plays their game. So, make up your mind. If you really want to work in a professional theatre with experienced professionals from whom you can learn something, put an end to the things you have been doing. If you want to spend the rest of your days marked as pitiable *farceur,* then reject my offer and go back to your friends."[4]

Olivier had not been spoken to so sternly since the days when his father used to hector him. Yet there was something different in the lecture he had just received—a detachment, a lack of anger, an earnestness that seemed almost to be affection—that impressed him, indeed overpowered him. He instinctively recognized that there was validity in Casson's remarks and, what's more, behind the bluntness, a sense of caring. But greater than that was the feeling of shame he felt at having been found out—the life he had so assiduously sought to hide from his father was obviously common knowledge after all.

"I may be wrong," Sybil Thorndike was to say later, "but my guess is that it came as some relief to young Larry to know that we knew he was up to some incorrigible things. I suspect that he was not very happy with himself for whatever he was doing but had been able to find no way to extricate himself. But when we brought it out into the open with him, it was as though he had conceded his foolishness to himself. He could then give it up and get on with more serious things. Oh, I don't delude myself into believing that he just dropped it like that and suddenly became a devoted student of the theatre. But he did take the job in Lewis's productions, and he did apply himself to it with humility and seriousness."

The jobs in *Henry VIII* and *The Cenci,* which carried Olivier into the early spring of 1926, exposed him for the first time to working daily with a group of experienced and thoroughly professional actors. Casson made good on his promise and cast Olivier in small parts—servants— in each play. But his principal duties were those of assistant stage manager—ensuring that the actors were called on time, looking after the props, supervising scenery and lighting changes, and keeping order generally backstage.

"Two important things happened to Larry as a result of that experience," says a member of the company today. "The first was that he learned in very quick fashion that well-known theatrical professionals took their work very seriously indeed. Jokes, pranks, pratfalls—the sort of thing he'd been used to—were not tolerated. He saw how responsible the actors felt toward their work, toward the script, toward their audiences. He was given a good bit of responsibility backstage and adjusted very rapidly to the earnestness and spirit of things.

"There was one moment early on in dress rehearsals when he fell down on the job—failed to have an actor ready for an entrance cue, something like that. Well, he was given a withering dressing down by one of the principal actors in *Henry VIII* in front of the entire company. After that he never again fumbled. In fact, he went in the opposite direction and became almost overbearing in his approach to the job.

"Also, he was exposed for the first time, I think, to the way in which professionals lived and breathed the theatre. There was a never-ending stream of talk among the actors about engagements past, engagements future, where who appeared when and in what part, who was going to this audition, who was going to that, who was being replaced in what West End production, and so on. Much of it was shop talk, but much was also serious discussion about various plays, Shakespeare, Restoration comedy, directors, actors, productions, what have you—all from actors' points of view and not in the sense of academic criticism or classroom analysis.

"Larry was often around to listen in on the discussions. I think he not only began to learn a great deal about the theatre in a practical sense, but he became genuinely interested in it for the first time. It was here that his theatrical intelligence and aptitude were first given life. Larry later confessed to me that he was something of a late bloomer, that until he came into that production of *Henry VIII* he hadn't really understood what the theatre was all about, hadn't understood it as a medium not just of entertainment but enlightenment. And, too, that it represented more than simply a forum for performers to feed their egos. He had had two years of fooling about in the theatre without getting any sense of his own direction. Now it began to dawn on him what he was up against —a long and great and serious tradition, and hundreds of other young actors seeking to excel within the framework of that tradition. I think you could say that period in *Henry VIII* gave him his first true sense of his calling."[5]

The second significant thing to happen to Olivier as a result of his job in the Casson company was, evidently, the final awakening of his masculine nature. Angela Baddeley, who fifty years later would become widely celebrated for her role as Mrs. Bridges, the irascible but warm-hearted cook in television's *Upstairs, Downstairs* series, was then a beauti-ful twenty-one-year-old cast in the role of Anne Bullen in the Casson production of *Henry VIII.* Although recently married, the young actress had a flirtatious manner and an infectious laugh that combined to at once entrance and confuse the nineteen-year-old Olivier.

A few tentative encounters with girls prior to his joining the Casson group had ended disastrously, thanks mostly to Olivier's timidity and conversational ineptitude. He was determined to press on, however. When he met Miss Baddeley, whose openness and playful cheeriness had a way of putting awkward young men instantly at their ease, he promptly fell in love.

"I never knew Larry's mother, of course," says the same company member, "but I heard from Larry that she had been a wonderful woman with a deliciously playful sense of humor when her husband wasn't around, and a great sensitivity to others. Well, Angela was very much like that as a young woman—a great, mischievous sense of humor, and a naturally affectionate way about her with people she liked, and she liked everybody. She might have been thought an outrageous flirt be-cause she was very ebullient and huggy. She always got up close to people when she talked to them and was forever touching them, men and women alike. But it was all done innocently, with males almost in a sisterly fashion.

"Well, Larry took it as something more serious than that. I don't know, one day she might have passed him in the wings, on her way to make an entrance, and squeezed his forearm or something. He had already begun to worship her from afar, I think, thoroughly discouraged

38

by his knowledge that she was already married, but adoring all the same
—probably because he saw so many of his mother's qualities in her. In
any event, that friendly squeeze on the forearm, or whatever it was,
Larry took as a silent signal that he had some special attraction to
Angela. It must have been like a jolt of electricity, for thereafter he
became like some old soppy-eyed basset hound trailing around in her
wake.

"This went on for weeks, all during the run of *Henry VIII.* All Angela
had to do was glance at Larry and you could see him stiffen, half-
embarrassed, half-thrilled. I don't doubt that Angela began to grow wise
to what was going on, and I don't doubt that recognizing how he felt
about her, she did tease him a bit with a little more touching and
hugging. But that just made him soppier and more adoring.

"All of this occurred in the busy-bee activity of backstage. Finally,
one day, Larry found himself alone with Angela in the empty theatre.
As I recall, she'd come in on Sunday morning to retrieve something
she'd left behind the night before, and he was there cleaning up the
dressing rooms. Apparently Larry found what she had come to retrieve
and she gave him a grateful kiss on the cheek, a 'dear boy' and all that.
He may have thought this a 'come hither' gesture and tried to kiss her
back, tried to smother her with kisses, all the while panting heatedly
about how much he loved her.

"Angela was a cagey old trouper when she told me the story, and
according to her, she didn't succumb to his advances but instead disen-
tangled herself from Larry's embrace, no doubt with dignity."[6]

6

The Birth of a Career

DENYS BLAKELOK was another struggling novice actor in mid-twenties London, six years older than Olivier but, like him, the son of a cleric. The two got to know one another in 1926 and struck up a lifelong friendship. Blakelok has written extensively about Olivier, and he once said: "Larry came out of that season of *Henry VIII* and *The Cenci* throbbing with a desire to make something of himself in the West End. Perhaps he was a wee bit overbearing, perhaps he believed out of some youthful conceit and impatience that he had learned all he needed to learn and was ready to explode full-blown onto the theatrical scene. I know he suffered a rude surprise. He was all over the place auditioning for roles, but he was turned down time and again. It was probably because of his looks. He had gained a lot of confidence in himself and was in the process of building up his body and working on his voice, but he was still thoroughly disheveled-looking and even wild in appearance—rough-hewn and with no sense for clothes. It was a time when the modern plays being done in the West End were all frothy comedies and fey farces, and the only actors producers were looking for were the slicked-hair, dashing, glib types. It's my understanding that he finally went back to Sybil Thorndike in despair and said: 'What can I do?' Sybil put him straight. She said: 'Forget the West End for a while. Have you heard of Birmingham?' "[1]

•

The Birmingham Repertory Theatre was England's most celebrated avant-garde theatrical organization. Founded before the war by businessman-turned-theatrical-impresario Barry Jackson in the industrial city of Birmingham, one hundred miles north of London, "The Birmingham," as it came to be called, had grown rapidly into a vigorous training ground for young actors, playwrights and directors. Entrepreneur Jackson had, by 1925, expanded the theatre's influence throughout the country by means of touring companies; he had also established a permanent theatre in London, where he put on a number of "experimental" new plays and modern-dress versions of the classics.* A singular array of distinguished English actors have had their basic training at the Birmingham, from Sir Cedric Hardwicke and Donald Wolfit in the repertory's early days to Richard Burton and Albert Finney in more recent years. Thanks to the advice of Sybil Thorndike, who was fast becoming his chief mentor, Laurence Olivier joined the ranks of the Birmingham.

"Had he not," said Denys Blakelok, "had he simply pursued a career as a West End actor, I doubt seriously that he would ever have achieved what he did in this country and become the theatrical institution he is. I was with the Birmingham for some time myself. It was much more than just a performing organization. Being there was like going every day to the most advanced school of theatre in the world. One was thoroughly immersed in the theatre and learned more in a week about acting styles and dramatic history than one would in years of plodding around the West End. The company was loaded with competition, and it created an atmosphere in which everyone tried to outdo everyone else, not just in performing ability but in theatrical knowledge and sophistication as well. Larry took to this competition like a fish to water. Some people were eventually defeated by it, but it excited him enormously

*The Birmingham Repertory was comparable in its impact on British theatre, in the 1920s, to the influence on the theatre in America of New York's Actors Studio during the late 1940s and 1950s.

and drove him on and on with ever more intensity to stand out."[2]

Sybil Thorndike knew Barry Jackson and recommended Olivier to him for a production the Birmingham was preparing to introduce in London in April 1926. An avante-garde mystery melodrama called *The Marvelous History of Saint Bernard,* the play had already been cast except for a few small roles. Olivier auditioned as a possible understudy and was hired, and given, in addition, the tiny part of a minstrel. The play, mounted at the Kingsway Theatre, was a critical success but was forced to close in June due to a nationwide work stoppage—known in Britain as the General Strike—that crippled the city for several weeks. Olivier was not noticed by the critics in his minor role. But he impressed Jackson enough to receive an offer to become a permanent member of the Birmingham.

"Larry almost turned it down," said his friend Blakelok. "It wasn't a matter of the low wages either. It was simply that instead of taking him straight up to Birmingham, Jackson wanted him first to go out and join one of the theatre's touring companies, which was spending the summer at a seaside resort. Larry had done that a year or two before, and he had no taste for another summer by the sea. Had he persisted, Jackson would probably never have allowed him into Birmingham. But then Larry discovered that Cedric Hardwicke was playing the lead in the touring play. Cedric was by then quite a star. It was an opportunity for Larry to rub shoulders with an actor of high reputation. So he finally agreed to go."[3]

The resort was Clacton-by-Sea, and the first person Olivier met the afternoon he arrived was an attractive actress in her early twenties named Muriel Hewitt. Still on the rebound from his experience with Angela Baddeley, but now with a little more confidence in himself, he once again felt the stirrings of desire after a few minutes' conversation with Miss Hewitt, who had told him most charmingly, "Call me Kit. Everyone does."

Olivier was given a day to work into the small part he had been assigned, replacing another actor, in the comedy the Birmingham troupe was performing at Clacton. Kit Hewitt volunteered to rehearse him in his lines the next morning, and Olivier was overwhelmed as much by her friendliness as her physical attributes. He spent the night alternately memorizing his lines and contemplating a romance with the young actress. When they met the next morning, Olivier was atremble with anticipation. He had been told often that his eyes were his most attractive feature and had already fallen into the habit of employing them to signal his desires.

"Those eyes!" another actress was later to say about Olivier as a nineteen-year-old. "They were excruciatingly seductive, but also jarring because they seemed somehow totally at odds with the rest of him. Bedroom eyes in a collier's [coal miner's] face, if you know what I mean. But in those days, as he grew to perceive the power of his eyes, their effect on people, especially on women, he learned to use them to great seductive effect. More than one young actress, including myself, succumbed at one time or another."[4]

Not Kit Hewitt, though. Olivier learned to his chagrin that she was married to another young member of the company, Ralph Richardson.

Notwithstanding that, within a few weeks Richardson and Olivier became fast friends, and Olivier looked forward to going back to Birmingham with "Ralphie" and his wife when the Clacton engagement ended. It was not to be, however. When the troupe packed up to return to Birmingham in August, Olivier, still an apprentice, was assigned by Jackson to tour for several months in one of the company's most popular commercial successes, a bittersweet comedy called *The Farmer's Wife.*[5]

Olivier's disappointment was assuaged when he was given the important part of Richard Coaker, the lovesick young farmer of the play's title. Having recently experienced successive bouts of lovesickness in his own life, Olivier, still only nineteen, was able to bring some verisimilitude to the role. In his first significant acting part since his school days, he acquitted himself well in the eyes of Britain's provincial audiences, although certain members of the touring company complained about his tendency to overact.

One of them said: "Larry was full of himself on that tour. He was fine under direction in rehearsals, but once out on the road, where there was no close supervision, he began consistently to come out of character and act for effect, experimenting with his lines at each performance and trying to milk the laughs with mugging and posturing. He felt, for the first time, I suppose, the power of playing a central part. And he was intoxicated by the ability that gave him to get reactions from the audience. In retrospect, I expect it was a good thing, for it did evolve into a great deal of the inventiveness and daring that later would become his personal stamp as an actor. But at the time it was totally undisciplined and indiscriminate, and was a pain in the backside to the other actors. Not that the others weren't given to hamming it up. But never as outrageously as Larry. Finally it got to the point that word reached Barry Jackson back in Birmingham, and orders came back for Larry to cease and desist. *The Farmer's Wife* was an enormously popular play, and those annual tours of it were great money-makers for Jackson and the Rep."[6]

Chastened, Olivier finished the tour just before Christmas of 1926 and was summoned finally to Birmingham by Jackson. The producer, recently knighted for his theatrical achievements, gave Olivier a stiff lecture on an actor's responsibilities. Many of the senior people in the Birmingham had been after Jackson to let Olivier go, he told the young actor. But he was inclined to give him another chance. That chance would consist of Olivier spending a probationary six months at the main theatre in Birmingham, where he was to apply himself to learning stage discipline as well as lines and acting technique.

Thereafter Olivier did better, although some of his contemporaries have said over the years that he did not warm very quickly to the task Jackson set for him. Cedric Hardwicke once recalled him as a "noisy young actor, forever drawing attention to himself with the most naive, overdone tricks—yet there was something about him that told you that once he got control of himself he would amount to something fine on the stage."

Ralph Richardson described him as "a cocky young pup" in those days, "full of fire and energy, and very badly needing of someone to calm him down. He later told me the reason he was so insufferable was because he was so afraid of being neglected, going unnoticed. His way of dealing with the competitive pressures at the Rep was to storm about making a racket in any role he was rehearsing. He drove Ayliff, one of our best directors, crazy with his antics and arguments over interpretation. Ayliff was the principal director that season, and I don't remember a production Larry was in that he didn't challenge the old boy on some point of stage business or line delivery."[7]

"Larry Olivier made himself generally obnoxious," Eileen Beldon, one of the Birmingham's leading actresses, recalled years later. "Frankly, I couldn't stand him. More than once I pleaded with Jackson to get rid of him. He was slovenly and hi-falutin. Of course, I realize now that he was just a young boy trying to prove himself, and that much of his behavior came from the fact that he was so scared and felt so far out of his element. At least, that's what Larry told me recently. I have no reason to doubt it."[8]

Not everyone found the young actor so impossible. "Larry was with us throughout 1927," says another Birmingham veteran. "He appeared in several of our productions that year. My memory of him is of a young man who was unaware of the enormous gifts he possessed. Why, all he had to do was walk onto the stage and the eyes and interest of the audience would automatically rivet on him. True, being unaware of his power, he often went to excesses in trying to make himself stand out. But he didn't really have to. He simply had this great physical presence and magnetism. I think the unkind comments you hear about him from others he worked with come more from professional jealousy than anything else. The boy was a natural and no one had to look at him more than once to realize it."[9]

Once Olivier was accepted by the Birmingham, his rise within the company was meteoric. He soon found his romantic fortunes changing too. "Part of the reason Larry was so resented by other male actors in the Rep," said actress Jane Welsh, "was because he was so attractive to the younger females. He had this naive, almost innocent exuberance and sensitivity that were very appealing. And he was very courtly in manner. He was an astonishing mix of boy and man, and many of us wanted to both love him and mother him."[10]

It was, in fact, Miss Welsh who turned out to be Olivier's first genuine romance. By all evidence, the affair began in mid-1927 in a series of fits and starts. But once they got over Olivier's inexperience, it became an intense relationship, albeit short-lived.

The break-up of Olivier's relationship with Jane Welsh came late in 1927, just as Barry Jackson was preparing to stage a series of new plays in London for the beginning of the 1928 season. Olivier pleaded with Jackson for a part in one of the London productions. Jackson offered him a small role in the avant-garde American play *The Adding Machine* by Elmer Rice. Olivier thereupon moved to London with the other Birmingham players who were appearing in the play and plunged into rehearsals.

The play opened at the small Royal Court Theatre in London's Sloane Square on January 9, 1928, and on this, his second professional appearance in the British capital, Olivier was noticed by the critics. Although his part was no larger than his minstrel in *Saint Bernard,* he had to play a key scene in a graveyard. All the actors were required to speak with American accents, and Olivier's character called for him to talk with a distinctively New York tinge to his voice. The play was generally lambasted in the press for the poor quality of its performers' accents. But Arnold Bennett, then one of London's leading drama critics, singled out Olivier as an exception, writing that the young actor had "by far and away the best Americanese." And St. John Ervine, another important critic, said in the London *Observer* that "Mr. Laurence Olivier as the young man who accompanies Judy O'Grady into the graveyard gave a very good performance indeed—the best, I think, in the play. He had little to do, but he acted."

Denys Blakelok later recalled that Olivier was particularly thrilled by these notices because he had worked so hard in researching and acquiring the proper accent—much to the derision of other actors in the play. "It was a vindication of his purposefulness and instinct for the correct way to approach his part. And it set the tone for his future career. Larry would almost always insist that his approach to a role was the right one, notwithstanding what others—directors, fellow actors— might have to say about it."[11]

Indirectly, Olivier had Blakelok to thank for his New York accent. Blakelok had been appearing in a West End production of *The Silver Cord* with the middle-aged American actress Clare Eames when Olivier came down from Birmingham to rehearse for *The Adding Machine.* Olivier had complained to Blakelok about the difficulty he was having in capturing the proper accent, whereupon Blakelok suggested he seek Miss Eames's advice and arranged an introduction. As Blakelok recounted it in his 1967 book, *Round the Next Corner,* Clare Eames was more than happy to tutor Olivier. And she was singularly impressed with the young actor's determination and intensity. "Clare Eames said to me at that time, 'Larry looks down at me with the eyes of a conqueror.' He was just beginning to be conscious of the dynamic power that was in him."[12]

Having been noticed by two of London's chief critics for his vocal proficiency, and having seen that proficiency equated in print by one of them to real acting, Olivier immediately went to work on improving his voice, which up to that time he had taken more or less for granted. At twenty-one, his voice was generally mid-register and tended toward a monotone, while his natural accent remained one of upper-class affectation such as he had first learned at home and in school, and had then refined to emulate the leading romantic actors of the West End. Vocal technique—accents, timbre, enunciation, lingual tricks, tonal idiosyncrasies—as a way of defining character rapidly became important to him.

Olivier's notices in *The Adding Machine* prompted Sir Barry Jackson to cast him in the Birmingham's next London production in February, a modern-dress presentation of Shakespeare's *Macbeth.* As a result, Olivier became aware of not just *Macbeth,* but also all of Shakespeare's verse writing as a useful tool for cultivating his voice. Consequently, while appearing as Malcolm in *Macbeth,* he began to spend an hour or more each day backstage declaiming speeches from that and other Shakespearean works, testing and exercising his voice, experimenting with vocal techniques of his own devising and expanding his lung power.

"If genius is ten percent inspiration and ninety percent hard work," Jackson said later, "then one can understand why many people have taken Larry Olivier to be a genius. Normally, up in Birmingham the actors were kept hard at work and had little time to relax. But when they came down from the Rep to appear in one of our London productions, they tended to spend their spare time on diversions, like soldiers on furlough. Not Larry. While other performers were out carousing in London's pubs, he would be back in the empty dressing rooms reading aloud from this, that or the next play. He became monkish about it, eschewing the companionship of the others in the company to spend long hours by himself working on his voice."[13]

It was not only his voice that he devoted long hours to working on. He continued to spend time in gymnasiums building up his torso and legs. By the time he appeared in grey flannel suit and felt fedora as Malcolm in *Macbeth,* remembered Denys Blakelok, "he had added a good amount of bulk. Larry reached only five feet ten or eleven in height, full grown. But when he appeared on stage, he conveyed a physical authority that made one think he was very much taller and quite real."

Macbeth in modern dress failed to please the critics, but again Olivier was noticed, this time more generously. A scene in which he played against Macduff was called by one critic "electrifying." Jessica Tandy, then a young actress in her first year with the Birmingham, remembered being startled by watching Olivier in the scene. "One left the theatre with an exhilarating feeling of having seen the beginnings of an actor of enormous potential."[14]

7

Leading Man at Twenty-one

D ENYS BLAKELOK said: "During
that Birmingham run at the Court, they put on a different play each month.
Larry was in just about all of them, but there was one in particular that
seemed to bring about his final metamorphosis from scruffy, homely ado-
lescent to dashing, handsome adult. He went to great lengths to get the
part, but once he got it and performed it, you knew that you were looking
at England's next star actor."[1]

•

The play was Alfred Lord Tennyson's clumsy fifty-year-old verse
tragedy, *Harold,* about the last Saxon king of England. It was the result
of poet Tennyson's desire to write a play in the fashion of Shakespeare,
but it had not been performed in years because of its inherent lack of
drama. Barry Jackson, however, insisted that it deserved a revival, primarily because of its language.

Although the play was a gloomy, undynamic blunderbuss, its principal character, Harold, was a dream-come-true for any actor with lead-ing-man pretensions. Harold, with more than three thousand lines, was onstage throughout; moreover, he was drawn as a highly romantic but doomed figure—an athletic warrior, a sensuous lover, a fiery ruler. The risk of such a desirable opportunity was that in the hands of any but the most skilled, experienced performer, the part could turn its actor into a laughingstock.

Olivier was still appearing in *Macbeth* when Jackson announced that the Birmingham company would stage *Harold* two months later, in April of 1927. "A strange thing happened," recalls Ralph Richardson. "There was a distinct absence of the normal jockeying among the Rep's actors to get the part of Harold. We all thought Jackson was out of his mind to include the play in the season, and everyone—well, almost everyone —was afraid of the role because of its ponderousness and the ponder-ousness of the play itself. But not Larry. He was aching for a lead role, and when he saw everyone's reluctance about Harold, he leapt eagerly into the breach."[2]

Persuading Jackson to cast him as Harold would not be easy, Olivier realized, since the Birmingham's head was already on record as saying the role demanded an experienced romantic leading man; indeed, he had begun a search outside the Repertory's ranks for just such an actor. While still performing in *Macbeth* and rehearsing his modest role in the London company's next production, *Back to Methuselah,* Olivier obtained a printed copy of *Harold* and started memorizing a few of the title character's key speeches. Late in March, a few days before *Back to Methuselah* was to open, the company held a full-scale dress rehearsal at which Jackson and the director assigned to *Harold,* H. K. Ayliff, were present. Present too was George Bernard Shaw, the author of *Back to Methuselah,* who was supervising the play's staging.

When Olivier made his first entrance, playing the part of Marcellus, instead of saying the Shaw character's lines he burst into a three-minute speech from *Harold.* At first everyone was outraged at what they took to be a childish prank. But their ire rapidly turned to fascination as they watched Olivier, dressed in his Marcellus costume, float about the set of *Methuselah* while speaking the verse of Tennyson's Harold.

When he was finished, silence descended on the theatre as Shaw, Jackson and Ayliff looked at each other and the actors on the stage milled about in confusion. Then Shaw, familiar with Tennyson's play, called up to Olivier, who was edging his way offstage in embarrassment. "Young man, you mispronounced the word 'deleterious.' " With that the tension was broken, and after everyone had a laugh the *Methuselah* rehearsal resumed. Afterward, Shaw and Jackson went backstage and confronted the contrite Olivier. "It's all right," Shaw said to him. "I've recommended to Sir Barry that you play Harold. He agrees. Now, I trust, you will return your full attention to Marcellus for the next month."[3]

Olivier had the part. During March, while playing Marcellus in the evenings, he rehearsed *Harold* in the mornings and afternoons, learning the remainder of his three thousand lines and countless cues in less than a week. "It's often jokingly said, but true," Ralph Richardson once remarked. "The first mark of a good repertory actor is his ability to memorize his part in no time. In this respect alone Larry was a genius —better than any of the rest of us. No matter how much other talent one has, one can not become an actor without the ability to memorize lines. It would have taken me a month to get a part like Harold down to the point where I could do an entire rehearsal without help. Larry did it in a week and was letter perfect."[4]

Harold was a bench mark in the budding career of Laurence Olivier. Cedric Hardwicke, still the Birmingham's leading actor, was starring in the production of *Back to Methuselah* while *Harold* was in rehearsal. "Larry Olivier took a great risk in going after the part of Harold," he commented some time ago. "In the first place he had to carry the unwieldy production. If he botched it up, the entire thing would come crashing down on his ears. He would have been ruined as an actor for years to follow. In the second place, even if he shone, the play was so bad that he would have received little credit. He had everything to lose and almost nothing to gain. But that was Olivier. He was a rather shy, diffident young man outside the theatre, but he was growing a great amount of self-confidence—hubris, even—within the company. In my considered opinion, he was stupid to play Harold because it provided him with too many opportunities to fall on his face. It just goes to show what my opinion was worth."[5]

Sir Barry Jackson later said, "Actually, I was criticized severely within the company for putting Olivier in the part. Everyone said he wasn't ready for it. What I didn't tell them was that after I was unable to find a more experienced actor, I decided that he would be a good gamble. Why? Because I knew by then that Larry was going to be an important actor. I also knew that the play was going to be a disaster to the critics. Now, I could have thrown an already-established actor into the role, but a familiar face, no matter how good, would have done little to dispel the critics' negativism about the play. But a new face! A young,

talented actor making his debut in a leading role—that would be something else. The theatre-going public in London went to the theatre
primarily to see actors, not plays. And although the critics maintained
a haughtier attitude, they in fact operated out of the same impulse. I
reckoned, then, that with a new face, a new name playing Harold, the
critics would be distracted from focusing on the faults of the play and
would concentrate most of their energies on the performance of the
unknown actor playing the lead. And I was right. That's just what
occurred."[6]

Jackson, somewhat of a theatrical purist, had never been accused
before of being a commercial showman. But it was a showman's strategy. Unfortunately he neglected another rule of showmanship—never
open on the same night as another play. *Harold* opened on the same April
evening in 1928 that the fabulously successful imported American
farce, Anita Loos's *Gentlemen Prefer Blondes,* premiered in London. As a
consequence, all the city's important critics missed Olivier's opening
performance; only a few second-string newspaper reviewers covered it.
"Of course," said someone who knew Jackson, "perhaps that was his
true showmanship—to keep the critics away from *Harold* altogether and
save himself, and Olivier, from embarrassment."

Jackson *was* right, nevertheless: the few critics who came to see
Harold largely ignored the drama's inherent inertia and concentrated on
the performances. They particularly lauded Olivier in the leading role
and heralded him as easily the best actor in the entire cast, although still
given to a tendency to overact—a defect they attributed to his inexperience. St. John Ervine, for instance, after seeing the play in its second
performance, had this to say in the *Observer:* "Mr. Laurence Olivier, the
Harold, varies in his performance, but he is excellent on the whole and
has the makings of a very considerable actor in him. His faults are those
of inexperience rather than of ineffectiveness. The good performance he
gave in *Macbeth,* added to the good performance he gives in *Harold,*
makes me believe that when romantic and poetic drama return to their
proper place in the theatre, Mr. Olivier will be ready to occupy the
position of a distinguished romantic actor."

About Ervine's review, Olivier said in 1973, "In those days with
the Birmingham it was our habit to disdain critics' notices, not even read
them. We all felt that the critics knew nothing about acting and that we
could learn nothing from reading their assessments of our performances.
But that was the public posture we held. Secretly we all read the notices
and were quite often grossly affected by them. When I read the *Observer*

notice, I was rather more insulted than pleased. It struck me as condescending and patronizing and I didn't like it at all. Oh, I knew I still had a good deal to learn, but the bit about inexperience stuck in my craw. And, too, the line about me having the potential to become a 'distinguished romantic actor.' In my view Ervine was doing nothing more than revealing his prejudice against the direction in which the theatre was going, his nostalgia for the theatrical pap of the old West End. More than anything else, I think, his classifying me as a potential romantic actor of the kind I viewed as old hat encouraged me to abandon any lingering wish I might have had to become a conventional West End actor. London had actors such as Martin Harvey and Henry Ainley, who were the darlings of the West End. I had admired them to a certain extent, but more for their success in the theatre than for their ability as actors. Indeed, I shamelessly copied them whenever I thought it appropriate. But after *Harold,* I no longer had any desire to do what they did —spend my life playing in treacly romantic dramas and comedies. I had been picking up an ever-increasing appreciation for the classic literature of the theatre, and reading what Ervine had to say pushed me further toward wanting to devote myself to the classics."[7]

Others say that Olivier's retrospective musings of 1973 were not how they saw the Laurence Olivier of 1928 who reveled in his limited *Harold* fame. "Larry was more than anything else intoxicated both by his achievement in carrying off Harold so decently and by the pure, egotistic sense of power he got from the role," thought a member of the company. "Although playing the lead in a quasi-classic drama may have inspired him to seek more classic roles later on, that was not what he got out of *Harold* in the immediate term. What he got out of it was his utter conviction that he was born to be a leading man and could not live without such status. The change in him during and after *Harold* was remarkable. It was like watching a playful, awkward lion cub change into a ferocious, powerful, full-maned adult lion overnight.

"The same thing happened to me when I got my first lead a few years later, so I know the feeling. It's a sense of power and self-importance and an I-can-do-anything-I-want kind of feeling that creeps into you, animal-like, and gives you a wallop of power and self-esteem you've never experienced before. People are actually coming to see you perform, are whistling and cheering, are ogling you enviously on the street. It hits every actor who gets a taste of being the center of attention on stage for an entire play, I suppose, with all the action and dialogue revolving about him. But it hit Larry with an extra force.

"Not that he became imperious or insufferably conceited or anything of that sort. But he *did* change before our eyes. He changed physically and vocally, of course, but most of all he changed in his entire style and personality, offstage and on. Where before he had been one-dimensional as an actor—rambunctious and busy and tending toward shouting—he suddenly became smooth and calm, yet in an authoritative style.

"And this extended to his offstage personality, so that you no longer had a sense of Larry Olivier the rather quiet boy and Larry Olivier the rather noisy actor. Playing in *Harold* gave him a new sense of himself, and the two different personalities merged into a single completely new one. It was a case of the whole becoming greater than its parts. He began to act offstage like a leading man, something of a star. This power he had acquired just took him over and transformed him into a whole new being, mentally, physically and spiritually. It was the fastest case of growing up and growing out I've ever seen."[8]

As high as Olivier soared during his month-long playing of Harold, he plunged just as abruptly when Jackson cast him in a minor role in the Birmingham's next and final presentation of the London season, a modern-dress production of *The Taming of the Shrew.* "I remember talking to him toward the end of *Harold,*" said Jane Welsh, "and he was most upset at having to take such a comedown part." She told of going with Olivier one afternoon to see Ronald Colman in the film version of *Beau Geste,* one of the frothiest romances of the day. Contrary to Olivier's own account, Miss Welsh recalled that Olivier was captivated by Colman's screen persona and the whole idea of becoming the "new Ronald Colman"—as suave and superficial a romantic actor as ever rose to stardom. A few weeks later she saw him in his small role in *The Taming of the Shrew.* He had only one important scene in the modern-dress production, she said, but "he played it like Ronald Colman personified, right down to the pencil moustache, slicked-back hair and syrupy voice. It was hard to tell whether Larry was playing straight or doing a parody. Whichever, he caught everyone's attention and almost stole the play."[9]

Evidently Jane Welsh and Olivier were on their way to a reconciliation during the month's run of *The Taming of the Shrew,* but it lasted no longer than the end of the run. With the closing of *Shrew* in late May, the Birmingham company was slated to return to the Midlands city to regroup and then scatter onto the summer tour circuit. Jane Welsh was cast in a comedy that was to tour during June and July among several seaside resorts in the southwest. She expected Olivier to join the troupe in a second-lead role—an expectation Olivier had encouraged when she arranged a party for his twenty-first birthday during the run of *Shrew.* But after *Shrew* closed, Olivier had second thoughts about spending another summer by the sea. He went to Jackson and begged off.

"For all practical purposes Larry was finished with the Birmingham," explained Peggy Ashcroft. "I was playing in another Birmingham production in London, *Bird in Hand,* and was about to leave to go into something else. Larry came by one day and began to complain about having to go back to Birmingham and undertake another summer tour. The girl who was to replace me was there when he came backstage, and I could see light bulbs going off in his head. Suddenly he started going on about how he had to stay in London, yet how he felt tremendously guilty about telling Barry Jackson that he didn't want to go back to the Rep. Did I have any ideas? He'd heard that Patrick Susands, who was playing opposite me in *Bird in Hand,* might be leaving. Did I think Jackson might replace Patrick with Larry? 'Larry,' I said, 'it's a silly part, no good for your career, no one will know you're in it.' But he grew adamant. 'I'll do anything to stay in London,' he said, all the while eyeing my replacement with profound curiosity while pretending not to."[10]

The replacement was an actress named Jill Esmond. Six months younger than Olivier, dark-haired and slim, she came from a well-known theatrical family, was a graduate of the Royal Academy of Dramatic Arts and had already achieved a measure of fame on her own in the West End as an ingenue. Olivier had seen her in one or two plays but had never met her. Now, close up, he felt familiar stirrings.

A few days later, he screwed up the courage to tell Barry Jackson that he wasn't going to join the Birmingham's summer troupe. He begged for the assignment to replace Susands in *Bird in Hand.* "It's not that I'm ungrateful for all the opportunities you've given me," he told Jackson. "But London's my home now and this is where I must try to make my career."[11] Jackson capitulated and Olivier moved into *Bird in Hand* in mid-June of 1928, learning the part almost overnight.

His role was an inconsequential one, but it afforded him the opportunity to be close to Jill Esmond, who played his female counterpart in the play. This time there were no husbands around to complicate matters. Nevertheless, Olivier learned very quickly that Jill was a fiercely independent young woman with a mind of her own and a tongue to match—at once sardonically witty and tender.

"It would be far-fetched to say that Jill was made in the image of

Larry's mother," a friend of both says. "But he did tell me later on that the reason he fell so hard for her was that she had many of his mother's personality qualities—a great sense of humor, a sharp intelligence that he thought was much more profound than his own, and a no-nonsense approach to life. Jill, although not a great beauty, was attractive enough —in her own way much more attractive than Larry, who still had many rough edges. Larry was just discovering himself sexually, you might say. Jill was rather more sophisticated about that and about life in general. Also she had a great style about her—sincerity, honesty, straightforwardness, none of the cloying sweetness, affectedness and helplessness that most young women of the day exuded. Her sweetness was in her direct way of looking at you and talking to you, in her frank approach to everyone she encountered. Anyway, he fell for all that, and fell hard.

"Jill took to Larry because, although he was still a bit awkward and uncertain of himself socially, he had many of the traits she had. He tended to be blunt and direct, and certainly he was honest and sincere, although he hadn't yet learned to express these qualities in as graceful a way as Jill. And he throbbed with a kind of innocent romantic yearning. For all Jill's realism and down-to-earthness, she was also a romantic with great dreams for herself and her future. She knew what she wanted, which was a life of independence but one she could share with those close to her. She recognized in Larry a similar streak of independence. As she gradually got to know him, she believed that they were cut out to be together. And so, in that very deliberate way she had, she allowed herself to fall in love with him."[12]

It was Jill Esmond's sensible, deliberate manner that caused the twenty-one-year-old Olivier his greatest romantic anguish yet. After three weeks in *Bird in Hand,* when Jill cautiously acknowledged a fondness for Olivier in the face of his repeated declarations of love for her, he demanded that she marry him. She resisted, saying, "Give me time, Larry, after all we hardly know each other."

And so their romance progressed in fits and starts through the summer of 1928. In the meantime the frustrated Olivier rapidly grew bored with his role in *Bird in Hand* and began to look around for something new to do.

An opportunity presented itself when, early in the fall, Olivier learned that producer Basil Dean was planning to mount an expensive stage adaptation of *Beau Geste.* Dean announced that he intended to stage his version with actress Madeleine Carroll in the female lead, and that he was launching a nationwide search to find the perfect young, romantic, athletic actor to play opposite her in the part of Beau.

It seemed an opportunity tailor-made for Olivier. Yet England was overflowing with romantic, athletic actors in their ambitious twenties, and they spilled out of the West End and out of the country's many outlying regional theatres in droves to audition for the part. Olivier had allowed the thin Ronald Colman moustache he had grown for *Macbeth* to thicken for his role in *Bird in Hand*. Now, with Jill Esmond's help, he shaved it back into a pencil-line sliver, oiled back his abundant, naturally curly hair into a smooth, shiny, pancake-thin carpet and plucked another harvest of hairs from his eyebrows. Then he went off to the theatrical offices of Basil Dean for his audition.

Olivier came away thoroughly convinced that he wouldn't get the part—"the competition," as he later said, "was too keen." What he didn't anticipate, however, was that Madeleine Carroll would slip into the Royalty Theatre one matinee afternoon a few days later to watch him perform in *Bird in Hand*, and that she would go back to Dean singing his praise.

Convinced that he was out of the running for *Beau Geste*, Olivier cast about for other opportunities. One came along in November in the form of an offer to perform the lead in what was intended to be a brief showcase staging of a new play that had already been turned down by a number of West End producers. The play was a melancholy World War I battlefield drama called *Journey's End* by an unknown writer named R. C. Sherriff. An equally unknown actor and aspiring director, James Whale, had acquired the rights to the antiwar play and was planning to mount it in a small auditorium during a weekend in the hope that it would gain the attention of London's theatre critics.

At first Olivier expressed no interest. It meant a month of rehearsals during his afternoons off from *Bird in Hand*, time he could better spend with Jill Esmond going to films, wandering through the city's museums and doing the other things a lovesick young man hungered to do to be with his beloved.

But Jill was made of sterner stuff. "She read the play script of *Journey's End*," says their mutual friend, "and she was captivated by its simple honesty and antiwar theme. She said, 'Larry, this is something you simply must do.' Playing a soldier in the trenches in a gloomy war drama was the antithesis of what Larry had in mind for himself in view of his romantic-idol ambitions, which had been fueled by his hope of getting the *Beau Geste* part. But Jill was insistent, telling him that he must expand his range and vary his image.

"I must say, Jill at that time was much more of a student of acting than Larry. She had the theatre in her blood because of her family.* And after four years at the Royal Academy she was much better versed in theatrical history and tradition than Larry was. She also had a much better sense of what Larry was suited for than he did himself. He was a natural, instinctive, intuitive actor; she was not. But she had a vast overlay of knowledge and appreciation for theatre that he lacked. She was steeped in the classics and had a firm intellectual grasp of their majesty and importance. He respected them, but he seemed to think more of them in terms of acting opportunities, vehicles upon which he could ride to performing virtuosity.

"Jill became Larry's teacher. She, more than anyone, infused him with a much larger perspective about the theatre than he had up to then possessed. Of course, much of his willingness to be taught came from his desire to please her. But it was she who taught him how to research roles, how to observe people, how to study portraits and probe character psychology, how to marry subtle gesture and movement and vocal intonation in a role. Jill was a formidable acting technician, and she schooled Larry in the importance of all these things so that they would jibe with his own natural gifts of stage presence and physical magnetism. Which was what was so sad about what happened later, when he left her. He owed much of his success to her, and although he never spoke of her unkindly, he never publicly acknowledged it either. Jill's problem was that she became too much of a teacher to Larry, and that tended to destroy the romance and affection. Once she had taught him, his genius and impetuosity carried him far above her acting level. She became teacher-wife instead of teacher-lover, and Larry began to feel hemmed in.

"In the event, Jill strongly urged him to take the part in *Journey's End.* And finally, to please her—for he knew it was the only way to please her at the time, even if it meant seeing less of her—he took it."

Olivier spent nearly a month of weekday afternoons and Sundays rehearsing the role of Captain Dennis Stanhope in *Journey's End* with the ragtag cast of out-of-work actors James Whale and author R. C. Sherriff had assembled to perform the play. Although once performed the play

---

*Jill Esmond's father, who had died six years earlier, was H. V. Esmond, an actor-producer-director-playwright. Her mother, Eva Moore, was a well-known English stage performer who later gained modest international fame as a character actress in British and American films.

would prove to be one of those rare "sleepers" of which show business legend is made, and it would serve as a springboard to fame and riches for many of its principals, Olivier remained unimpressed by it during rehearsals. But then, Sherriff and Whale were unimpressed by Olivier. Sherriff later said that Olivier had been their fourth or fifth choice for the part, and that they had offered it to him only after several other better-known actors had declined it and they had seen him in *Bird in Hand.* On stage, Olivier had a very strong masculine presence, said Sherriff later, "neither fey and arty" in the fashion of the day "nor rugby-playerish."

Sherriff thought he would be good in the part of Stanhope. But then, during rehearsals in a chilly studio over a shop in the West End, Olivier gave Sherriff a different impression. "Of course, offstage, he lost that presence. He looked much less imposing. In addition, he was on the withdrawn side and had little to contribute to the discussions about how the play could best be acted. Altogether he appeared bored and restless, and Jimmy Whale and I began to think we'd made a mistake."[13]

Another cast member was young actor Maurice Evans. "One had the feeling early on," he says, "that Larry was just going through the motions, that he resented being there and couldn't wait to get it over with. I remember him telling me that he must be crazy working for nothing in a play that would only perform for two nights and that no one would come to see. Later I learned that he was madly in love with Jill Esmond at the time and was in a constant state of yearning over her. He eventually played his part well—no, make that proficiently—but he never became engrossed by it, or by the play, the way the rest of us did."[14]

It was true. *Journey's End* had its first showcase performances on Sunday and Monday, December 9 and 10, 1928, when the rest of London's theatres were dark. It aroused the critics to accolades, one calling it "the greatest of all war plays." And it would, a few weeks hence, reopen for a long and distinguished run in a West End theatre.

In 1980, Olivier confessed to having often had "terrible artistic judgment in the choice of roles I have gone into in my life." He might have added that his judgment was often as bad with respect to the roles he refused to go into. When *Journey's End* was preparing to move in January of 1929 to the West End, where it would run for almost two years and provide its cast members with decent incomes as well as bright futures, Sherriff and Whale expected Olivier to go with it. In the meantime, Basil Dean, on the strength of Olivier's performance in the play, offered him the lead in *Beau Geste.* Since Olivier was still more interested in becoming a matinee idol than a "serious" actor, he opted for the role in *Beau Geste* and told Sherriff and Whale to find another actor to play Captain Stanhope.

The actor they found was the unknown Colin Clive, who would capitalize on his success in *Journey's End* to become, soon after it closed, a lavishly paid leading man in Hollywood. Olivier, on the other hand, would find *Beau Geste* a colossal failure, and he would not only remain unimportant to Hollywood for another ten years but would watch his London stage career sail into the doldrums for almost as long.

8

Jill Esmond Olivier

CATHLEEN NESBITT, an English actress and friend of Jill Esmond and Laurence Olivier, said once: "Larry and Jill were in many ways made for each other. But at the same time they weren't. In the beginning Jill did rather better than Larry professionally, and she was also rather smarter and more sensible, more practical about herself. Larry loved her, but there was always a slight undercurrent of resentment on his part too, as though he couldn't stand the fact that she was so bright and often so right about things. It encouraged a sense of competition in him, which was understandable but foolish, since Jill was not competing with him. But, you know—male pride and that sort of thing."[1]

•

Beau Geste opened and closed within four weeks during January and February of 1929. In an effort to recoup his losses, Dean slapped together another production and offered Olivier the lead. The play was

The Circle of Chalk, and Olivier, nearing twenty-two, played an Oriental prince in love with a slave girl. Overdoing his makeup and adopting a pattern of eccentric gestures, he was roundly lambasted in the press, and the play, itself dramatically uninteresting, also folded within a month. Those who knew Olivier began to remark on his lackluster approach to his performances. "Here he had become what he had always wanted to be," said one, "a leading man in the West End. And he was practically throwing away the opportunity to expand himself. It wasn't that Larry was bad because he had insufficient talent and couldn't help it. It was as if he was being bad deliberately."[2]

Years afterward, Olivier explained this dark period to a friend as one caused by a combination of confusion and loneliness. For one thing, he had come to regret having left *Journey's End* for *Beau Geste.* He had done it against Jill Esmond's advice, and now he was forced to watch Colin Clive receive all the acclaim he might have gotten, and thought he deserved, for having created the role of Dennis Stanhope.

What's more, plans for the filming of *Journey's End* had been announced. After the collapse of *Beau Geste,* Olivier had gone back to James Whale and offered to return to *Journey's End* as Stanhope. He had been none too gently rebuffed by Whale, then shocked to read in a newspaper a few days later: "Rumors that Mr. Laurence Olivier, originator of the Captain Stanhope characterization in *Journey's End,* would be returning to the role were set to rest yesterday by Mssrs. James Whale and Maurice Browne, producer and manager respectively. Mr. Whale indicated that Mr. Colin Clive, presently appearing, is now so widely identified in the public mind as Stanhope that the public would be loathe to accept Mr. Olivier. 'In point of fact,' said Mr. Whale, 'it is my opinion that Clive is the far better of the two actors in the part. We were never entirely happy with Mr. Olivier.' "[3]

People close to Whale recall today, however, that Whale was furious at Olivier's earlier defection.

Though prevented from returning to *Journey's End,* Olivier had still harbored the hope that he would be offered the chance to play Stanhope in the film version. Now that hope was shattered too. Whale had added, "When it comes time for the motion picture to be made, I have every expectation that Mr. Clive will be its star. Why, after all, tamper with success? Mr. Clive *is* Captain Stanhope."

Olivier would say years later, self-deprecatingly, "That entire experience taught me a great deal. It taught me never to lust after a part that genuinely belonged to another actor. Such lust can succeed in doing nothing but to eat you up and make you miserable. . . . It also taught me, though it took some time to really learn the lesson, that playing even a small role in an important play is ever so much more rewarding than a major role in an inconsequential one. Jill had been preaching that to me for as long as I'd known her, but I was too thick-headed to let it sink in. I began to realize it with *Journey's End,* but it still was years before it actually took."[4]

Jill Esmond was the other major cause of Olivier's "year of drear," as he once called 1929. London was at the height of its post-World War I prosperity that year. Actors, writers, producers and managers were no longer considered a breed apart by the upper reaches of society. As author Graham Greene observed in a later magazine article, "London in 1929 was a frenzy of gaiety and money-spending and the breaking down of social barriers. There was a time only shortly before when people who engaged in theatre found their friends and husbands and wives only among themselves. But by the late twenties that had all changed. Actors and actresses and producers were marrying the daughters of barristers and the sons of bankers, and even an occasional Lord or Lady crept into a theatrical family tree. And vice versa."

Olivier was not immune to the new trend. Jill Esmond, socially prominent and comfortable with people other than those involved in theatre, had given him a taste of "getting along" in society in general. Not that he suddenly wanted to marry a barrister's daughter. That was the problem. He was more desperate than ever to marry Jill. And she was more insistent than ever that they wait.

Jill had complicated matters at the beginning of 1929 by accepting an offer to go to the United States to repeat her role in a New York production of *Bird in Hand.* By that time Olivier had left the play and was preparing to open in *Beau Geste.* He was stunned by Jill's decision, and some speculate that it was the cause of his less-than-sterling performance in the Foreign Legion play. He tried to argue Jill out of it, but she was not one to sublimate her own career to the romantic needs of her lover—particularly when he had ignored her urgings that he not abandon *Journey's End* for *Beau Geste.*

Thus Olivier was forced to spend the winter, spring and early summer—almost six months—without his beloved. His despair showed in his performances.

In addition to *Beau Geste* and *The Circle of Chalk,* Olivier appeared in one other play during the period. The play was *Paris Bound,* a lank domestic comedy that opened in May, a few weeks after *The Circle of*

Chalk had closed. *Paris Bound* closed just as quickly, and Olivier was once again taken to task by the critics for a portrayal that, in the words of one, was "beyond our endurance." Herbert Marshall was in the cast, and he would later say, "It was an inoffensive little play, but it could have been better had Larry taken more interest. As it was, he moped about, forgot lines, and was totally undisciplined. There was no chance of ensemble playing with him in it."[5]

With his twenty-second birthday behind him, Olivier went from *Paris Bound* into another production at the Garrick Theatre, *The Stranger Within.* Here, playing a character named John Hardy in a suspense drama, his notices were better. But the play was without merit and was forced to close in a few days for lack of audiences.

"Lack of audiences," a well-known actor explained to me recently in an interview about his old friend Olivier. "That's when Larry began to get the message. I was with him a good part of that year, and he got to realize that audiences weren't coming to see him. The cult of the actor was at its peak then. Audiences patronized the theatre primarily to see the performers, not the plays. But there were dozens and dozens of theatres and scores and scores of productions every year—much more than the market could bear. London was theatre-crazy, but out of that mania there grew a certain amount of discrimination. A well-known actor or actress might appear in four different productions in a season, and—you know—the actors became like family to the audiences. Almost every actor was getting horrifically overexposed. Familiarity bred contempt or, if not contempt, indifference.

"Now, the standard most leading men had to go by was the audiences they could pull in, notwithstanding the play they were featured in. But all that began to change in 1928, 1929. The public was sated with actors, and it began to demand better plays. Which is why a play like *Journey's End,* totally populated by unknowns, was such a resounding hit. Oh, there were certain star performers who could still pull them in —Noel, for instance. But he was an exception because he was so, well, eccentric and witty. But your standard leading men—the matinee idols? Forget it. They were all in trouble, and doubly so the up-and-coming ones. And that's when Larry Olivier realized that being a leading man in the West End wasn't all it was cracked up to be. He was getting plenty of exposure, but he wasn't drawing.

"He told me later on, he said, 'Yes, that was it for me. I decided if I was going to make anything of myself as an actor I was going to have to do plays, real plays.' And he said, 'I'll become a character, like you.'

And I said, 'Rubbish, Larry, you're much too good-looking to be a character actor. Why don't you specialize in the classics? There you can be a character actor and matinee idol all wrapped into one.' And he said, 'Aye, the thought's occurred to me. Well, I'll have to do something, won't I?' And that's when he began to abandon his matinee-idol ambitions and started to see his future in a different light."[6]

That "different light" *was* the classics. But Olivier didn't quite know how to go about it. He had acted in a few Shakespeare plays but he had always viewed them basically as acting exercises—part of his training, much as he had recited Shakespearean speeches over and over again to improve his vocal techniques.

But become a Shakespearean actor? The idea still seemed far-fetched, particularly in view of the fact that another young actor, a few years older than Olivier, was then making a name for himself in London as a Shakespearean specialist. His name was John Gielgud.

"Larry was going through an unhappy time that year, despite the fact that he was appearing in play after play and had finally started to earn some real money for a change," actor Roland Culver observed. "A lot of his unhappiness derived from external factors, such as his being separated from Jill Esmond and the business about *Journey's End.* But much of it sprang from internal things too, the principal factor being his confusion over the direction he was going. Acting in flop after flop that year, I think, enabled him to come to the realization that he had a huge talent but was wasting it, was unable to fully exploit it, in the conventional theatre.

"I remember going with him to see Johnny Gielgud in something. Now Larry at that time was very much involved in masculine pursuits because of his relationship with Jill and he had little tolerance for homosexuals and such. He went to see Gielgud thoroughly prepared to despise and ridicule him as an insult to the theatre. What happened was that he was transfixed by Johnny's performance—by the grace of it, by the insight that flowed from its understated eloquence. Gielgud was not at all the effeminate actor we had expected to see. Feminine, yes, but not effeminate. But the femininity he released, coupled with his masculine persona, was what made him so effective—that contradiction. It was a great insight for Larry. And having a lot of feminine qualities himself, which he had theretofore always tried to hide, Larry began to think differently about himself as an actor. He had been rigorously suppressing his feminine impulses on stage for fear of being laughed at. Then he saw Gielgud letting his own femininity flow free, and he was thoroughly impressed by the way it enhanced Johnny's performance, giving it complexity, surprise and a mysterious depth.

"Larry learned something central about himself from watching Gielgud. It was as though he had found a key to unlocking a previously sealed vault in his talent. And it was then that he started to talk about wanting to become a classical actor. 'In modern plays, that feminine underlay in an actor will only get him in trouble with an audience,' he said. 'But in Shakespeare it works. It really helps.' "[7]

It would be a while before Olivier would have a chance to test his newfound aptitude for the classics. His major concern remained his longing for Jill Esmond, who was still in New York and was under contract to remain for almost another year in *Bird in Hand.* After *The Stranger Within* failed in June, Olivier looked for a play to get into for the 1929 fall season. Then he learned that *Murder on the Second Floor,* a long-running London hit, was being sent to New York for a September opening on Broadway. He pleaded with the producer for a part in the New York production and got it. Late in August the British stage company sailed for the United States on the steamship *Aquitainia.*

According to another actor who made the trip, Olivier was at once nervous and enthusiastic about going to America. It was his first journey out of Britain. He had heard from Jill about the difficulty of playing before New York audiences and about the fast-paced, crassly commercial life of the city of skyscrapers. But most of all he was anxious about his reunion with Jill. A few weeks before, a British actor just returned from a Broadway engagement had told him that Jill was being seen around New York with a well-known American performer. The news filled Olivier with jealousy and misery. As the ship approached the American coast, a fearful anticipation bubbled in him.

Another actor on that Atlantic crossing was Richard Bird. Bird, ironically, was on his way to New York to take the role of Captain Stanhope in the Broadway production of *Journey's End.* He tried repeatedly to engage Olivier in discussions about how best to play the part, but he found the original Stanhope uncommunicative, almost rude. "It was as if he personally resented me as Stanhope," Bird later said. "I then found out that he might have had reason to. I learned that he'd tried to get the New York production for himself and was rejected for it."[8]

Olivier's fears that he would find Jill Esmond involved with someone else proved unfounded, and their reunion was a happy one. It was made all the more happy for Olivier when, after several weeks of pleading on his part, she agreed to marry him, but not until she returned to England. She insisted on being married with all her friends and family present, an impossibility in New York.

The two were inseparable in New York except when they were performing in their respective plays. More important, they filled each other with the insights they had learned about themselves while separated. Olivier told Jill about having seen John Gielgud and the ideas the experience had triggered in him. He also told her of another revelation he had had—something that had been drilled into him by a veteran actress with whom he had appeared in one of the failed West End plays the year before. "Young man," she had told Olivier, "you are a gorgeous creature on stage, but you are altogether too predictable in what you do. You play for the obvious effects when you should play for the subtle ones."

She had gone on to give him a concise lesson in acting. "When you have a long speech, do not pause to take your breath when you would ordinarily. I am surprised you have not learned this. What you do is standard declamation—the audiences expect it. But audiences love to be surprised, to be shocked. So do not take your breath when they expect it. Break up the speech so that you take your breaths at the most unconventional places. For instance, in this scene you tell the inspector: 'As I rounded the turning, I saw there was a carriage blocking the road, and through the glass, its reflection glinting in the gas-illumined mist, I spied the familiar ring on the hand of my mother.' As you say it now, you take your breath pauses at all the usual places. But try it this way: 'As I rounded the turning I saw there was a—pause for breath—carriage blocking the road and through the glass, its—pause—reflection glinting in the gas-illumined mist, I spied the familiar ring on the hand—pause —of my mother.' This gives your speech a more natural flow, and it surprises the audience. It is a different rhythm than they're used to hearing from actors, and it draws their attention to you. They don't know what to make of you.

"You should practice this in all you do," the veteran actress had continued. "Do not make the conventional stage gesture to convey an emotion. Do something different. Instead of putting your hand to your brow to convey your concern over the news you have just heard, slip your hand into your suit-jacket pocket and let it wring nervously beneath the fabric so that the audience can see it. Rather than move left to confront your accuser with angry words of your own, which is what the audience expects, turn your back to him and speak your words to the lamp. Surprise, my dear boy. Always keep your audience in a state of suspense over what you will do."[9]

At first Olivier had scoffed at the old woman's advice, for he had been taught that above all an audience must feel comfortable with a leading man. But when he saw Gielgud, he gained an appreciation for the virtue of surprise in acting. Gielgud was all tricks of voice and gesture, which, along with his natural delicacy, fascinated audiences. "It was at about this time that Olivier began to unite in his mind ideas about femininity and physical eccentricity as useful acting techniques," said Felix Barker, who wrote an early biography of the actor. "In many ways the revelations he experienced in 1929 were his Road to Damascus. It would take him another four years to apply them fully, but they elevated his potential from that of a fine natural actor to that of a great actor."[10]

Others would disagree with Barker's assessment. "Rubbish," says a friend of Jill Esmond. "Larry's problem at that time was that he was a great imitator. His idea of acting was to borrow different things from dozens of other actors and put them all together into a stewpot that turned out to be his own characterization. Jill, on the other hand, was an original and highly inventive actress, quiet and understated, but bursting with technique. Added to that, she was much more intelligent about acting than Larry, and much more articulate. He was very respectful of her intelligence and knowledge, and he soaked it up like a sponge.

"Larry only began to become a really good actor after he got involved with Jill. She taught him so much. I have no doubt of the influence first seeing John Gielgud act had on Larry. But whatever he felt he was unable to clarify in his mind or give voice to until Jill, in her offhand way, explained it to him. Jill was the prism through which Larry began to see and understand how little he knew and how much he could learn. True, once his mind was put to it, he was a fast learner. But it was Jill who actually put his mind to it. She gave him the ideas and articulated what they meant so that Larry could carry them out. She was mature beyond her years, while Larry was still struggling out of his boyhood."[11]

Olivier's and Jill Esmond's stay in New York was short-lived, since Olivier's play, *Murder on the Second Floor,* turned out to be a flop with Broadway audiences and closed a few weeks after its opening night. The box office for *Bird in Hand* was weakening too. Jill was under contract to continue in the play on a tour of the United States during the winter of 1929–30. Hoping to tour with her, Olivier tried to get his old part in the play back but was rebuffed by Actors' Equity, the American stage performers' union. Under Equity rules, no producer could hire a foreign actor to play in more than one production within a six-month period. Thus Olivier was unemployable on the American stage until at least March of 1930. With Jill on the road and he himself unable to work, he had no choice but to return to London.

When Olivier departed from New York, he left little impression on the local theatre community. A producer who met him at the time said: "Olivier was here for only a few weeks, but he was nothing like the Olivier I later got to know. He was reclusive and lost here, uncomfortable and distrustful and dour, like many Englishmen on their first visit. He was so wrapped up in Jill Esmond that I don't suppose he cared about anything else. Certainly no one who met him felt they were in the presence of some future great actor. As far as we were concerned he was just another English actor, somewhat shy and self-contained and not very friendly."[12]

Olivier arrived back in London at the time of the great American stock market crash of October 1929. The crash reverberated throughout Britain and Europe, triggering the beginning of a worldwide economic depression that was to last well into the 1930s. The economic mood in London turned gloomy. Unemployment rose sharply and finance money for commercial theatrical production suddenly dried up. Olivier got a part in a West End production in December, but like his previous plays, this one closed after a few weeks and he was left with no prospects for the new year. Existing productions with only marginal audiences had to close down, and dozens of plays, planned for the early months of 1930, were canceled.

As it turned out, Olivier would not work again on the stage for eight months. He turned to movies—then considered hack work by most actors—and made two cheap pictures to support himself. Although they earned him enough money to keep going, he found film work tedious and boring. The only bright spot of the period came when Jill Esmond returned from America in April. When she arrived with tales of New York, Chicago and other cities in the United States, her star was brighter than ever and the tabloids lavished great attention on her. She was hired immediately to go into a long-running play, *Nine Till Six,* as a replacement for the female juvenile lead.

The fact that Jill so easily found work while he couldn't only deepened Olivier's dissatisfaction. Nevertheless, with her salary of twenty-five pounds a week to support them, he and Jill were married at All Saints Church in London on July 25, 1930. Olivier was twenty-three, Jill still twenty-two.

9

Private Lives

$\mathbb{A}$ friend of the Oliviers at the time, who wishes anonymity, says today: "Jill and Larry's marriage got off on the wrong foot and never quite recovered. Oh, yes, there was a great deal of superficial happiness at first—it was a wonderful, gay wedding. But internal tensions set in early on. Because the Depression was causing a severe slowdown in activity in the theatre, Larry could find no work. It gave him a great deal of insecurity, which was compounded by the fact that Jill *was* working, earning a tidy sum, and getting a great deal of public notice in the bargain. Larry was old-fashioned and honorable, even a bit staid in his values, and he felt deeply unsettled over the fact that Jill was having to support them. As well, he was inflicted with the actor's usual larger-than-ordinary ego. The attention Jill was getting, coupled with his own neglect, began to gnaw at him and exacerbate his guilt. Feeling contempt for himself, he began to take it out on Jill in sudden explosive rages over the most trivial things. Too, Jill was very outgoing and had many friends, whereas Larry was basically introverted. Secretly, I think, he was jealous of Jill's easygoing familiarity with so many people, many of whom

Larry had no use for because of their—as Larry thought of it—superficiality. Larry was going into the very-serious-about-the-theatre period in his life—a period, I might add, that was more due to Jill's influence than anything else.

"Jill was an intellectual while Larry was not. Yet he was trying hard to become one so as to be a match for her. Anyway, he began to see two sides to Jill and resented this contradictory aspect of her nature. One was the intellectual side, which he approved of. But the other was her ability or willingness to suffer the many fools and superficial idiots she had among her friends. They were not bad or evil people. But Larry found them profoundly boring, and he couldn't understand what Jill, his great love, could possibly see in them."[1]

•

Actually, Olivier's marriage to Jill Esmond set the stage for a rapid turnaround in his fortunes. The wedding was widely reported and pictured in the press, one paper describing the bride and groom as the year's "dream couple" and gushing over the number of theatrical celebrities, mostly friends of Jill and her family, who attended. Among them was Noel Coward, the immensely popular writer-performer whose racy personal life and professional wit were at once the outrage and delight of English society.

According to his account, Coward found himself in conversation with Olivier at the wedding reception and felt sorry for him. As another guest later observed, "Larry, for all the surface happiness he tried to project, seemed melancholy and uncomfortable on his wedding day. I think he was embarrassed by being surrounded by all these successful stage people when he couldn't find work on the stage. It would have been perfect for him had he been starring in a play at the time of his marriage; it would have made it all seem complete. As it was, he felt—well, a bit of a pariah. He was not working, so he was not one of them. He probably resented their solicitude. With the bad notices and flop plays he'd been through, he was wondering if he hadn't totally mucked up his career. And he was wondering if all those bright, glittery people weren't thinking the same thing—that he was already a has-been."[2]

Coward evidently entertained such thoughts and appointed himself Olivier's rescuer. "Look, young man," he said to Olivier at the wedding party, "I know how you're feeling because I've been in your position myself. I'm putting on my new play in the fall—starring myself and Gertie. It's time you appeared in a hit for a change, else you'll become anathema to the managers. My play will be a hit, and there's a part you can play. What say?"

Olivier had already heard about the play from Jill, who had read an early script. Called *Private Lives,* it had been dashed off by Coward in a few days and was a standard, elegant, quick-witted Coward marital comedy, created mainly as a vehicle for himself and the actress who was to be his co-star, the beautiful, witty Gertrude Lawrence. The part Coward offered Olivier was that of Victor Prynne, the dull, pompous husband of Gertrude Lawrence. His function in the play was solely to serve as an object of the lead characters', and audiences', derision. It was strictly a secondary role, a routine acting job, and not one designed to advance the career of a young actor with a passion for stage romance and heroism coursing through his blood.

Almost insultingly, Olivier declined Coward's offer. A few days later, Jill entered the picture. She insisted that Olivier take the part— after all, Coward was a family friend and, moreover, one of the hottest commercial properties in London. Besides, he had offered fifty pounds a week.

"The part's no good," Oliver argued, having just read the script himself. "There's another play going into rehearsal in October that's got a good part for me. I'll wait for that. Anyway, Noel's offer smacks too much of charity. I won't take charity, damn it."

"Rubbish!" exclaimed Jill. "It has nothing to do with charity. Noel wants you for it. You're an actor, aren't you? How can you pass up an opportunity to work with Noel? It's sure to be a success. You'll learn so much from Noel. And the money!"[3]

Against his better judgment, Olivier agreed to play the role. As Coward later said, "Poor Larry, he was so sure he was doing the wrong thing, he had such a hangdog, defeated look about him. But I really wanted him for it. Victor Prynne was an oaf, but in order to make his marriage to Amanda [Gertrude Lawrence] believable, he had to have something going for him. Otherwise why would smart, witty Amanda have married him, you see? He had to have something that redeemed his doltishness. What else but that he be extremely good-looking. And that's why I wanted Larry. He was so damned physically attractive on stage that he would give an extra dimension to Victor. Larry, of course, never really enjoyed playing Victor. He thought he was wasting his time. But in the end, it did him a lot of good."[4]

Even Olivier later conceded the point, paying tribute to Coward's influence on him during his 1967 BBC interview with Kenneth Tynan. He told Tynan, "I think Noel probably was the first man who took hold of me and made me think. He made me use my silly little brain. He taxed me with his sharpness [during the rehearsals and successful run of *Private Lives*] and shrewdness and his brilliance. He used to point out when I was talking nonsense, which nobody else had ever done before. He gave me a sense of balance of right and wrong. . . . He would make me read. I never read anything at all. I remember he said, 'Right, my boy, *Wuthering Heights, Of Human Bondage,* and *The Old Wives' Tale* by Arnold Bennett. That'll do, those are the three best. Read them.' I did. I also read *The Forsyte Saga.* I began to read a bit of Dickens. . . . Noel was a tremendous influence. He made me quite a bit more sensible than I had been up to then. . . ."[5]

Already a leading man at twenty-three, Olivier was still stage-struck but no longer starstruck. Thus he was not overly impressed by the theatrical celebrities he saw regularly around London. Yet as the energy and magnetism of Coward's personality revealed itself to Olivier during rehearsals in August, he held the older performer in increasing awe. On another occasion he would say of Coward, "He more than anyone else put me onto Shakespeare and classical acting. After acting with him and experiencing his comic genius, I realized that I could never hope to become a comic actor of any consequence. And I had lost my ambition just to repeat myself over and over again as a standard romantic actor in contemporary dramas. I had been wanting to play Cyrano, a combination of comedy and pathos and romance and poetry and stage heroics—a great, funny, ham role. I went to Noel one day and told him about it. He said, 'Shakespeare, my boy, Shakespeare. Read Shakespeare, read it all. That's where you belong. It's got everything you want to do. Rostand is nothing but tenth-rate Shakespeare.' And so I started reading Shakespeare, but seriously and earnestly this time. And of course, Noel was right."[6]

Coward was his own director and producer—manager, in the parlance of British theatre—and he believed in investing his professional productions with as much elegance and refinement as he put into his personal life. *Private Lives* embarked on a pre-London tour of the provinces late in August. But this was not the tour of soot-bathed trains, seedy hotel rooms and lumpy cafeteria foods that confronted most touring companies. "The touring days of the past belonged to another world," wrote Coward in *Present Indicative,* a 1937 book about his earlier career. The entire tour was "swathed in luxury" as the company traveled by car, stayed in only the best hotels and ate in the best restaurants. "Assurance of success seemed to be emblazoned on the play from first; we had few qualms, played to capacity business and enjoyed ourselves thoroughly. We felt, I think rightly, that there was a shine on us."[7]

On Coward and the others in the production, yes. But not on Olivier. Interviewed while on tour by the Manchester *Evening Chronicle,* he was pictured by the reporter as "a virile youth who is older than his years in spirit . . . sad to relate, but he is unusually pessimistic, almost cynical."

When the reporter asked Olivier to account for his gloomy mood, the actor responded, "Only fools are happy. . . . I suppose it is because they don't really know what they want in life, and so every little pleasure that comes along they regard as a paradise of happiness. I somehow can't get that way. I always examine things so very closely that immediate pleasures are dwarfed by my insistence on ultimate benefits."

When the reporter wondered how a young man who had had so much success in the theatre, and who was now playing an important role with Noel Coward, could be so negative in his outlook on life, Olivier responded, "All that may sound very well, but I have with very few exceptions always had parts that I have not liked. . . . I hate the part I'm playing now."[8]

"When that interview appeared in the Manchester paper it mortified Larry," says a friend. "I mean, he was embarrassed by the dour, funless image the reporter projected of him. I said, 'But Larry, did you say those things?' And he said, 'Well, yes, but I never thought I sounded like such a sod.'

"But that *was* Larry—not a sod, but a generally cheerless, moody character unable to take any pleasure out of life. The article caught him exactly as he was in personality. For him it was like looking in a mirror and despising what he saw. He started to change after that, to make an effort to get some pleasure out of life and be more personable. Noel, of course, helped him along quite a bit as he exposed Larry to his own fun-filled, charming life.

"That was Larry up to then—the typical parson's son expounding darkly on the sins of joy and pleasure, as though he was taking his oral examination for graduation from the seminary. He was infused with guilt, not the least of which were his guilt at having had some success and his guilt in playing in a role he felt was beneath him, and I suppose his guilt over being an actor in the first place. One always felt with Larry that he carried a cloud about with him from which, every once in a while, an admonishing finger would thrust and point at him accusingly, and from which a spectral voice would resound, 'Why hast thou forsaken me, Laurence Olivier?' "[9]

Private Lives opened at the Phoenix Theatre in London in September 1930 to effusive praise. Olivier's gloom while on tour was assuaged, evidently, by the fact that he was finally in a hit. The fact that it was a Noel Coward hit gilded the lily. For although Olivier could not pretend he was anything more than the play's "second banana," and a fairly expendable one at that, he saw his stature rise because of his association with the popular Coward. The feeling, he conceded later, was heady. But after a few days it only sharpened his dissatisfaction—perhaps made of envy—that he was riding on someone else's coattails.

"Larry did all the right things after *Private Lives* took London by storm," says another witness to the period. "He and Jill started to go to parties, they socialized with Noel and his celebrity crowd, Larry took some of the money he was making to buy elegant clothes, and so on. I remember meeting him on the street one day shortly after *Private Lives* opened. He was no longer the Larry of old, baggy, mismatched clothes, unruly hair, and all. He cut a dashing figure in a trim new custom suit, gleaming white shirt and fedora. He was barely recognizable. Thank God, he hadn't changed otherwise, though. He was still old Larry, apologizing for his new look and sheepishly blaming it on Jill."[10]

Private Lives was so popular that it could have run for at least a year to full houses. But Noel Coward didn't like long runs—"Leave them panting for the next one," he was fond of saying. He decided to close the London production after three months and move it to New York for another three before going on to something new.

There were problems. One was that Olivier didn't want to go to New York—he wanted to stay in London to capitalize on his success. The other was Adrianne Allen, the young actress who played Olivier's female counterpart in the play, Sibyl. She was pregnant and could not go. How to replace both performers who, although not essential to the success of the play, served as pleasant and believable contrasts to the fast-paced patter of Coward and Gertrude Lawrence?

Coward begged Olivier to go to New York. "I can't replace both of you, Larry; it would mean simply too much work, breaking in two new principals."

"But I can't leave Jill," Olivier protested.

"Jill!" Coward exclaimed. "Of course, what a lovely idea? Why didn't I think of it?"

"What's a lovely idea?"

"She'll take over for Adrianne."

"Don't be daft, Noel," said Olivier. "Jill's a brunette. Adrianne's a blonde, Sibyl's a blonde, everyone expects her to be a blonde."

"Haven't you heard of wigs, dear boy?"

"But, Jill—"

"Yes?"

"She's used to better parts than Sibyl, Noel. And anyway, she wouldn't feel right for it. She wouldn't consider taking it on."

"She would if you asked her. Just think, both of you in New York again, playing together on Broadway, international exposure, who knows what might come of it for both of you?"

When Jill unexpectedly expressed her delight with the idea, Olivier had no choice but to consent to the New York trip. Recently Jill had made her first movie for a British film studio and was eager to do more. She told Olivier she'd heard that British actors were in demand in Hollywood now that sound movies, or "talkies," were becoming more common. The two films Olivier had made the summer before, just before his marriage, had left him dubious about acting in movies.

"I don't want to go to Hollywood," he said. "That's not acting. I don't give a damn if I never see a film studio again."

"My darling," said Jill, "you may change your mind when you learn what they pay in Hollywood."[11]

So Olivier and Jill went with *Private Lives* to New York in January of 1931 for a three-month stay. The trip changed Olivier's life in more ways than he could have imagined.

10

Hollywood

ANew York producer-director—
then a young Broadway actor—who got to know Olivier and Jill Esmond
during the New York run of *Private Lives* early in 1931 says: "From what
I could see they had a stormy relationship—one day lovey-dovey, the next
Larry sulking about something and Jill refusing to speak to him, then a huge
making-up and all lovey-dovey again until the next time. Larry struck me
as reserved and slightly superior in his attitudes most of the time, while Jill
was very personable and outgoing and somewhat actressy. I think both
were bored in the play, for they were really nonentities compared to
Coward and Gertie Lawrence. . . . Now that I think of it, that's what got
to Larry and Jill—what I just said. He seemed to get exercised about Jill's
'actressy' nature. I would see them at an occasional party. Jill would be
in the middle of things, chatting in her English-actress fashion. Larry would
be off in a corner, looking self-important with a drink in his hand and trying
not to glower at Jill. Larry was very good at acting on stage. But he felt it
unseemly to reveal himself or to be lavish with himself off.

"That's it, he used to think what Jill did—all her outgoingness among people she hardly knew—was unseemly. It embarrassed him, and then he would take it out on her. And Jill, being the independent woman she was, dished it right back at him. 'Pack it up, mate.' That was one of her favorite expressions. Larry would nag at her for a while about her behavior, then she'd finally turn on him. 'Oh, pack it up, mate, I've heard enough of your rot.' Larry would feel so guilty at having made her angry that he'd brood for a time, hurt by her indifference and mad at himself for taking it. I never saw the final explosions and making-up because they saved those for the privacy of their digs. But they must have been something.''[1]

•

With talkies becoming well established in 1930 as the wave of the future in American motion pictures, the Hollywood studios had talent scouts combing Broadway for new "talent"—actors and actresses who not only were attractive but whose voices were congruent with their looks. (Many silent film stars' careers had collapsed with the advent of sound; their voices were simply all wrong for the silent images the public had of them.) Acting ability was a secondary consideration. What mattered to the studios were photogenic appearance and vocal quality, and it was a bonus if a performer had an English accent. The movie moguls were impressed by English accents. Moreover, the convention among the studios had been to base a large part of their "product," i.e., movies, on the literary classics. English actors and actresses were thought to be best suited to such films. Already Hollywood had established a large stable of British actors—Basil Rathbone, Ronald Colman, Clive Brook, Aubrey Smith, Herbert Marshall and Nigel Bruce among them. But as the demand for, and profits from, talkies expanded, the need for further British talent increased as well. Especially, in 1931, for actresses.

Olivier and Jill Esmond opened in the New York production of *Private Lives* in January of that year. Although both had appeared on Broadway two years earlier, so far as Hollywood was concerned they were new faces. The popularity of Coward's comedy drew talent scouts and movie producers to the play like flies to flypaper. Within the month, both Oliviers were spending their free afternoons making screen tests for Hollywood in the dingy studios of New York's Hell's Kitchen.

Among the companies most interested were M-G-M, RKO and Paramount. At the time there was no such thing as a free-lance movie star. Actors and actresses, if they wanted to work regularly in movies, were required to sign contracts binding them to a particular studio for seven years, with renewal options, at starting salaries of two hundred and fifty to five hundred dollars a week, depending on the studios' views of their potential and usefulness.

Paramount was interested especially in Jill Esmond Olivier, since its executives had already seen the movie she had made six months before in London—a sound production directed by Englishman Alfred Hitchcock, and distributed by Paramount, called *Skin Game.* David O. Selznick, Paramount's head of production, recommended that they sign Jill. Jill and Olivier, however, had decided that one wouldn't go to Hollywood without the other. She made a contract for her husband a condition of her signing. Selznick refused. He might have acceded to the twin contract demand, he later said, but the salaries the Oliviers were holding out for—one thousand dollars a week each—were simply unthinkable, "way out of line for beginners."

An M-G-M executive, confronted by the same demands, said, "These dumb Limeys—they think they can come over here with no experience and no names and get Gloria Swanson salaries? They can go back and rot in London, for all I care. They're not even that good-looking!" And a Columbia Pictures vice president exclaimed, "Don't they know there's a Depression on? They'll be lucky to get two hundred and fifty a week if they get anything. I don't know who's advising them. But whoever it is, he ought to be locked up."

The man who was advising Olivier and Jill was none other than Noel Coward. "He had listened to Jill and Olivier argue long and hard about going to Hollywood," said New York producer Saul Colin. "Jill wanted to go, Larry didn't. So they went to Noel to settle the argument. He convinced Larry that a Hollywood contract would be worth its weight in gold for the right money. 'It's a chance for both of you to become international film stars,' he said. 'You could make millions.' And Larry said, 'But what if we don't? What if we just end up as supporting players? I don't want to spend my life as a supporting player in films.' And Noel said, 'Dear boy, you get your money in advance. You demand two hundred pounds a week, both of you do. Any studio willing to pay that sum is sure to work its backside off to make you stars. And even if it doesn't happen, you've still got all that money in the bank for yourselves when your contracts are over.' And then he said, 'Don't worry, my dears, you just go and do your tests. Let me handle the rest.'

"Noel handed the whole problem over to his agent and lawyer. I recall that Jill wasn't very happy with the solution. She feared it would jeopardize her chances at a movie career. She was willing to take much less. 'After all,' she said, 'how could we spend two thousand dollars a week between us?' But she went along with the idea of them both having to get contracts. She wasn't so ambitious that she wanted to spend all her time in Hollywood while Larry was back in London.''[2]

RKO was a smaller studio than M-G-M, Paramount and Columbia. Under the financial control of David Sarnoff's Radio Corporation of America (RCA) in New York, it was in the process of expanding. Like the other studios, at first it had rejected the Oliviers' contract demands. Then, one night shortly after *Private Lives* opened in January, Sarnoff himself attended a performance. Just the day before, he had seen the results of the Oliviers' screen tests. Although he had liked Jill Esmond's, he agreed that she was not worth more than three hundred dollars a week. He was less impressed with Olivier's test.

His mind changed abruptly after seeing the two on stage. He was startled by Jill's sophistication, but even more so by Olivier's stage presence. "The kid's in a lousy part," he told a companion, "but he still gets your attention just by being there. Isn't that what makes movie stars?"

The next morning, Sarnoff instructed RKO chief Hiram Brown to sign the Oliviers up. "If we don't get them," he said, "one of the others will. Or else they'll go back to Britain and become stars there. Then we'll have to pay through the nose when we want to use them."

Brown reminded Sarnoff that the Oliviers were demanding a thousand dollars a week each. "I don't care," the RCA head replied. "They could be the next Lunt and Fontanne. Offer them five hundred."[3]

A deal was soon struck. Although Olivier was still reluctant, he gave in to Jill's wishes and agreed to sign at a compromise figure worked out by Noel Coward's representatives: seven hundred a week for each of them to start, with yearly increases of fifty dollars a week for two years, the contracts to be renegociated at the end of that time.

The Lunt and Fontanne Sarnoff had referred to were, of course, Alfred Lunt and his wife Lynn Fontanne—the celebrated "first couple" of the American theatre who were almost equally popular with audiences in England. One of the selling points Noel Coward had used in urging Olivier to consider Hollywood was: "Just think, Larry, you and Jill could do for motion pictures what Alfred and Lynn have done for the stage—you could be a tremendously popular cinema team."

Coward and the Lunts were good friends. According to a friend of the Oliviers, Coward introduced the Oliviers to the Lunts soon after the

Private Lives company arrived in New York, although another friend says the introduction occurred in London. Whichever the case, Lunt and Olivier took an immediate liking to each other—"Alfred was the first American actor Larry met whom he felt inferior to," recalls the first friend.[4]

Alfred Lunt was a living encyclopedia of theatre history and acting technique, as well as a skilled actor. Unlike most performers, acting filled every crevice of his life. "Alfred loved to cook," producer Herman Shumlin once said of Lunt. "That was his only hobby. But even when he cooked it was like watching a performance."

"Olivier was deeply impressed and influenced by Lunt," said Saul Colin. "Larry was just getting a sense of himself as a theatrical personality, although he was still woefully lacking in what you might call a well-rounded grasp of the theatre. Under the influence of his wife, under the influence of Noel Coward, he had developed his theatrical intelligence to a certain degree, certainly. But basically he was lazy. Not about himself as an actor—there he was very self-absorbed and ambitious. But he was not terribly avid intellectually, and he did not apply himself very avidly to educating himself.

"All that changed, however, when he met Alfred Lunt. Alfred was a tremendous naturalistic actor, and he loved to talk acting with anyone who would listen. He was a teacher, besides. And when he started talking to Larry, Larry became utterly fascinated and totally the student. Alfred talked to him about truth in acting and how to get it. He filled him with ideas and tips about technique that Larry had never thought of before. But more than that, he astonished Larry by his wide intellectual grasp of the theatre as a whole, referring to what so-and-so did in a performance of *Hamlet* on such-and-such a date a hundred years before, and what another actor did in *Coriolanus* fifty years before, and so on.

"Between being filled with ideas of himself and Jill becoming the next Lunt and Fontanne and seeing at first hand the stuff Alfred was made of—how hard he worked and how unrelenting was his theatrical knowledge and curiosity—Larry became fired by a desire to be like Lunt, to imitate him. I don't mean to imitate his acting, but to imitate him as a man of the theatre. Larry had been getting a lot of information in bits and pieces but he had never really been motivated before to follow them up and form them into a cohesive theatrical intelligence. When he saw how such an intelligence enhanced Alfred Lunt, how it gave him grace and style and such substance and authority, he was motivated to do the same."[5]

If Olivier had felt himself above acting in movies prior to signing with RKO, he felt even more superior when he and Jill arrived in Los Angeles late in the spring of 1931 to start fulfilling their contractual obligations. Lunt had discouraged him about going into films for the same reasons Lunt had, for the most part, avoided them—"It's not acting, Larry, it has nothing to do with acting. It's posing and nothing more." Olivier had replied, "I know, I know. But Jill wants to have a crack at it."[6]

Lunt's was not the only warning Olivier received about Hollywood when he and Jill embarked by train for the West Coast. Others had recited tales of the greed and indifference to art of most of the movie company executives. "You'll find yourself caught in a vicious circle out there," one veteran told Olivier. "The movie moguls live like Oriental potentates and they think of actors only as meal tickets. Expensive meal tickets, sure, but meal tickets just the same. They'll pay you plenty of money, but only for so long as you do their bidding, like privates in their personal armies. They've got it all figured out, and if you try to change anything they'll stamp you out like an ant at a picnic."[7]

Olivier, then, thought he was well armed on his arrival; he was, in fact, prepared to serve his duty as a "private" quietly. The main surprise he found was in the topography and climate of Los Angeles. The almost perpetually sunny and temperate climate, and the lush, flowery landscapes of Beverly Hills, were in stark contrast to what he was accustomed to. As were the steep hills surrounding the Los Angeles basin with their narrow, dusty canyons and their brand-new terraced housing tracts. Another surprise was the rapidly expanding colony of English actors and actresses that had established itself in Hollywood during the previous few years. Olivier knew many of them, and their presence softened the cultural shock both he and Jill experienced on their arrival.

There was another kind of shock that he didn't get over so easily. Although they were new arrivals from London and Broadway, the Oliviers aroused little interest in the mainstream movie-industry society. What interest there developed centered mostly on Jill; she came with the bigger reputation, inflated by the fact that RKO's press agents had emphasized her in their release announcing the studio's signing of the two. There were no allusions to a new Lunt-Fontanne team, however. And one morning, shortly after their arrival, Olivier was astonished to read in a local gossip column: "As for Miss Esmond's husband, Laurence Oliver [sic], he comes to Hollywood evidently in the hopes of knocking Ronald Colman off his perch as England's champion movie leading man. As one talent expert at M-G-M was heard to say the other night, 'He has no chance. Maybe he's trying to look like Ronny, but his face is too strong and his looks are too rugged, rather than weak and suave. When it comes to rugged actors, we don't need Englishmen. We've got plenty of Americans around to handle those parts.' "[8]

Olivier couldn't figure out whether the piece was more of a rap against Ronald Colman or against him. He was incensed, and he immediately dispatched a letter to Colman assuring him that he had not come to Hollywood to compete with him. Colman phoned him at the house RKO had rented for the Oliviers in Beverly Hills. Having also seen the item, he expressed his amusement.

"Welcome to Hollywood, old boy," he said to Olivier. "Got your note. Absolutely no need to apologize. That sort of thing is standard fare here. Why don't you and your wife come round for drinks Thursday next. I'll give you both a lesson in growing the thick skins you'll need if you expect to stay here."[9]

Colman, whom Olivier had indeed set out to imitate a few years before in London, became his first Hollywood mentor. Their initial get-together for drinks turned into weekly dinner dates between the Oliviers and Colman and his wife Benita. "Ronnie gave me a crash course in getting on in Hollywood," Olivier would say later. "He and Benita became great friends, although frankly I never understood how they could stand living there all the time—even with their riches. Well, on second thought, I could. After all, Ronnie was a big film star, a great heart throb. That was enough for him."[10]

But not enough for Olivier. Or was it? Had he become a Hollywood "heart throb" in the early thirties, would he have been content to settle in Hollywood and today be remembered as just another faded, aged reminder of a distant era? "Not on your life," he recently told an interviewer who asked the question. "Hollywood was not for me. I can honestly say that I was unimpressed with that kind of adulation. I was young, but unimpressed. I saw what it did to so many great talents— Barrymore, for instance. And it remains the same today. Look at your Montgomery Clift, your Brando. Thank God, I never got into that."[11]

Olivier spent most of his time with his English actor pals while in Hollywood. "They were a notoriously cynical lot about film acting and the people who ran the studios," says a man who was there. "Some of them anti-Semitic, but always happy to be friendly to their Jewish employers on the set and in public. Years later Larry played Shylock in *The Merchant of Venice,* and I'm sure he modeled his characterization on some of the studio heads he first encountered in Hollywood."[12]

One such mogul who did not quite fit the stereotype was David O. Selznick, the man who had turned thumbs down on Olivier and Jill Esmond for Paramount several months earlier. A producer with artistic aspirations , as well as a hard-headed businessman, Selznick quit Paramount during the early summer of 1931 to join RKO as chief production executive. It was his job to cast the studio's contract players in various productions, always with the goal of keeping the public happy with its established stars and turning its newer, less well-known performers into stars in their own right—all for the ultimate purpose of keeping movie-house turnstiles spinning.

Selznick was brought into RKO by David Sarnoff to revive the studio's sagging fortunes and make it competitive with the giants. Rather than allow contract stars to remain idle while they were collecting weekly paychecks, the studios made it a practice to "loan" them out to other studios. This is what happened to Jill Esmond after the Oliviers arrived in Hollywood. RKO loaned her to Paramount to make a movie called *Once a Lady.* Olivier, in the meantime, was assigned a part in an RKO production called *Friends and Lovers,* an adventure-romance set in India.

"It was apparent right from the start that Olivier was completely out of his element acting in movies," Victor Schertzinger, the movie's director, said. "He had absolutely no camera sense—my God, we often had to stop takes because he'd look at the camera in the middle of a scene. And he acted the way he did on the stage—all broad gestures and a face forever busy with expressions. He was totally unnatural, an amateur. When I finally got him toned down, he became very stiff and tight-lipped and soft-voiced, barely audible. He was uncomfortable being asked not to 'act,' but just be himself."[13]

The RKO brass were appalled when they saw Olivier's performance and arranged to loan him out to the Fox studios for his second picture, *The Yellow Ticket.* "We felt Larry could be a good actor," Hiram Brown later said. "But let him get his education at other studios' expense."

The Yellow Ticket, in which Olivier co-starred with Lionel Barrymore as the villain and Elissa Landi as his romantic interest, was set in Russia, though filmed on the sound stages and back lot of the Fox complex.

Here Olivier was up against the traditionally hammy acting of Barrymore. Cautioned by director Raoul Walsh to underplay his role as a naive Western journalist wandering through postrevolutionary Russia, Olivier came off as anaemic and uncertain in contrast to the boisterous Barrymore.

By the time Olivier finished *The Yellow Ticket,* Selznick had joined RKO. One day late in 1931 he called the young actor into his office and said, "Larry, we're spending a great amount of money on you and so far you're not working out. Jill is doing much better, and she has a good chance to become a star. So do you, but your attitude's all wrong. You're not trying. I think you owe it to us to try."

"But of course I am trying," Olivier protested.

"Maybe you think you are. But I know some of these fellows you're hanging around with—your countrymen. And I know what they think about acting in movies. They're a bad influence on you, Larry. Even Jill agrees."

"Jill? You've spoken to her about this? How dare you?"

"We have an investment in you, Larry. As head of the studio I have to help decide whether to continue with it or drop you at the end of your contract."

"What if *I* decide to drop *you,*" Olivier said belligerently.

"Fair enough," said Selznick. "But it would be a pity, either way. What I want is to see you make it big in this industry, the way I think Jill's going to make it big. But there are certain things you're going to have to do. First, you must use some of the money we're paying you to get your teeth fixed. Second, get out and meet some different people. I mean, people who are important in this industry—producers, directors, writers. Stop shutting yourself off with those English actor friends of yours. Look how Jill is beginning to fit in and blossom out." That had already become a sore point between Olivier and his wife. He resented the fact that she seemed happy to be doing movie work and enjoyed the many Americans she was meeting.

"Finally," Selznick went on, "I want you to take some special acting instruction. You're without any naturalness on screen, you come across as stiff and weak. You've got to learn that acting in front of a camera is completely different from stage acting."

This was the ultimate insult. Laurence Olivier in need of acting lessons? "No," he said. "I'll get my teeth fixed. I'll try to socialize with other people. But I'm not going to have anyone teaching me how to act. I *am* an actor."

Selznick regarded Olivier benevolently for a moment. "Larry," he said, "do you know what the *O* of my middle initial stands for?"

Olivier shook his head.

"It stands for nothing. I just decided to stick it in there one day when I was younger. I did it to distinguish myself from an uncle of mine, David Selznick, whom I despised. But when people ask me what it stands for, I tell them 'Oliver.' Now, why do I tell you this? Because your name is Olivier. Yet half the people in this town don't know it. Just the other day I had a call from someone over at M-G-M asking me if Laurence 'Oliver' was available to work in a film they're making about Canada. And yesterday one of our producers was in here going over our list. He said, 'This Laurence Oliver, is he the one who was in *Friends and Lovers?*' Christ, man, one of our own and he doesn't even know how to say your name. Do you see my point?"[14]

Olivier got his teeth straightened. During the next few months he ventured outside the English colony to become friends with such other young actors as Douglas Fairbanks, Jr., and Robert Montgomery—both intense Anglophiles. But still he refused to take special instruction in film acting.

"Larry is growing more and more depressed about his film career," said Fairbanks to a fan magazine. "But at the same time he's come out of his shell and has proved to be great fun to be with. A lot of us were surprised to learn that he has such a great rollicking sense of humor."[15]

Fairbanks was married to Joan Crawford, but the marriage was in the process of breaking up. "Doug was on the prowl," recalls a friend, "going to different parties and nightclubs every night and acting generally the way the public imagined that unattached Hollywood stars lived their lives. Larry was often with him, leaving Jill at the home they had in the hills to study lines for her next day's work. Doug was basically unhappy at the time. He still lived under the cloud of his father [Douglas Fairbanks, Sr., the famous silent film star and husband of Mary Pickford] and he was upset about the Crawford business. He was living his life kind of hysterically and bitterly, loudly warning all his friends never to marry actresses, especially movie actresses. 'Their ambition kills your manhood,' he liked to say.

"Jill wasn't too crazy about Larry's relationship with Fairbanks. Larry had gone from hanging out exclusively with his English friends to hanging out with Americans who were trying to be more English than the English. That was Doug's thing, and his attraction to Larry—well, he saw in Larry something he wanted desperately to be, an Englishman with a marvelous voice and a Bond Street cut to his jib. Larry was fascinated for his part by Doug's athleticism and debonair style. Doug was very proud of his physical dexterity. He taught Larry to play a passable game of tennis and showed him loads of gymnastic tricks. Larry got a lot of his later stage athleticism from Doug Fairbanks."

Jill's ambitions for herself would soon foment a marital crisis. Olivier made his next film for RKO in the winter of 1931–32. Called *Westward Passage,* it co-starred the strong actress Ann Harding. Once again Olivier came across as a less than commanding presence, an insipid young man who projected little of the sex appeal and romantic mystique written into his character. The film was not only a failure financially, like his two previous ones, but it convinced the heads of RKO—Selznick excepted—that he had no future. They decided not to use him in any further productions and allow his contract to run out. Nor were rival studios interested in borrowing him.

As Olivier sat idle in Hollywood during the spring of 1932, different plans were being hatched for Jill Esmond. Selznick had obtained the motion-picture rights to the long-running and controversial English stage hit *A Bill of Divorcement,* by Clemence Dane (a nom de plume for the colorful writer and painter Winifred Ashton). This was a "woman's story" on the theme of insanity as grounds for divorce, and the role of Sydney Fairfield, the young heroine, was coveted by dozens of established movie actresses. Selznick, who was to produce the film personally, decided to give the part to a relative newcomer after signing the aging John Barrymore to play the heroine's father. It was a movie that would make whoever played the female lead a full-fledged star, meaning that RKO would not only benefit immediately but would have another star in its bank for future films.

Selznick first considered Katharine Hepburn, a fresh young talent from Broadway who was highly favored by George Cukor, the film's director. But Hepburn's agents were demanding the unheard-of salary of fifteen hundred dollars a week to start—far beyond what RKO's chief executives would allow Selznick to pay on a picture they were not altogether enthusiastic about in the first place because of the insanity theme. So Selznick settled on Jill Esmond, with an ulterior motive. He once said, "Everybody at RKO was down on Larry Olivier except me. And even I was disappointed that he had progressed so slowly and didn't seem to care. I thought this might be an effective way to light a fire under him so that he'd get his contract renewed. I knew Jill could handle the part of Sydney. And I knew if the picture succeeded and made her the star I thought it would, it would serve to inspire Larry and get him to work on his own acting. My ultimate plan was to star them together in a later picture, after Jill hit it big."[16]

Selznick's decision to give the role to Jill had just the opposite effect on Olivier. Without knowing of Selznick's grand design, he became displeased by the idea of Jill becoming a movie star while his chances continued to fade. He was without the prospect of a future film, whereas Jill was already busy formulating her characterization of Sydney Fairfield. His displeasure was then unwittingly compounded by Selznick.

David Selznick's older brother Myron was one of Hollywood's leading movie talent agents—a profession he had almost single-handedly invented in the 1920s after giving up his own producing career. In preparing Jill Esmond for her leap to stardom in *A Bill of Divorcement,* David Selznick recommended that she engage Myron as her agent. Myron Selznick thus became Jill's representative and, indirectly, Olivier's too. When he met them, they were already arguing over Jill's desire to play the part of Sydney. Intervening one day, Myron accidentally let slip the news that RKO intended to make no further use of Olivier and to let his contract expire. He offered to try to make a deal at one of the other studios.

But the news was too much for the unhappy Olivier. Hollywood wanted his wife, but not him! That did it—he was finished with Hollywood and was going back to England. Jill could stay if she wanted to, he told her. But if she did, she could consider their marriage over. He had wasted enough time acceding to her wishes. He may have been washed up in Hollywood, but he still had a career at home on the stage.

Jill, once the initial turmoil died down, weighed the alternatives. If she refused to yield to her husband's demands, she could well become the star she had always hoped to be but would probably lose him. If she agreed to give up the part and return to London, she would hold onto Olivier but would lose what might be her only chance for stardom. Independent she was, but not that independent. She acknowledged some merit in Olivier's arguments. He *had* been sacrificing his own stage ambitions for her movie ones; they would not have come to Hollywood in the first place had it not been for that.

Jill decided that her husband was more important than stardom. She went to see David Selznick. "Is it true that you're not going to renew Larry's contract?"

"That's the way it looks," he said. "Does he know?"

"He heard it from your brother."

"Damn!" Selznick exclaimed. He started to explain what he had been planning.

"It doesn't matter," Jill interrupted. "He intends to return home immediately. He insists that I go with him. I'm afraid I must."

"But, Jill, do you realize what you'll be giving up?"

"I do. But Larry comes first."[17]

By the terms of her contract, Selznick could have forced Jill to play the role. But he was not interested in having a reluctant actress star in a film he was producing himself.

"I ended up using Hepburn instead," he said later. "She cost me fifteen hundred dollars a week and I was almost thrown out of RKO because of it. All because of my stupid brother and his big mouth."

11

Garbo

$\mathbf{M}$AYNARD MORRIS, a leading American talent agent, said about Olivier in 1961: "The reason Laurence Olivier never became the great movie star many people thought he should have been was not due to his so-called contempt for film acting, his high-handed, above-it-all attitude toward movies. It was not because he did not want to be a star. It was because he had no screen personality. It's personality that makes movie stars. Yes—looks, voice, movement, acting ability, are all important. But if these were the prime requisites, hundreds of thousands of people could be stars.

"When young actors and actresses come into my office to audition, they think the only thing I'm concerned about is the way they look and talk and do their scenes. Those are the remotest things from my mind. As soon as they come in the door I'm looking for personality. By personality I don't mean amiability and gregariousness, such as in, 'Oh, she has a terrific personality.' I mean the natural projection of a wide variety of human colors that, taken all together, form an irresistibly unique person. This is one's personal energy, that quality that flows out and draws or commands people's attention. It can't be forced, for then it is transparently phony. After Marlon Brando came on the scene, I used to see thousands of young actors who did everything that Brando did in order to be like him. The only trouble was that even with his mannerisms, they didn't have his uniquely complex personality.

"Olivier, for all his great stage acting ability, has little in the way of a screen personality. In real life he is quite different than he appears on stage. In real life he is quiet, taciturn, phlegmatic, slow to anger, slow to laugh. He is thoughtful, deliberate, without idiosyncracy or eccentricity. He could be taken for a rather good-looking professor or engineer instead of an actor. He transforms himself on stage magnificently, it is true. But for movies, all that comes through is his basic personality, which is without electricity and appeal. I once heard him ascribe his ability to act great roles to the fact that as a real-life person he is a 'hollow man.' I think he's probably right. That hollowness may be just right for a stage actor, who uses his roles to fill himself in. Who knows, perhaps it is Olivier's personal hollowness that compels him to act in the first place. But it is his hollowness that the camera captures, not what he fills it with. And that's why he has never become a movie star."[1]

•

Olivier may have heard words similar to those during his first stay in Hollywood. According to an English friend, he returned to London with Jill in August of 1932 filled with bitterness about Hollywood specifically and film acting in general. "Largely he talked about the assembly-line aspects of American filmmaking," says the friend, "but he also let slip once or twice that people out there had complained about his inability to make an impression on the screen. I'm sure he heard things about himself that he didn't like purely because they assaulted his conception of himself as an actor. He couldn't understand these notions of screen persona and magnetism. He thought acting should be acting, whether on stage or screen, and he couldn't see what personal magnetism had to do with it."[2]

Olivier's rancor was sharpened by the fact that when he and Jill arrived in London, it was once again she who got most of the attention. She gave out interviews freely about life in Hollywood and the combined excitement and tedium of making movies, while he remained dourly uncommunicative on the subject.

Shortly after the couple's return, however, Olivier was offered another chance to act in a movie—this one a fairly important one. The famous Gloria Swanson had formed her own production company and, through it, was preparing to appear in her first talkie to be made in Britain. Swanson was a star celebrated for her insistence on dominating the screen. She had fought vigorously against the Hollywood studios whenever they assigned an actor of any substance to share the screen with her. By producing her own movies, she expected to have control over the choice of her co-stars. For her first sound movie she chose a humorous story about the problems of an English married couple trying to live separate lives. With herself as the glamorous wife, she cast as her co-star her then real-life husband, Michael Farmer. The picture was called *The Perfect Understanding.*

Although Swanson was assured of a weak screen presence in Farmer, he proved to be altogether too feeble to be believable when the first rushes were viewed. Both director Cyril Gardner and United Artists, the Hollywood distribution company financing the production, complained to Swanson that the picture would be a disaster with Farmer as the male lead. Not only was he excessively weak compared to the imperious Swanson, but he couldn't act.

"All right," Swanson said finally. "Get me someone else." Michael Farmer was shunted off to a minor role as the production shut down and a search was launched to find a replacement. Cables flew back and forth between United Artists in Hollywood and Swanson headquarters in London suggesting available actors. Swanson rejected them all. Then came a cable from Myron Selznick: Laurence Olivier, the young English actor who had made two pictures for RKO, was in London and available.

Olivier knew nothing of the cable—he was touring West End theatrical offices looking for a play with which to revive his stage career. In the meantime Swanson, anxious to resume production on *The Perfect Understanding,* obtained a print of Olivier's movie *Westward Passage.* OLIVIER MIGHT DO, she cabled United Artists after viewing the film.

Olivier was having no luck in finding a stage vehicle for himself— the Depression was still on and the British public was getting most of its entertainment in cheap-ticket movie houses rather than in the more expensive theatres of the West End. Then he received a cable from Selznick: GO SEE GLORIA SWANSON AT DORCHESTER. CO-STARRING ROLE IN HER PERFECT UNDERSTANDING. FOUR WEEKS WORK UNDER YOUR CONTRACT RKO. DON'T PASS UP.

Without telling Jill, Olivier went to see Swanson, who kept him waiting for two hours in the hall of her suite at the Dorchester hotel, overlooking Hyde Park. In contrast to her sultry screen image, she was all business. She told him that she had made a great mistake in casting her husband opposite her in the picture. "He's a darling man," she said, "but he's just not strong enough for the part I'm playing. I need a strong, strong actor, one who will challenge me throughout the picture. That's what audiences love, they love to see me get my comeuppance. Will you do it?"

Olivier, flattered, quickly agreed. "Larry, of course, was unaware of what Gloria was up to," said an executive of United Artists who was present. "She had no intention of having a strong leading man. She had seen *Westward Passage* and perceived that Larry came across as a light-weight compared to Ann Harding in that picture. She knew he could act passably, but what was more important was that, after talking to him, she knew that she could dominate him. I mean, if he fell so easily for that 'strong actor to give me my comeuppance' bull, he was putty to be molded. There was a director on the picture, but he was just a hired hand. Gloria was the real director with her constant 'Now, I'd like this scene this way' business. And Larry was still out to prove that he could be a movie star. I sincerely believe he secretly thought that acting opposite Swanson in the picture was going to rocket him at last to the top of the movie industry."[3]

Gloria Swanson dictated every scene and, true to form, throttled all attempts by Olivier to project any strength or masculine determination. "I remember one scene," said the U.A. executive, "in which Larry was supposed to swivel his head around in a reaction shot to some outrageous thing Gloria said. The reaction called for in the script was one, I think, of glowering anger, to be followed by a single word—'rot,' or 'rubbish,' or something like that. Well, Larry did it fine on the first or second take. But then Gloria stepped in and said to Gardner, the director, 'Let's try it this way.' And then she forced Gardner to do about a dozen more takes while she directed Larry to give a different expression of reaction each time, ranging from puzzlement to raised-eyebrow questioning to a kind of Dagwood Bumstead befuddlement.

"When Larry inquired about the necessity of all the different takes, Gloria said, 'Darling, I've been in the business for ages, leave it to me, trust me.' And Larry trusted her. And each time he trusted her, she gained more control over him—just as she wanted her character in the picture to do over him. Larry fell right into the trap without knowing it. He knew it later, though, when the movie was released. As producer, Gloria had the final say on the editing process. And whenever she could, she put in the sequence that gave her the most power and made Larry look like some simpering idiot. I won't say that the reason the movie was a flop was because of this, but it would have been much better if Gloria had allowed Larry's character to have more strength and substance."*

Unexpectedly, the fact that Olivier was making a movie with the world-famous Swanson earned him more publicity in the British press than he had ever received from his stage work.

"Larry became a celebrity in London in a way he never had been before," actor-friend Jack Hawkins once told me. "But it was not something he took any pleasure in. In fact I think he felt guilty and annoyed by it, because he came to believe what he was doing in the Swanson film was worthless, a charade. I remember having him and Jill round for drinks one night, and his arguing with Jill, 'If this is motion-picture celebrity, I don't want any part of it. Why should people look up to you for being a film actor? It's all a sham.' "[4]

Film producers decided to capitalize on Olivier's sudden fame. At first he resisted, still looking for a play. But with no play yet in sight, he gave in once more to financial considerations. He and Jill had been living in a flat in the West End since their return from Hollywood. Now, at the beginning of 1933, they learned that the lease on a fashionable house in Cheyne Walk, overlooking the Thames in Chelsea, was available. The house had been owned in Victorian times by the artist James Whistler. Noel Coward urged them to take it—"You can never live too well, my dears. When you live well, people want to know you."

Since their RKO contracts were on the verge of expiring, the Oliviers needed money to buy the leasehold. Coward had a solution to this, too. He knew a film producer who wanted to make a picture starring Gertrude Lawrence. "Gertie's dying to do it," said Coward. "But it needs two strong co-stars, a younger man and woman, to get the financing. I've recommended you both. I hope you don't mind. And of course Gertie would adore having you."[5]

The film was *No Funny Business,* a sophisticated, romantic sex comedy that was a precursor of the droll British film comedies that became so popular in the 1950s. In 1933, though, English movie audiences were

---

*Interestingly, Olivier had a reverse experience when he made *Westward Passage* a few months before in Hollywood. Ann Harding, his leading lady in that picture, went out of her way to ensure that Olivier had the most advantageous lighting and camera angles in his scenes with her. Because of Harding's generosity, he was inclined to trust Gloria Swanson's motives.

not yet ready for the comic sophistication of a Gertrude Lawrence. The film was only a modest success, and Olivier came across again as nothing more than a vapid foil for the picture's female star.

"Making *No Funny Business* did not serve to improve the relationship between Jill and Larry," commented the movie's co-director, Victor Hanbury. "There was a good deal of competition between them on the set, a lot of clenched-teeth spatting. Jill was fully committed to film acting, whereas Larry was halfhearted about it all. She resented his attitude and at least once accused him of trying to upstage her in a scene by deliberately underplaying, by not putting any energy into their dialogue. Jill was very assiduous, impeccable in her approach to film acting. Larry was rather slovenly and cynical, full of wisecracks and then pretending surprise if anyone caught him up. He struck me as not very happy doing what he was doing—embarrassed and defensive."[6]

In April of 1933, a play finally came along. Called *The Rats of Norway,* it was a melodrama about life at an English boy's boarding school that was to be directed by, and have as its star, the Canadian actor Raymond Massey. Olivier and Massey had met in California the previous year. Massey remembered Olivier's having told him tales of his school career at St. Edward's, and when he heard that Olivier wanted to return to the stage in London, he called him. The part he had to offer—that of a teacher at the school—was a secondary one, but the character was vital. Olivier took it. And, as he said over thirty years later, "That's when I realized finally that playing a good subsidiary role is just as important to an actor as playing the lead. In a way, a good, meaty character part offers the actor many more opportunities to be creative and inventive than a lead part. When you're in a lead part, the production succeeds or fails on your interpretation. But when you are in a character role, when you are only a supporting player, you are freed of that grave responsibility and can concentrate fully on the great fun of acting."[7]

The play had a modest run. Olivier's part called for, as one critic described it, "naturalistic acting at its most natural, no emoting, no grandiosity, but just plain quiet acting." Olivier measured up in the eyes of most who judged his performance, although two reviewers complained that he was frequently quiet to the point of inaudibility. Said one, "It is known that Mr. Olivier has in recent years devoted himself to performing in moving pictures. His return to the stage is welcome indeed, but he might be cautioned to speak up. Has he forgotten that there are no microphones on the stage, as I understand there are in moving picture studios?"[8]

"Larry was betwixt and between in that play," Raymond Massey said later, "and it was perfectly understandable—I have the same problems switching back and forth between picture acting and stage acting. I think it's the reason so many stage actors who go on to become film stars are afraid to return to the stage. In the first you are accustomed to the broad movement, the pronounced gesture, the projected voice. Then you go into films and you have to learn that everything you are accustomed to looks artificial and ridiculous on screen. You learn to tone yourself down, radically. . . . John Barrymore described it perfectly to me once. He said it's like husking an ear of corn. Pick an ear of corn from a stalk and you've got a stage actor. Husk it for cooking and you've got a film actor. The only problem is, once the husk is off, you can't put it back on the ear.

"That was Larry. He had spent a year or two off the stage trying to become a film actor. He had been told over and over again that he must tone himself down. In *The Rats of Norway,* a lot of that influence penetrated his acting—he was almost too subdued. It caused him a great deal of confusion during rehearsals—he was extremely cautious about overacting, as if he was embarrassed to get caught out, as if he felt the presence of a film director out in the seats always ready to shout, in exasperation, 'Cut!' I told him the Barrymore story about cornhusks. 'My God,' he said, 'do you mean I'll never be able to put the husk back?' Once he'd gotten his character in the play set, he stayed with it. But he thought about that Barrymore analogy a great deal. I think it brought him to a point where he said to himself, 'I can't be a stage actor and film actor at the same time. One destroys my feel for the other. I must choose one and reject the other.' My impression then was that he was going to give up films for good."[9]

If Olivier was about to choose the stage, as Massey implied, his resolve was compromised by the events that followed. *The Perfect Understanding* was released in the United States while he was still early in the run of *The Rats of Norway* in London. It was released also at a time when, in Hollywood, M-G-M was busy preparing a new vehicle for its biggest star, Greta Garbo. The movie was to be the story of Queen Christina of Sweden and her romance with a Spanish diplomat.

Garbo, the eccentric Swedish beauty, unlike others had made the transition from silent films to talkies with ease; indeed, her popularity had soared with the coming of sound. She not only earned six thousand dollars a week in 1933, but she had the right to choose her leading men. During the silent years, her principal co-star had been the handsome

John Gilbert. But Gilbert's tinny voice had lost him his popularity when sound began. Louis B. Mayer, head of M-G-M, had convinced Garbo that with *Queen Christina,* she should have a new co-star to play the Spanish diplomat.

Many leading actors had already been considered and rejected by Garbo as being too strong or masculine. She, like Swanson, needed to dominate the screen. Not only that, but whatever character she played had to dominate, indeed enslave, the men who played opposite her—this was the core of her film mystique to which millions of female moviegoers so raptly responded. Her new co-star had to be handsome and vibrant in order to make her interest in him believable, yet pliant enough to enable Garbo to overshadow him.

It was Myron Selznick who planted the idea of Olivier in the minds of Mayer and *Queen Christina*'s producer, Walter Wanger. In June, Selznick put together a special screening of Olivier's movie with Gloria Swanson and said, "There, you see? He's got everything you need for Garbo. He'll be sensational as her lover."

The movie was shown to Garbo. According to *Queen Christina*'s director, Reuben Mamoulian, she gave her conditional approval. But final approval would have to await a screen test between her and Olivier so that she could better gauge how she looked opposite him.

Selznick negotiated a deal with Mayer for a one-year contract for Olivier at forty thousand dollars, to be paid even if Garbo decided against him for the part of Don Antonio. In June he cabled the news to Olivier along with a steamship ticket, telling him to return to Hollywood. Simultaneously, through his press agent, he released the news that the English actor had been chosen to co-star with the great Garbo in her next movie.

"Larry couldn't turn it down," said Raymond Massey. "The news was all over London and the tabloids printed excited stories about Larry as Garbo's screen lover. It was as if Larry's having been selected did something special for the nation's honor. Had he turned it down, he would have been the most unpopular man in England, at least among the female population. He was chagrined when he came to me one day and asked to be excused from the play. He said that he wasn't all that enthusiastic about returning to Hollywood, but his wife was. Jill wanted to go back, and I suppose Larry said to himself, 'Oh, what the hell, I'll give it one more try.' "[10]

His return to Hollywood was to prove Olivier's greatest embarrassment yet as a budding film star. As he told it to Norman Zierold, Garbo's biographer, in the late 1960s, he never felt comfortable with the film queen and had the distinct feeling that she was uncomfortable with him. During rehearsals before the shooting of the picture's principal love scene, scheduled to be filmed at the start of the production, Olivier, as Don Antonio, was to discover that Christina (Garbo), who had been disguising herself as a boy, was actually a woman.

"The director explained that I was to come forward, grasp Garbo's slender body tenderly, look into her eyes and, in the gesture, awaken passion within her, that passion for which she is later to give up the Swedish throne. I went into my role . . . but at the touch of my hand Garbo became frigid. I could feel the sudden tautness of her, her eyes as stony and expressionless as if she were marble."[11]

What occurred thereafter has been the subject of considerable dispute. What was certain was that M-G-M issued an abrupt announcement: Olivier had been fired and replaced by John Gilbert. Louis B. Mayer claimed that Garbo had come to him and demanded Olivier's dismissal—"He does nothing for me," he reported her as saying. Reuben Mamoulian said that the decision was his, that Olivier betrayed himself at the start by his acting inexperience and immaturity. "I could see immediately that he would never be able to handle Garbo." Myron Selznick, perhaps recalling his client's fiasco with Gloria Swanson, publicly proclaimed, "He was too strong for Garbo, he impinged on her presence." Several wags insisted that Olivier had been the victim of a publicity stunt by M-G-M, or a power ploy by Garbo herself. "It was M-G-M's way of pumping up the picture," declared one insider. "It was Garbo's way of proving to M-G-M that John Gilbert was the only actor for the part in the first place," disagreed another.

Whatever the case, Olivier was out. And his release was handled in a way that left him humiliated. He and Jill fled to Hawaii for two weeks to escape reporters anxious to know what had really happened between him and Garbo. (Garbo, typically, remained silent on the matter.)* While Olivier was in Honolulu, M-G-M wired him with an offer to double his salary if he would return and make a different picture. He refused to reply.

*Years later, in the 1940s, Garbo entertained the possibility of making a screen comeback by starring in a movie to be based on the life of George Sand. According to biographer Zierold, she would have asked Olivier to play opposite her. But because the necessary financing could not be arranged, she never got a chance to.

12

Coming of Age

SAID ACTOR James Dale about Olivier's Garbo period: "Larry was absolutely finished with movies—at least with Hollywood movies—after his Garbo experience. He felt he had been knifed in the back by everyone. As he got older, he tended to brush it off by saying they were right to fire him, that he was really inept against Garbo. But when it happened he was in a high dudgeon. He railed against Louis Mayer, against Mamoulian, against Wanger, even Myron Selznick, his agent. He wanted nothing more to do with them. He thought they were all playing around with his life and career. He was even mad at Jill. He blamed her more and more for the rotten experiences he was having in films. 'Goddamn,' he would shout, 'if it wasn't for you and your blasted ideas!' But even Jill was sympathetic. She agreed that it was a terrible bust-up thing they'd done to him. 'All right, Larry, no more Hollywood,' she said.

"Jill was in a vise too. She loved Larry, of course, but her ambitions for herself kept intruding. I think it was then that she made some sort of secret decision to give up her Hollywood hopes. *A Bill of Divorcement* had just been released with Katharine Hepburn in the role Jill would have had. It made Hepburn an overnight star. Jill was melancholy, but she resigned herself to it. She had none of Hepburn's startling screen personality. She was inclined to concede that if she had played the part, the outcome might not have been the same. It might not have made her a star. And with that, she became content within herself to recommitting herself to Larry."[1]

•

James Dale had become friends with Olivier seven years before when both were in the Birmingham Repertory's London production of *The Marvelous History of Saint Bernard.* In August of 1933, Dale, in New York, had agreed to appear as co-male lead in an English play called *The Green Bay Tree,* which was going to be produced and directed by the notoriously contentious American theatrical impresario Jed Harris. After Harris had searched unsuccessfully for weeks for an actor to play the other male lead, Dale said, "What about Larry Olivier? He's been having a devilish time in Hollywood."

The reason Harris had been unsuccessful in his search was because every actor who knew or had heard of him detested him. Possessed of a hyperactive ego and the soul of a tyrant, he treated actors the way medieval lords treated their serfs. A blunt, roughhewn type with a quicksilver mind and the manners of a foundry worker, he was especially contemptuous of British actors and their formal, punctilious and —he thought—superior ways. Why he had taken on an English drama to produce and direct in 1933, no one could divine. Unless, as one Harris hater put it, "He decided he absolutely needed a vehicle to take his aggressions out on the British."

There *was* a more compelling reason. *The Green Bay Tree* was a drama that contained strong undercurrents of homosexuality. Harris loved nothing better than to shock. In 1933, anything approaching overt homosexuality was taboo on Broadway. Need more be said?

Harris remembered Olivier from Noel Coward's *Private Lives.* "In fact," he said to me prior to a 1980 television appearance on the Dick Cavett Show, "I took him to be one of those British fags, that's how good he was in the Coward thing. I'd forgotten he was married."

Olivier would be "okay for the part of Julian" in *The Green Bay Tree,* Harris decided. "It was a part for a queer, but he could play that easily enough. I wasn't too happy about having a guy who'd just struck out

99

in Hollywood. But what the hell, I hadn't been able to find anyone else to play the goddamn part."[2]

Olivier was back in Hollywood when he received the call from Dale. "There's a good part for you here in New York," Dale said. *"The Green Bay Tree,* Julian Dulcimer, playing opposite me. Heard about your troubles. Why don't you take it? The director's a right common bastard, but so what? We'll have some fun. And there's a part for Jill if she wants it."

Olivier and Jill Esmond agreed to take the parts if for no other reason than to "save them from having to go back to London so soon after the Hollywood debacle," as Dale said. "It was headline news in London when Larry got dismissed from the Garbo picture, and he was loath to go straight back and face the folks."[3]

The Green Bay Tree, which opened on Broadway in October of 1933, was a resounding hit but a profoundly dismaying experience for the already disgruntled Olivier. Rehearsals were an actor's nightmare. The hot-tempered Harris directed by fiat rather than persuasion, constantly insulting his cast and belittling the actors to the press. He was particularly contemptuous of Olivier. Even forty-five years later, after Olivier had been showered with honors, Harris derided his ability.

"The importance of acting is grossly overrated in our theatre society," he told me. "All actors are overrated, and Olivier is a prime example. Actors are children—self-indulgent, petulant children who think only of themselves. In order to function at all in the theatre, they need strong directors to be their parents and show them the way. I've heard Olivier complain about me as a director. But I'll tell you, he and all these other actors who get anywhere labor under the delusion that they are responsible for their success. That's horseshit. The reason Olivier was halfway good in *The Green Bay Tree* was because I made him good. I took none of his childish shit about 'forming' his character and his 'choices' in reading lines. I just told him to read his lines my way, and if he didn't like it to get the hell out of the play—I'd get somebody else. Actually he was plenty scared and he wouldn't have dared challenge me—he wanted the job too badly.

"That's the way you have to be with actors. You've got to realize they're scared children and take no nonsense from them. They don't care about the play. They have tunnel vision and care only about themselves, their own parts, how they are going to look. I've heard Olivier castigate me and even tell me how he fought with me to—quote—maintain the integrity of his characterization—unquote. Garbage. His performance in that play was all my doing—he just supplied the body and voice. That's all any actor does, provide the body and voice. Look at Olivier's career. You'll see that his best performances always came when he had a strong director, like me."[4]

The New York Times critic, Brooks Atkinson, and dozens of others hailed Olivier's portrayal of the cocky, effeminate, but ultimately pathetic Julian Dulcimer. One paper described the play's climactic scene, in which Julian was beaten into slavish submission by his benefactor's abnormal attraction for him, as "too terrible to bear." It added that Olivier's performance was "not acting, but an exhibition of emotional collapse so painful to witness that the eyes of the audience are torn away."

The reviews were probably the best and most unanimous Olivier had ever triggered as an actor. But he hated the entire experience, not only because of Jed Harris's despotic direction but because he despised the character of Julian. "Julian went against my entire nature," he would later say. "He was weak, indecisive, despicably without backbone. I never felt comfortable playing him, and I began to despise myself for his disagreeable qualities."[5]

According to Harold Clurman, though, playing Julian Dulcimer had a "turning-point effect on Olivier's career." Clurman, then a leader of New York's Group Theatre and later a distinguished director and critic, saw Olivier in the role many times during the play's run. "In view of Larry's later career," he told me, *"The Green Bay Tree* was a watershed experience. First because of Jed Harris. Harris worked him like a horse, and although he was brutal to work for and Larry clearly abhorred him, he gave Larry a sense of discipline and seriousness about the theatre he'd not had before. Larry was somewhat of a casual actor until he met up with Harris. Jed was a taskmaster only because he believed so passionately in the seriousness of the theatre. It was this passion that gave Jed his 'there-is-only-one-way-to-do-it—my-way' fury. And Larry absorbed this passion, possibly in spite of himself. . . . It was ironic that he should have his greatest acting success in New York rather than London. But I think he later recognized the irony and realized that at that time, at least, American theatre people were much more avid about their work than the British. They worked harder, they demanded more, they were uncompromising in their visions. That rubbed off on Larry, mainly via Harris, and he began to bring the same attitude into his own work.

"And then there was the matter of the part itself. Larry was playing a role that went completely against type. This is what made it so interesting, and so fascinating to playgoers. Although Larry said he hated the part, I think it was a great enlightenment for him. You know what I mean, the movies had been trying to make a matinee idol out of him. . . . Most of the stage work he had done before was of the same ilk—toward developing this romantic leading-man image. It had been Larry's whole orientation to what acting was all about. But here he was cast against type. To sustain it, he really had to do some hard acting, summoning up feelings and attitudes to create a character that were foreign to his sensibility. It gave him the wonderful experience of seeing how rich and complex acting can be when what you are doing is recreating yourself in an entirely hostile image.

"I told him this one time, twenty years later. I told him that the character he played back in the thirties in *The Green Bay Tree* was what first gave him the impetus to expand his acting horizons and start taking chances. He agreed. He said, 'You're right, as much as I couldn't stand playing the part, it took hold of me and made me want to sink my teeth into more such roles. It taught me a great deal about acting.' "[6]

Olivier's reputation as an actor of distinction was solidly cemented in New York, and he thought briefly of remaining in the States to take a starring role in a new play scheduled for the fall season. But in March 1934, Noel Coward offered him a co-starring role in the London production of S. N. Behrman's American comedy hit *Biography,* which Coward intended to finance and stage but not perform in. The role was that of Richard Kurt, a boorish American book editor.

Olivier had seen the play in New York. He had formed vivid opinions about the worst aspects of the American character, and he was anxious to sink his teeth into more roles that went against his nature and type. He exercised his option to leave *The Green Bay Tree* after six months. At the end of March he and Jill sailed to London.

With Coward directing and Olivier starring along with the popular American actress Ina Claire, everyone connected with *Biography* was sure it would be a hit. Olivier played Richard Kurt to the hilt of vulgarity, modeling his characterization closely on Jed Harris and producing a perfect New York accent. But, as an observer would later remark, "Larry overdid it. His Richard Kurt was a burlesque, a parody. Not even the usually anti-American London audiences believed that Americans could be so one-dimensionally repulsive. It was a great comedown for Larry. He had taken the easy route in building his character—all mannerisms and so on. He thought it was brilliant, but the audiences saw through it. It wasn't acting, it was impersonation."[7]

Biography was forced to close after a few weeks, costing Coward thirty thousand dollars. But the writer-performer refused to be defeated by the failure of his first producing venture, and he had another American comedy waiting in the wings. This was *The Royal Family* by Edna Ferber and George S. Kaufman, a rollicking satire based on the famous acting family, the Barrymores. Having changed the title to *Theatre Royal* to avoid the impression that it might be a takeoff on England's royal family, Coward had cast actor Brian Aherne in the role of the pyrotechnic John Barrymore character.

Coward had intended to stage the Ferber-Kaufman play during the fall of 1934, well after *Biography* had settled in as a long-running hit. But in order to recover his losses from the failed Behrman play, he rescheduled *Theatre Royal* for an earlier debut. Brian Aherne, however, was in Hollywood until the fall. Coward needed someone to fill in for him until he was free to return to London.

Olivier was already doing some filling in of his own as Coward contemplated the problem. When *Biography* closed in May, his friend Ralph Richardson had been rehearsing the role of Bothwell in a play called *Queen of Scots*—a vehicle penned by mystery writer Josephine Tey for one of England's best-known actresses, Gwen Ffrangcon-Davies. Richardson, basically a droll character actor, was doing badly in the romantic, athletic part of Bothwell and he knew it. When he heard that Olivier was out of *Biography,* he went to him and asked him to take over the part. Olivier agreed and spent the beginning of the summer as the showy Bothwell in the limited-run debut production of *Queen of Scots.*

As Richardson was to say, "It was a lark for Larry. It gave him an opportunity to try himself out in some of the swashbuckling bits he'd learned from Doug Fairbanks in Hollywood. He was just then learning how he could use his body to captivate audiences."[8]

Olivier quickly got bored with the play. "It involved too much in the way of daily making up and costuming for such an inconsequential part," he recently remarked. His boredom may well have been sharpened when he learned that Coward needed someone to step in for Brian Aherne as the John Barrymore character in *Theatre Royal.*

Olivier had met Barrymore during his first visit to Hollywood three years before. The legendary actor was then on the downhill slope of his career—a tempestuous alcoholic, a half-crazed genius, but still larger than life in everything he did. Olivier had been "frightened by Barrymore's excesses but entranced by his outrageously bravura personality and ego."

Prior to the opening of *Biography,* when Olivier learned that Noel Coward had purchased the British stage rights to *The Royal Family* and was planning a fall production, he had said to Jill Esmond, "Damn, I'd love to play the 'John' part. Why didn't Noel tell me? I would have skipped Richard Kurt and waited for that."

Now, out of *Biography* and performing boisterously but indifferently in *Queen of Scots,* Olivier went to see Coward. "I know you've got a contract with Brian," he said. "But let me play it until he gets here."

Coward said later that he had already thought of asking Olivier to fill in but had resisted the urge because "I thought Larry would be insulted by being asked twice in a row to take over someone else's part. And even more offended by then being asked to give up a part he would have, for all practical purposes, created. I knew about the regrets he'd gone through after he relinquished Stanhope in *Journey's End.*"

Coward was thus delighted when Olivier made the approach. He immediately agreed, but with the warning that he had a contractual obligation to Aherne and that "Larry definitely would have to step out when Brian returned."[9]

"Larry was still young and naive in many respects," said Valentine Dyall, his understudy in *Theatre Royal,* "but he was no dummy when it came to getting himself the part of Tony Cavendish [the John Barrymore character]. Nor, of course, was Noel ignorant of what was happening. I had seen Larry act before, and he'd always struck me as a competent, if archetypical, English leading-man type. But he attacked Tony Cavendish with all the explosiveness and acrobatics he could muster. He was out to make sure that once in the part, no one else could play it. He wanted to make it so much his that when Brian Aherne showed up, he would beg out of his contract."[10]

That was precisely what happened. In rehearsals, Olivier turned Tony Cavendish, written by Ferber and Kaufman as a moderately broad-scale theatrical buffoon, into a riot of vocal tricks and physical gymnastics. Although Coward, directing, could see that he was overplaying shamelessly, he was still anxious for the comedy to be a hit. Olivier's pyrotechnics might just guarantee that. So breathtakingly daring were some of his stage maneuvers that audiences might throng the theatre just to see them.

"Noel tried to tame Larry down," said Jack Wilson, an intimate of

Coward's, "but Larry would have none of it. This was a new Larry— it was the first time anyone had seen him so obsessed with a part. He was riding a whirlwind, I suppose because he felt he had nothing to lose. Later he said, 'No, I've just caught the essence of Barrymore.' But what he was really saying was: 'No one else can play this part, damn it! It's mine!' And it was."[11]

But Olivier's performance was not just reckless, youthful showing off. "On the surface," said another member of the cast, "it was all outward and physical. But it was much more than that. Larry really got into the character and made him remarkably true to life. It was not just a circus performance, but a chillingly real-life one."

By the time Brian Aherne returned from Hollywood to fulfill his contract with Coward, the play was on its pre-London tour in Glasgow. "I went up to Glasgow," Aherne later said, "and was stunned to see what Larry had done with the role I was supposed to play. There was one scene where he made this horrifying leap from an upper landing and over a bannister onto a stairway below. And that was just one of the more bizarre tricks he pulled off. The audiences went wild. After observing all that, I went to Noel Coward and gracefully, you might say, bowed out. I wasn't about to follow Larry into the part. It was a great role for any actor, and I would have loved to have played it—my way. But by then it was Larry's creation and I had the good sense to acknowledge it."[12]

Theatre Royal opened in London at the Lyric Theatre in the early fall of 1934. The play's debut was an overwhelming success, and not just audiences but critics too were rapturous in their praise of Olivier. "A hair-raising performance," wrote the usually dour dean of West End newspaper critics, James Agate. "The portrait is lifesize and life-like."

Among those in the first-night audience was John Gielgud, just a few years older than the twenty-seven-year-old Olivier. Since the day in 1929 when Olivier had gone to see Gielgud act in Shakespeare, the two had become casual acquaintances. Gielgud was entranced by Olivier's Tony Cavendish. In 1934 the brightest young star of the English classical stage, he saw in Olivier's performance a whole new side to acting, one that not even he had considered before. "It made me envious," he said recently. "Larry's marvelous use of physical technique and his mastery of timing were breathtaking. It widened my perception of my own art and definitely had an influence on my future work. An ironic twist—wouldn't you say?—since Larry would tell people that seeing me at the Old Vic a few years before had had a great influence on him."[13]

But it was more than just a complementary influence that Olivier's performance in *Theatre Royal* had on Gielgud. "I had a sense that Larry was suddenly my rival. He was younger than I, and I had the disagreeable notion that he was now in a position to surpass me. I didn't like the idea one bit, and I felt that I had better let out my sails."

A few nights later another young performer came to see *Theatre Royal.* As she watched Olivier dash and soar about the stage, she was mesmerized. Her name was Vivian Hartley Holman, although as an actress she had started to call herself Vivien Leigh.

Olivier settled into what he expected to be a long and glorious run of *Theatre Royal.* Audiences packed the Lyric at every performance and ticket orders were backed up for six months. But one evening in the late fall, two months into the run, Olivier came a cropper. Executing his by then celebrated leap over the balustrade, he made a misstep when he landed on the stairs below. The result was a severely fractured ankle. At the top of his form, he had to leave the play.

13

Gielgud

"**L**ARRY came out of *Theatre Royal* with his leg in a cast," said his friend Jack Hawkins, who was acting at the time in a West End revival of *Hamlet* with John Gielgud in the title role. "But nothing encased his ego and self-assurance. *Theatre Royal* had made him a bona fide star in London, and his horizons seemed unlimited. There was so much he wanted to do, felt he could do, and the only thing that got in his way was his impatience. Plus his injury. He had to sit around for a while, and I fear this made him even more grandiose in his ambitions for himself. Our production of *Hamlet* was a great success, thanks principally to Johnny's performance, and I remember going to visit Larry and him telling me that he'd like to give old Hamlet a try, to see if he couldn't do it better than Gielgud. It was a bizarre idea, really, since one didn't think of Larry in Shakespearian terms—he just didn't have the voice."

"And then there was his other idea, which also seemed rather bizarre. Larry was still only twenty-seven, but he was talking about becoming a manager, taking out a lease on a theatre and putting on his own productions with himself and Jill. He asked me if I'd be interested in joining the small company he had in mind to put together."[1]

•

As Olivier later described it to Kenneth Tynan, his abrupt departure from *Theatre Royal* was as nerve-racking as quitting cigarettes. He had been fine-tuned not only to his performance but also to the adoring appreciation of the audiences. Most evenings he had gotten at least a dozen curtain calls and had gloried in them unabashedly. It was an immensely satisfying way to salvage a reputation damaged by the publicity surrounding his Hollywood embarrassments. But the sudden cutting off of nightly performing brought him weeks of withdrawal pains. He became itchy, restless and, as he put it to Tynan, "perhaps a trifle overambitious."[2]

His managerial ambition manifested itself in his purchase of a pair of plays he intended to present himself. The first was a drama called *The Ringmaster*. Its principal attraction resided in the fact that the lead character was a crotchety invalid confined to a wheelchair—the condition Olivier suffered from at the very time he first read the script. The second play was a comedy entitled *Golden Arrow*.

Olivier organized the production of *The Ringmaster* while his leg was still in a cast, assigning the lead to himself and asking Raymond Massey to direct. Jill Esmond took a subsidiary role. A friend said, "Jill was worried about appearing in a play Larry was producing. She thought people might resent it as nepotism. But Larry insisted she take the part."[3]

The Ringmaster was a failure, closing after ten performances. Olivier suffered an added fillip of bitterness when the critics for the most part praised Jill Esmond's acting and dismissed Olivier's. Again, notice was made of Olivier's tendency to mumble his words when striving for naturalism. "After his rousing, colorful performance in *Theatre Royal,*" wrote one reviewer, "Mr. Olivier disappoints here in a role calling for realistic acting. He seems to equate realism with unintelligibility." James Agate took similar exception: "I wished [Olivier] would not clip his speech and throw away the last words of a sentence; it was a continual strain to hear him."

Olivier hoped to recover his financial loss by putting on the other play he had bought, *Golden Arrow*— this as director as well as producer and star. But a final accounting of the books of *The Ringmaster,* and a settling of debts, revealed that he could not finance the comedy alone. To his rescue came Maurice Browne, the man who had backed the unpromising West End production of *Journey's End* six years earlier. Browne offered to put up the needed money in exchange for half the profits. Olivier hastily agreed.

A man who was close to the production said: "It was ill-conceived from the start. Larry was all wrong for the part, and it was his first real directing experience as well. He would say, 'No one gets anywhere in this world without taking risks.' But if this was a risk, it was not well thought out on Larry's part. He was, I'm afraid, suffering from an excess of hubris—producing, directing *and* starring was an enormous amount of work for even the most experienced theatre man. Larry was not up to the task."[4]

There were two reasons Olivier chose to wear all three hats, according to others. One was Gielgud's success in the West End with *Hamlet.* The Old Vic actor was not only starring in the production but had directed and presented it himself. Gielgud had become an actor-impresario at thirty-one, and Olivier felt challenged to eclipse him.

The second reason had to do with Olivier's domestic life. With regard to this, there are only hints from surviving witnesses. The hints suggest that during his stint in *Theatre Royal* he met a young, beautiful, redheaded actress from Ireland who had recently started working as bit player in the London company of the Birmingham Repertory Theatre. Constantly at odds with his wife, Olivier is said to have become infatuated with the twenty-year-old. Whether his infatuation turned into a genuine love affair, no one is willing to say. If it did, Olivier undoubtedly would have kept it secret from his friends, since his friends were Jill's as well. What his friends were sure of, though, is that he became the young actress's mentor. He couldn't put her in *The Ringmaster,* but "he desperately wanted her close to him when it came time to start work on *Golden Arrow,*" according to one friend. The conclusion is that Olivier only decided to produce *and* direct *Golden Arrow* so that he would be in a position to give the young woman a part.

"Much of Larry's attraction to her," adds the same friend, "had simply to do with the fact that he was tired of living in Jill's intellectual shadow. He wanted for once to be the dominant figure in a relationship. He needed a woman who would look up to him, adore him, hang on his every word. Jill loved him, but she wasn't worshipful and obedient, and she certainly didn't hang on his every word. Larry was growing into a very proper Englishman who, one got the impression, believed that obedience, or obeisance, was the essential function of a woman in a man's life."[5]

In staging *Golden Arrow,* some recall, Olivier divided his attention between the play and the young actress. Maurice Browne became unhappy with the progress of the production and decided to remove his support halfway through the rehearsal period in April of 1935. Olivier was faced with the threat of having to abort the production unless he could come up with further funds to see it through; he still didn't have enough money of his own. So he took a step that he'd been resisting.

In 1935 the British film business, until then somewhat of a cottage industry, was in the process of being revolutionized by a showman-entrepreneur named Alexander Korda. Born and raised in Hungary, Korda had settled in London in 1931. A year later he made an enormously popular movie, featuring the eccentric actor Charles Laughton, called *The Private Life of Henry VIII.* The film's international success gave Korda the financial means to satisfy his ambition of establishing his own motion-picture production company in the fashion of the great Hollywood studios. And in the fashion of Hollywood, in order to provide himself with a stable of talent with which to make the many movies he had planned for the future, he had begun to sign local actors and actresses—famous and unknown—to long-term contracts.

Korda had offered Olivier a contract during the actor's run in *Theatre Royal.* Olivier had declined, insisting that he had no further interest in making movies. But now, six months later, needing fresh money to bring his production of *Golden Arrow* to the stage, Olivier changed his mind. He agreed to sign on with Korda's studio, London Films Ltd., in exchange for a contract that provided him with a generous immediate cash advance. With that money in hand, he was able to complete his presentation of *Golden Arrow.*

Golden Arrow was even more of a box-office disaster than *The Ringmaster* had been. Denys Blakelok, who was in the play, mourned it in his 1967 book *Round the Next Corner.* "I wish there were something more positively interesting to record about that . . . production," he wrote. "But the play, though witty and entertaining, was very lightweight and did not give [Olivier] much chance to stretch his imaginative powers. His own performance was immaculate as ever. So were his clothes. Olivier was then at his most smart and sophisticated—quite a different personality from what we know today."[6]

Critic James Agate was less charitable when he wrote in the *Sunday Times:* "Throughout the evening Mr. Olivier had not one single word to say that was worth speaking or hearing."

The play closed in ten days. With it, apparently, went Olivier's relationship with the young redheaded actress he had introduced to the West End. Her name was Greer Garson, and within a few years she would be one of Hollywood's hottest stars.

Olivier was financially bloodied but unbowed spiritually by his first experience as an actor-manager. "His commercial daring at so young an age drew a lot of clucking of tongues," recalls a friend. "And when it turned out to be a failure, there were a lot of self-satisfied 'I-told-you-so's by a lot of small-minded people who were nothing more than envious of Larry—of his wife, of his house, of his talent, of his already secure place in the theatre. But his real pals rallied round him —people like Richardson, Coward, Massey, Gertie Lawrence, and such. They'd all been through their own failures and welcomed Larry to the club. Since they had gone on to great success, they convinced Larry that his greatest achievements were still ahead of him. Someone else might have crept into the woodwork and hidden after going through the embarrassment Larry had. But he—well, I suppose that's the measure of a man, how he handles a defeat. Larry was momentarily discouraged, but never defeated.

"Indeed, the experience served, I think, to round out Larry's character. In a way it inspired in him the idea that taking great personal chances was the great fun of life. And it was that idea that he began to put into his acting, the idea of doing what no one expected him to do, of doing what everyone was sure he could never pull off. He forever after wanted to show the world that he could pull off whatever he set out to do, and he put that compulsion into his acting. It made him, of course, the super actor he became. And it derived, I'm sure, from the calamity of *The Ringmaster* and *Golden Arrow.*"[7]

Olivier later recalled that his determination to succeed as an actor-manager was so fierce that he couldn't wait to have another go at it. Ralph Richardson was of the same mind, and the two resolved to find a play they could present and appear in together. "It's the only way to go," Richardson said. "Be your own boss and stop being at the mercy of half-witted managers and producers and incompetent actors."

But before Olivier could return to the rigors of self-production, he had to begin fulfilling his contract with Alexander Korda. In July of 1935, a few weeks after the closing of *Golden Arrow,* he was summoned by Korda to Denham, where the Hungarian producer was in the process of establishing a large movie production studio. The financial linchpin of any motion-picture company of the day was to make as many movies within a given amount of time as possible; only in that way was the cash flow sufficient to support the companies' overhead and the opulent lifestyles their chief executives maintained. By 1935, Korda's London Films was churning out film after film, most of them costume dramas, using the large stable of local acting talent he had put together. For Olivier's first movie, Korda ordered a quick remake in English of a successful French film of the year before. Called *Les Nuits de Moscou,* Korda retitled it *Moscow Nights.* (It was exhibited eventually in America as *I Stand Condemned.*)

"Korda took an instant liking to Larry," says a onetime associate of both men. "Alex was trying hard to lose his Hungarian image and become a proper Englishman. He was impressed by Larry's very British style. But he was more impressed by the fact that Larry was a man of the theatre—not just another actor, but a man who had ambitions of being an impresario himself, who had tried and failed but was keenly game to try again. Alex was your usual Middle European despot when it came to doing business with most people. But with Larry he always trod softly, respectfully. He wanted Larry to be more than an employee —he wanted him to be a friend.

"As for Larry—well, at first he remained aloof, suspicious of Alex and resolved, I'm sure, only to go through the motions of acting in his films. But Alex had a charm and persuasiveness that were irresistible— even to rather stuffy Englishmen. That is, when he wanted to use it. He used it on Larry, and Larry warmed to him quickly.

"Alex was frank. He'd heard about Larry's attitude toward films and his bad experiences in Hollywood. 'I want you to become a star,' he told Larry, 'because it will help make you rich, but even more so because it will help make me rich. So why shouldn't we collaborate on each of us getting rich?'

"Alex had had some bad experiences in Hollywood before he established himself in London, and he had his own special contempt for many of the bigshots who ran the studios. He would regale Larry with stories about the Hollywood bigwigs and their vulgar tastes and unethical business practices. Well, this sold Larry on Alex. The two established a conspiratorial fellowship based on their mutual contempt for the Hollywood moguls. 'I want to give the world something better than the *dreck* Hollywood produces,' he would say to Larry, 'but I need your help.' And Larry responded. The longer he worked for Alex, the harder he tried to put his best into film acting."[8]

Moscow Nights marked the first step in the revision of Olivier's attitude. Although the finished product was unmemorable, the making of the movie proved to be a valuable lesson in film acting for Olivier. Anthony Asquith, the director, was a man who understood the power of the camera better than most film makers. He was a stickler for natural acting, which he called "playing yourself."

He told Olivier: "On stage, an actor has to 'become' his character. But in front of a camera, the actor must let the character become him. On stage you use voice, mannerisms, gestures and expressions that you think define the person you are playing. On screen you must not allow this to happen, because the camera lens is so unsparing in its ability to focus the eye on actuality. The camera reveals that kind of acting as acting. You must be content to restrict your voice, expressions and mannerisms to those that are natural to you. Unless you do that, no one will believe your character."[9]

Asquith directed Olivier in *Moscow Nights* with an insistent but sympathetic hand. When the film was finished, Olivier had a new appreciation of film acting. It was heightened when the movie was released. Although *Moscow Nights* was not a critical success, the reviewers lauded Olivier's presence in it as its best asset. "Such pleasure as I got from *Moscow Nights* was largely due to Mr. Olivier's recurrent appearances on the screen," wrote the *Observer* critic.

Another influence on Olivier's changing film sensibility was the actor Robert Donat, who had recently become a top star of British cinema with his performance in Alfred Hitchcock's *The 39 Steps*. The film, aside from being a spellbinding tale in itself, climaxed the transition from silent movies to talkies. No longer would movie audiences tolerate the one-dimensional silent-movie acting styles that had lingered through the early stages of sound. Olivier saw Donat's performance in the Hitchcock thriller and was, for the first time, impressed by the ability of the camera to capture a feat of acting.

Watching Robert Donat perform, though, had a more significant impact on Olivier than merely helping to change his attitude about screen acting. Donat enjoyed his cinema success but still thought of himself primarily as a stage performer. He had already made a solid name for himself in London as a classical actor. When he and Olivier met at Denham, Donat had just received an offer from John Gielgud to play Romeo in a Gielgud-directed Old Vic production of Shakespeare's *Romeo and Juliet* in the West End. The production was to be a follow-up to Gielgud's highly popular *Hamlet*, which had recently closed after one hundred fifty-five consecutive performances—a near record for a Shakespeare play.

Donat and Gielgud were friends, but other commitments prevented Donat from accepting Gielgud's offer. The time was early September, 1935. Gielgud and his financial backer, Bronson Albery, had a lease on the New Theatre, but they would have to abandon it on November 1 unless they could get their production of *Romeo and Juliet* on the boards well before. When Donat declined, they began to hunt desperately for someone else to play Romeo. Unable to find anyone, Gielgud considered playing Romeo himself, although his original intention had been to play the lesser role of Mercutio to Donat's Romeo. Donat, hearing of his difficulty, contacted Gielgud and said, "What about Larry Olivier?"

Gielgud was doubtful. He had thought briefly of Olivier after Donat was forced to decline Romeo but had dismissed the idea on the ground that Olivier was too showy and boisterous an actor to play the broodingly complex Romeo.

"This was simply my own prejudice at work," Gielgud said years later. "I was looking for someone whose primary acting virtue was his ability to speak Shakespeare's verse. One didn't think of Larry as suited to Shakespeare in those days, as his voice was—well, one thought his voice was not up to the job. The most consistent criticism Larry had received as an actor was not so much his lack of vocal technique as his misuse of it."

Donat partly changed Gielgud's mind. "The man is a chameleon," he said. "He can use his voice in any manner you ask him to. He would look smashing as Romeo. All he'd need would be some strong technical direction from you."

Donat brought the two men together for lunch at The Ivy, a fashionable restaurant in the West End. Afterward Gielgud offered Olivier the part, although he retained strong reservations. He still believed that Olivier was "a trifle too coarse in his projection of himself" to be the sensitive, fragile Romeo he had been hoping to put on stage. By that time, though, he had no alternative other than to play the part himself. As it was, he decided, he would have to learn it anyway, so that he could step in should Olivier not work out.

His offer to Olivier was put in those terms. "You can take on Romeo. But you must also learn Mercutio so that we can switch immediately if the critics should find excessive fault with you."

Olivier, although eager to test his adult wings in Shakespeare, was offended, and he disputed the proposal. "Look here, dear boy," Gielgud told him, "it's our money we're putting at risk, and quite a bit of it. We must have insurance."[10]

It was Jill Esmond who was the ultimate influence, albeit a reverse one, in persuading Olivier to accept the proposal. Her marriage to Olivier had begun to founder the year before as he gained an increasing sense of his power as a stage actor in *Theatre Royal.* No longer was he willing to have her serve as his intellectual mentor and the engine of his ambition.

"Jill was still seeking to change Larry, I'm afraid," says a friend. "To get him to do, see things her way. She gave him quite a razzing over his attempt to become a manager with that disastrous comedy he presented after he had to leave *Theatre Royal.* It was all against her advice, she often complained to people. Well, Larry didn't cotton very well to that, just as he didn't cotton to Jill's other efforts to make him follow the course she thought he should.

"There was also that Greer Garson business, which Jill resented mightily though she put up a good front about it. The marriage was no longer a happy one, and Larry seemed particularly disgruntled. And then, of course, Jill came along and said, 'You'd be a fool to play Romeo in Gielgud's company. You're all wrong for it. Johnny Gielgud and the rest of his group will wipe the stage with you.' Or something to that effect. Well, that just made Larry all the more determined to play the part."[11]

That and the fact that he knew Gielgud had misgivings about him. "Larry came into rehearsals with an 'I'll-show-them' attitude," said a member of the cast. "And at first he confirmed John's worst fears. He did not come in pandering to John, slavishly following his every suggestion. John as usual went for the linguistic effect in his direction. Larry was like a meteorite flashing through a firmament of fixed stars. I mean, he could have been acting in another play."

The three weeks of rehearsals were filled with tension and bitter arguments between Olivier and Gielgud. Olivier was forging the character of Romeo not as the sweet, lovesick teenager of tradition but as an earthy, athletic romantic who compulsively blunders, rather than being forced by innocence and fate, into his tragic end. As another cast member said, "Larry was out to dominate the play by sheer force of his presence, to ride roughshod over the rest of us as we went about things in our rather restrained Gielgudian fashion. And that's exactly what he succeeded in doing."

The Gielgud production of *Romeo and Juliet* had its premiere at the

New Theatre on October 17, 1935—preceded by behind-the-scenes press gossip about violent differences between Olivier and Gielgud over Olivier's interpretation of Romeo. Indeed, the press inflated the opening night into the theatrical event of the year: the arrogant Shakespearian newcomer versus the much-respected veteran interpreter of the Bard. At first blush, Gielgud was the clear winner.

Olivier's performance was roundly castigated by the critics. Predictably, his handling of Shakespeare's verse was the focus of most of the agitation, one reviewer writing that Olivier's "blank verse is the blankest I have ever heard," another saying that Olivier "plays Romeo as though he were riding a motor-bike." And James Agate bewailed: "Mr. Olivier's Romeo suffered enormously from the fact that the spoken poetry of the past eluded him. In his delivery he brought off a twofold inexpertness which approached virtuosity—that of gabbling all his words in a line and uttering each line as a staccato whole cut off from its fellows."

There was, however, another side to the controversial characterization that was also reflected in Agate's critique. In fact, Agate's might be the best description of Olivier's technique to survive over the intervening forty-five years. After taking exception to Olivier's speech, he wrote: "Apart from the speaking, there was poetry to spare. This Romeo looked every inch a lover, and a lover fey and foredoomed. The actor's facial expression was varied and mobile, his bearing noble, his play of arm imaginative, and his smaller gestures were infinitely touching. Note, for example, how lovingly he fingered first the props of Juliet's balcony and at the last her bier. For once in a way the tide of this young man's passion was presented at the flood, and his grief was agonizingly done. . . . Taking the performance by and large, I have no hesitation in saying that this is the most moving Romeo I have ever seen."

It was to this aspect of Olivier's portrayal that the public—notwithstanding the almost unanimous critical condemnation—responded so enthusiastically. The play ran for one hundred and eighty-six performances, a record for *Romeo and Juliet.*

One theatre-goer who saw the production as a twenty-year-old recalled it for me recently: "Olivier was electrifying. A lot of it had to do with the fact that his performance was so daring, and thus shocking to a public brought up on Romeo as an effete, hapless boy. Olivier played him as you might imagine a real Italian young man in the 1930s to be—swaggering, cocky, bold and possessed with his masculinity, yet vulnerable and sensitive. What made it so exciting was that he did it all through gesture and movement and stance. I often thought afterward that he should have played the role mute, without his lines. He told everything through the pictures he painted with his body as he moved about the stage. If ever a picture was worth a thousand words, Olivier put it together in this role. He gave Romeo incredible truth, and the speeches were secondary. If anything, they intruded on the truth of the characterization."

Often it is neither the critics nor the public that makes a performer's career. It is through one's fellow performers that news that a genuine star has arrived first enters the awareness of the press and the entertainment world in general, then captures the attention of the public. This was very much the case with Olivier. Had he not played Romeo as he did in the 1935 Gielgud production, he might well have remained nothing more than a journeyman West End actor. And had he not provoked the awe and envy of his fellow actors, he might never have been given the further opportunities that enabled him to rise above them all.

Not every colleague gloried in Olivier's Romeo. Alec Guinness, for instance, then a twenty-one-year-old member of the *Romeo and Juliet* cast, remarked to David Frost on television in 1970 that he had resented Olivier at the time. He felt sorry for Gielgud, who up to then had no rival in the English theatre. "Larry Olivier was undoubtedly glamorous," Guinness said, "but he seemed a bit cheap—striving after theatrical effect and so on—and making nonsense of the verse."[12]

But most actors who saw Olivier as Romeo, as well as directors and producers, were rhapsodic about the performance. Ralph Richardson, admittedly not objective, said, "A miracle. It's astounding the way he just stands there against the balcony with such an extraordinary pose that his animal magnetism and vitality and passion come right over . . . no words are necessary. You just look at him and feel this great outpouring of sympathy."[13]

Alexander Korda said to the *London Daily Telegraph:* "I have never seen anything like it in the theatre. If anything, Larry Olivier transcends Shakespeare in giving a true glimpse into the soul of a man."[14]

Said actor Robert Newton to another publication, "No actor, after having seen Olivier as Romeo, can again play the part without copying him. The public just won't stand for anything less than the gusto and truth Larry brings to the role."[15]

Newton was wrong. As a result of the critics' condemnations of his opening night performance, Olivier went to Gielgud and Albery and offered to leave the play. Albery had a better idea. In order to foster interest in the production, he announced that Olivier would play Romeo for six weeks and then would exchange roles with Gielgud. In that way, audiences and critics could return and judge for themselves the virtues of one acting style compared to the other when applied to Shakespeare.

"It was a capital publicity ploy," says another London producer. "The public were excited about Olivier. But Johnny had a large and loyal public of his own. I was in New York in the 1950s and I remember hearing from Talullah Bankhead about the daily controversy put up by the papers about who was the better baseball player, Mr. Mantle or Mr. Mays. Evidently it was a heated issue amongst local baseball aficionados. Well, that's what Bron Albery got going when he had Olivier and Gielgud switch roles. He built it up with the press as a theatrical *mano a mano,* and it paid off handsomely. Except that once Johnny took over the part, playing Romeo in his usual highbrow manner, the controversy fell somewhat flat. There was no doubt that Larry Olivier's portrayal had a power and majesty that Johnny's lacked. It was a great mistake on Gielgud's part from an acting point of view. Suddenly he was forced to face the fact that his equal as a Shakespearean actor, possibly even his better, had arrived on the scene. Yet Johnny was the type of fellow who could say, 'Well, there's room for both of us.' "[16]

Word of Olivier's eccentric brilliance in *Romeo and Juliet* quickly spread to Hollywood. He was immediately offered, and accepted, the part of Orlando in the M-G-M film version of Shakespeare's comedy *As You Like It.* He made the picture during the mornings and afternoons late in 1935 at a studio near London while he played first Romeo, then Mercutio, at night at the New Theatre. Although Shakespeare still did not appeal to the movie-going masses and the film was a financial flop, Olivier shone as the colorful, athletic Orlando.

As a result of his Romeo, he also glittered ever more brightly in the eyes of the twenty-two-year-old actress who, entranced, had watched him cavort so electrically about the stage the year before as Tony Cavendish in *Theatre Royal.* The story has it that when she saw him as Cavendish, the actress turned to the woman she was with and whispered, "That's the man I'd really like to be married to."

Now it was no longer an idle fantasy. After seeing Olivier as Romeo, Vivien Leigh is said to have turned to her companion and exclaimed, "God, I have got to meet him."

14

Vivien Leigh

"**W**E didn't know it then," says a woman who was once a schoolmate of Vivien Leigh's, "but then how could we? It was there, though. Vivien would get along fine for a few weeks, a few months—be perfectly normal and friendly and involved in her activities. Then, suddenly, a complete turnaround. Sometimes it would last only a few hours, other times a day or more. But when it happened, we'd see a completely different girl—moody, silent, petulant, rude, often hysterical. None of us understood it, not even the schoolmistresses. At first we credited it to longing for her family—they were living out in India, you know. But as we got to know her better, we realized that she was quite happy to be at school and didn't seem to miss her family at all. . . . Knowing what we know today about these things, one would definitely have to say that Vivien was a disturbed young girl, disturbed in some way that she had no control over. Had she been a child today, someone undoubtedly would have taken serious notice and sent her to a doctor to be examined. Who knows what he would have discovered—a chemical imbalance, a genetic defect? It's impossible to say, I don't know if there's a name for what Vivien suffered from. But she definitely suffered from some mental peculiarity that on occasion put her severely out of sorts. . . . It was frightening when it happened, almost on the order of a dual personality."[1]

•

Vivien Leigh had been born Vivian Mary Hartley in Darjeeling, India, on November 5, 1913. She was the only child of Ernest Hartley, a young Englishman who had settled in India a few years before as a financial broker, and his wife, Gertrude. Hartley, originally from the northern English county of Yorkshire, engaged in amateur dramatics as an avocation. His wife, also from Yorkshire but of Irish-French ancestry, found her avocation in religion. A staunch Catholic, she was said to have conducted her marriage as a kind of war between her own doctrinaire beliefs and her husband's moral fecklessness. She won, but at the cost of losing Ernest Hartley to a life of infidelity and hedonism. With that, she turned her rigid Catholicism on her daughter.

After witnessing several childhood years of domestic turmoil at her parents' home in India, Vivian was sent at seven to a Catholic girls boarding school—a convent, really—at Roehampton, a suburb of London, to be educated. At thirteen, her father having become well-to-do, she continued her education at a series of similar convent schools in France, Italy and Switzerland, becoming fluent in French, Italian and German, and revealing an aptitude for dramatics that was complemented by her remarkably good looks.

The only aspect of Vivian's life that seemed flawed was her constant physical clumsiness. While in Switzerland she had been eager to learn how to ski and ice-skate, but she was bedeviled by an inability to stay on her feet. Nor could she ride a bicycle without tumbling to the ground after a few pedals. Sent to a doctor at sixteen to discover the reason for her ineptness, she and her parents were told that she had a balance problem—something to do with her inner ear. She would, the physician assured them, grow out of it.

Vivian's developing beauty as a teenager was in stark contrast to her appearance as a child and a cause of wonder to her parents. As a child she had been chubby and knock-kneed, with a moon-round face whose eyes were buried like small marbles in a fleshy field of cheeks and brows. But at sixteen her face was angular, bearing high, streamlined cheeks and large, lustrous, grey-green eyes. Her forehead was boldly shaped, her nose delicate, her mouth full and sensuously curved. Her at once fragile and strong face was framed by a shimmering aureole of chestnut hair, and her head was supported by a neck that was swanlike in its sinuous grace. A lithe, supple torso and shapely legs completed the figure of a young woman extraordinarily endowed.

In the summer of 1931, when Vivian was seventeen, she completed the last year of her studies in Switzerland and returned to London, where her father and mother had settled temporarily after leaving India. With the Depression tightening its grip on London and diluting the value of Ernest Hartley's wealth, he moved Vivian and her mother to a rented estate in the countryside of Devon. There the Hartleys spent the winter.

Vivian, living with her parents for the first time in ten years, quickly grew impatient and irritated. She saw at first hand how her mother's preoccupation with Catholicism had turned the older woman into a joyless, self-righteous wife to her father. She understood for the first time his openly hedonistic, philandering life outside the house. She was torn between a dutiful sense of loyalty to her mother and a thrilling secret admiration of her father. Although he no longer engaged in amateur acting, Ernest Hartley, then forty-seven, still enjoyed regaling Vivian with stories about the theatre. He himself was astonished at his daughter's blossoming beauty. One night, over dinner, possibly to needle his wife, he said to Vivian, "You know, Vivling [his pet name for her], you might make an actress yourself."

Gertrude Hartley angrily registered her objection to the suggestion. As Vivian watched her parents argue, she thought: "Why not? I've got to do something to get out of this place."

Vivian had been steeped in the precepts of Catholicism by nuns and pious schoolmistresses for ten years. But except for the exquisite manners and mental discipline her education had instilled in her, its religious aspects hadn't taken. Vivian had begun to rebel against the social structures of Catholic doctrine during her last two years in Switzerland. Her sense of rebellion was only heightened by her mother's slavish devotion to religious ritual.

Vivian mulled over her father's playful suggestion during the winter of 1931–32. Residing far from London, she had little to do but read. One of the books she studied was a biography of Lillie Langtry, the actress-socialite whose career had been a source of scandal and sensation in England's Victorian era. Another was the fiercely controversial

121

Lady Chatterley's Lover by D. H. Lawrence—a new novel considered salaciously graphic in its portrayal of a contemporary woman's sexual self-fulfillment.

"It was those two books," said a friend from that period, "that filled Viv with her desire to get out into the world. She had been brought up by her mother and educated by the nuns to believe that sex was a necessary evil invented by God solely for procreation. Intellectually she had already dismissed that as a lot of rubbish. She was still a virgin, but she instinctively knew that sex and womanhood and all the rest were just as important as fine table linens and vases full of flowers in a woman's life. At least it was going to be that way in *her* life. After she read *Lady Chatterley*, I remember her coming to me and telling me how desperate she was to find out what sex was all about, firsthand. 'God,' she'd then say, 'I would have loved to have been Lillie Langtry.' "[2]

But it was someone she had known personally, not through the remove of a book, that ultimately decided Vivian Hartley to take up her father's suggestion and try for an acting career. When Vivian had been at the Roehampton convent school, one of her schoolmates had been an auburn-haired Irish girl, two years older, named Maureen O'Sullivan. Vivian remembered her as a girl with a driving ambition, when she was ten, to become an actress. Now, ten years later, Maureen O'Sullivan, barely twenty, was a rising star in Hollywood. Vivian journeyed into London in February of 1932 to see her onetime schoolmate's first movie. When she returned to her parents, she announced that she wanted more than anything to study to become an actress. Overruling her mother's further objections, her father arranged for her to enroll at London's Royal Academy of Dramatic Arts.

February of 1932 was a fateful month not only for Vivian's career ambitions, however. Within a few days of declaring her desire to study acting, she met at a weekend ball in Devon a thirty-one-year-old barrister from London whose family owned an estate nearby. Handsome, urbane, strait-laced and social-minded, educated at Harrow and Cambridge, H. Leigh Holman—as he called himself, his first name being Herbert—was immediately attracted to Vivian and she to him. Later in the spring, when she moved to London to start at the Royal Academy, they began to see one another regularly. By July they were engaged and in December they were married, taking up residence in Holman's bachelor flat in London's St. John's Wood. Vivian was nineteen.

During their courtship, Vivian attended the Royal Academy of Dramatic Arts daily. As several of her friends were later to say, her initial urge to act became a hardened determination after only a few weeks of study. But Leigh Holman had no enthusiasm for her ambition. After their marriage, or possibly as a condition of it, he demanded that she withdraw from the Royal Academy and set about being a proper barrister's wife.

Vivian did so. "She imagined herself to be helplessly in love with Leigh," said one of her friends. "But it was more of an idealized love than a real one. Leigh, with his sandy hair and impeccable manners, resembled Leslie Howard [one of England's leading actors]. He was twelve years older than Vivian, rather on the serious side but socially desirable.

"Viv fell for Leigh because she was ready for a great love. She wanted to taste all the mysteries of womanhood and he came along at a convenient time, so she fantasized him into being something he was not. He was pleasant enough, but plenty dull and humorless. She could have had an affair and let it go at that. She told me later that by the time of her wedding, she realized she was not madly in love with him. But she married him anyway because he was her escape from living with her mother. I suppose, also, because he *was* a good catch.

"It was the thing for girls to marry young in those days, and of course one's success was always measured in terms of the qualities of the husband one caught. Viv was highly susceptible to this way of thinking, and Leigh Holman was a proper catch indeed. He had all the superficial social requisites. But he had none of the internal things that Viv obviously needed, although she hadn't yet come to recognize them. He had no fire, no imagination, no passion. He was well practiced at containing his feelings, if he had any, while Viv was just in the process of discovering the joy of expressing her feelings."[3]

After three months of growing restlessness in their small St. John's Wood flat, Vivian pleaded with her husband for permission to return to the Royal Academy. He agreed to part-time attendance. Before Vivian could take up her studies again in earnest, she became pregnant. She gave birth to a daughter in October 1933. Soon thereafter the Holmans moved into a small but elegant house—once inhabited by Lynn Fontanne—in the heart of Mayfair.

"It was that house that really resparked Viv's desire to act once and for all," says another who knew her at the time. "And, in fact, in an indirect way it was the house that inspired her to pursue Larry Olivier." The house, at 6 Little Stanhope Street in Mayfair's quaint, ancient Shepherd Market, needed much in the way of decoration and furnishing. Antique furniture was a subject that interested Leigh Holman, and together he and Vivian devoted their energies and imaginations to outfitting their new home. "It was the happiest Viv ever was with Leigh," recalls her friend. "Having the baby and fixing the house really brought them together for a while. The only trouble was that it didn't last. Leigh hired a nanny for the baby, plus they had a cook and a housemaid. After a few months, Viv had nothing to do all day but go out to lunch with the pals she had made at the Royal Academy.

"She and Leigh gave a lot of parties at the house. There was one night when they had a furious row. Viv was so proud of the house, of her lifestyle, of everything. The thing she bubbled most about was that the house had once been Lynn Fontanne's—I mean, not a visitor came without being told about that in great detail. After they were there for a while, Viv started talking to her friends about going back to the Royal Academy. If Leigh had been mildly against it before, now he was firmly opposed. The subject came up at a party. Viv sort of half-jokingly said she wanted to resume with her acting but Leigh wouldn't let her. You could tell from the way she said it and the way Leigh reacted that it was a bone of contention between them. Viv was trying, in a not too subtle way, to get Leigh to agree to it in public—she thought he would be embarrassed to say no in front of their friends. But he—well, he didn't exactly blow up. He made this stentorian announcement, something to the effect that now that he had bought her the famous Lynn Fontanne's house, she didn't need to act. That she could never be as famous as Lynn Fontanne and would have to settle for living in Fontanne's house and forget about acting. I recall that it was all rather patronizing, and Viv ran from the room in tears."[4]

Vivian spent much of 1934 trying to forge a change in her husband's attitude. Finally, toward the end of the year, he softened. He realized that Vivian had little interest in being other than a show mother to their year-old daughter Suzanne. Also, she had begun to drink in a fashion that was less than healthy, and she occasionally experienced strange, temporary mood changes that alternately puzzled and frightened Holman.

It was his good friend Oswald Frewen, however, who finally persuaded Holman. Frewen, a cousin of Winston Churchill and a man who moved easily among society and theatre people, had grown as fond of Vivian as he was of Holman. Vivian soon turned him into a mediator between Holman and herself.

"Let her have her fling with acting," Frewen advised Holman over lunch one day. "Once she gets it out of her system, she'll be all right."

From Holman's later point of view, it was the worst advice he ever followed. He agreed to let Vivian "have her fling." But she never got it out of her system. For all practical purposes their marriage was over.

Armed with her husband's reluctant approval, Vivian, through friends, got a tiny part in a film called *Things Are Looking Up* in September 1934. On the strength of that and her looks, she obtained a talent agent who tried to sell her to Alexander Korda's London Films. Korda, then signing up talent left and right, was impressed by Vivian's beauty but found her wanting in type—her features were too regular, almost too perfect, to have character, he claimed.

Vivian's agent, John Gliddon, was undaunted. What was needed first, though, was a name change. Vivian Holman was prosaic, Vivian Hartley stuffy, and movie moguls put great value on mellifluous names. "Vivien Leigh" was the name Gliddon settled on, borrowing Vivian's husband's middle name for her professional last name and changing the *a* in Vivian to an *e* to give her first name a more feminine aspect.

Two more bit parts in movies followed. Then, in February 1935, Gliddon got Vivien her first stage role in a fifteenth-century costume drama called *The Green Sash,* which opened at a small theatre in South London. The play was a failure and closed in two weeks, but Vivien was praised highly by the second-string critics for her appearance and acting. Only her voice came in for negative comment—some thought it too thin for the stage.

By that time, Leigh Holman thought his wife should have gotten her acting desires out of her system—three unremarkable film parts, a rejection by Alexander Korda and a stage failure were sufficient grounds, in his mind, for her to abandon her dilettantish ambitions. Oswald Frewen once recalled that just after the closing of *The Green Sash,* Vivien and Holman visited him for a weekend at his country estate in Sussex. Vivien was thoroughly bitten by the acting bug, Frewen said, and had no intention of giving it up. "She spent the weekend filling my ears with her delight over what she had so far achieved. All, of course, out of earshot of Leigh." As for Holman, "He moped around, thoroughly dissatisfied with Viv's continuing glow over her accomplishments, which he thought were nil."[5]

"It was not so much vanity or a need for self-gratification that propelled Vivien into acting," said David Horne, an actor who became a close friend for a while. "It was the excitement and variety of the acting world that got to her—the passions, the hard, often tedious work, the sense of comradeship among players. The theatre in London was like an extended family, all these eccentric, interesting, self-absorbed, highly amusing and exhibitionist people. It was in such contrast to the orderly world of barristers and bankers that her husband was immersed in. It brought out passions in her like lava from an exploding volcano. Once the lava started to flow, it could never be put back."[6]

According to others, the lava flowed with a special urgency when Vivien Leigh first glimpsed Laurence Olivier during his stint as Tony Cavendish in *Theatre Royal* in the fall of 1934. "Viv was entranced by Larry," says one. "She was dying to meet him, but afraid to as well. It was then she realized once and for all that her marriage to Leigh had been a mistake, that she did not love Leigh. She was madly in love with Larry, even if it was only from afar. She used to tell me that she imagined being in bed with Larry instead of Leigh. She went to see Larry in *Theatre Royal* on eight or nine occasions, matinees, all by herself. Leigh would come home and ask what she'd done that day. She would invent a story about having done something else. Larry became an obsession with her."[7]

Says another, "Vivien might well have become discouraged with her acting and given up the whole idea, as Leigh wanted her to do, had she not become aware of Olivier. But once she became aware of him, there was no stopping her. 'I must become an important actress so that when I meet him we will be equals,' she said once to me. 'Who knows, perhaps we'll marry one day and become the new Lunt and Fontanne. Wouldn't it be fantastic to be another Lunt and Fontanne, and then live in the very house Lynn Fontanne lived in?' That was just one of her fantasies about Olivier. She had many others. When she was reminded that Larry was already married, and to a famous actress, she shrugged it off. She started asking around, asking anyone who had the slightest knowledge of Larry and Jill Esmond, asking what their marriage was like, whether they were happy together, that sort of thing."[8]

Olivier's marriage was definitely not a happy one in 1935, though that fact remained concealed from all but his closest friends. His failures as an actor-manager with *The Ringmaster* and *Golden Arrow*, following his great success in *Theatre Royal*, had put his career at odds with itself. And although he had delighted the London theatre world with his performance in *Romeo and Juliet*, it had been at the further expense of his relationship with Jill Esmond.

Jill, the theatrical purist, had been appalled and embarrassed by her husband's interpretation of Romeo. Yet she recognized that his unorthodox portrayal might have been in reaction to her warnings about acting with Gielgud. She was relieved when in December 1935, Olivier yielded the role of Romeo to Gielgud, took over as Mercutio and gave a more conventional performance in that part.

With Jill's relief came a resolve to do something to rescue their troubled marriage. "Jill realized," says a friend, "that she no longer had a hold over Larry as an actor. She saw that he was going to be a big star with or without her. Indeed, he had already eclipsed her, and she sensed that she was forever going to be relegated to a back seat. As for their developing together as a husband-wife team, as had more than once been suggested, that idea was no longer discussed. Larry was all theatre now, he was obsessed by acting and by the notion of reaching greater and greater heights. He'd made it clear to Jill by his attitude that there was no room for her in his rocket ride to the top.

"Jill accepted this, I think, and was content to exist in his shadow. But she didn't want to lose him. So she took measures that she thought would rebind him to her in other ways."[9]

Jill's principal measure was to become pregnant. Reports vary on whether Olivier had any say in the decision. All agree that he and Jill had put aside thoughts of having children during the first few years of their marriage because of their need to establish themselves. Some say that by 1933 Olivier wanted a child but that Jill had resisted the idea, and it was for that reason Olivier first became discontented. Others claim that by the time Jill was ready to have a child, it was Olivier who resisted the idea, contending that his own childhood had been so unpleasant that he didn't want to inflict a similar fate on another child.

Whatever the case, Jill became pregnant at the end of 1935. Ironically, it was during the evening of the day that Jill told Olivier of her pregnancy, when he took her to dinner to celebrate the occasion, that he and Vivien Leigh first met.

Vivien was no longer an unknown by then. After her first stage appearance in *The Green Sash* the previous February, she had gotten several more film assignments. These brought her to the increasing notice of the local entertainment world. Then, in May, she had won another stage role—the female lead in a comedy of German origin called *The Mask of Virtue*. Vivien's performance made her an overnight sensation in London. Playing a young prostitute posing as a lady of virtue in order to lure a nobleman into marriage for the purpose of publicly disgracing him, her portrayal of the dual character was termed "expert" and "shining." "London has a new star," proclaimed one newspaper.

In the audience on the opening night of *The Mask of Virtue* was Alexander Korda, who had come as a courtesy to Maxwell Wray, the play's director and once a Korda functionary at London Films. Korda was as impressed by Vivien as everyone else. A few days later, conceding that he had been wrong about her when he met her the year before, he announced that he'd signed her to a five-year, $250,000 film contract calling for her to make two movies a year. Her first Korda film, in the fall, would be in the co-starring role of Roxanne in the popular *Cyrano de Bergerac*, with Charles Laughton playing the comic-nosed Cyrano.

Vivien Leigh was no longer an overnight stage sensation. Now, with the imprimatur of a coveted Korda contract, she was a genuine star.

A star without work, however. Producer Sidney Carroll, seeking to capitalize on Vivien's sudden fame, moved *The Mask of Virtue* to a much larger theatre. The play was not enough of an attraction to support the move, and he was forced to close it in August. In the meantime, the film version of *Cyrano* was postponed after Korda got into a quarrel over production details with the temperamental Charles Laughton. Forced to wait in the wings for the dispute to be settled and unable to take on another play, Vivien was left with little to do during the fall of 1935.

According to Eve Phillips, then a young actress and fashion model who was assigned a job as a stand-in for Vivien in her first few Korda movies, "She was bored and itchy. Her husband was furious at all the attention she was receiving and withdrew from her in a huff. I know it's the accepted wisdom that Viv went straight from her husband to Olivier, but that wasn't the case at all. She was mad about Olivier. But she didn't even know him and she carried on her infatuation from a distance. I know she went to see him in *Romeo and Juliet* on a number of occasions, and she talked about him incessantly. But what could she do? He was married. Not even Viv was that daring.

"She was daring enough, though. She met a great many theatre and movie people that year, and she was so beautiful that the chaps were falling over themselves trying to seduce her. Her love life with her husband was practically nonexistent, she told me. I think her feelings about Olivier aroused some deep animal feelings in her that she'd not been aware of before. Anyway, I know for a fact that she had two secret affairs during the time she was waiting for *Cyrano* to get off the ground. The reason I know is because she used my flat. I knew one of the chaps —he was an actor, married. The other—I only knew who he was, I didn't know him at the time. Alexander Korda."[10]

Korda, then forty-two, was already a legendary womanizer in London, as well as the city's foremost movie mogul. He had shed his first wife, a Hungarian actress, several years before, and was hoping to marry Merle Oberon, one of his earliest discoveries. This did not keep him from lavishing his attention on others, however.

Vivien had just celebrated her twenty-second birthday when she received a call from Korda on November 13, 1935. Expecting news that *Cyrano* was finally ready to start, she was surprised to hear Korda ask her to join him for a private lunch so that he could toast her birthday and discuss other business. She immediately came to the alert. Korda was the man who had put her old schoolmate, Maureen O'Sullivan, into her first featured movie role during his brief stay in Hollywood five years before. She had since heard from Maureen that he made it a practice to try to sleep with every actress he put under contract. "It's something he feels they owe him," Maureen had told her. "He claims it's good for business—it's the only way he can decide which actress is best for which part. He must know an actress completely before he can really use her in films. At least that's what he says."

It was with such forewarning in mind that Vivien met the smooth-talking, seemingly world-weary Korda for lunch. Korda was not an especially attractive man physically, but his personality was compellingly authoritative. He spoke to Vivien of the difficulties he was having in resolving his *Cyrano* problems with Laughton. Whom, he asked, would she like to see in the role of Cyrano in the event Laughton failed to work out?

Laurence Olivier, she replied without hesitation. Under Korda's subtle questioning, she confessed her infatuation with Olivier.

Korda was keenly sympathetic. He also revealed his interest in the idea of starring Olivier and Vivien in another picture. "I have gotten to know Larry well," he said in his heavily accented English. "A gorgeous man. And I can tell you, my darling, he will be available soon."

"To work?" Vivien asked, misunderstanding.

"In every way. He will not stay married much longer. I see something for the two of you in the future. I will make it happen. But you must trust me. Do you know what I mean?"

Vivien didn't, quite.

"I understand you too are unhappy in your marriage, my pet."

Vivien, now viewing Korda as both a father confessor and her most direct route to Olivier, conceded that he was right. "I feel so fettered and tied down with Leigh. He's a dear man. But we have nothing in common, I'm afraid."

"Larry is the same way," Korda said. "He has only to meet you and —I promise—fireworks! You can become two great stars together. Perhaps you will even marry. Let me handle it. Trust me, my darling. In the meantime, I must get to know you better. You know what I mean, of course."

"You mean . . . ?"

"Yes, my darling . . ."[11]

"It was a brief affair," said Eve Phillips. "Two or three times, that's all. Viv used Korda as much as he used her. He kept promising to arrange an introduction to Olivier. In the meantime she got involved with this actor. That romance was a little more serious. Viv was aching to fall in love, and she tried with the actor. But she couldn't. It was just sex. Viv was discovering sex. She was saving her passion and love for Larry."[12]

It must have seemed to Vivien, despite Korda's veiled assurances, that her passion for Olivier would have to remain suspended forever. One night early in 1936, she agreed to have dinner with John Buckmaster, a son of actress Gladys Cooper. Buckmaster took her to the Savoy Grill, a popular gathering place of theatre people. There, sitting at a nearby banquette, were Olivier and Jill Esmond. Buckmaster waved, the Oliviers waved back. Vivien pleaded for an introduction. As the Oliviers were leaving, Buckmaster beckoned them to his table. The introductions were made.

Olivier remarked that he had seen Vivien in *The Mask of Virtue* and politely congratulated her on her performance. "Alex Korda tells me he's thinking of putting us in a film together," he added smoothly, holding her gaze.

Demurely, Vivien said that would be nice, but that "she didn't think she was in the same league as Olivier," as Buckmaster has frequently told the story.

"Nonsense," chimed in Jill Esmond. "Larry's a fish out of water when it comes to film acting."

"She's right," Olivier agreed. "I'm frightfully bad."

After another moment or two of small talk, Olivier announced to Buckmaster that the evening was an occasion of celebration for himself and Jill—she had just told him that she was going to have a baby. As Buckmaster engaged in a long congratulatory speech, Vivien Leigh's heart sank. Having finally met Olivier, she had experienced a surge of attraction greater than anything she'd known before.

After the Oliviers departed, according to Buckmaster, "Viv suddenly went quiet, then became testy. Larry had shaved his moustache for *Romeo and Juliet,* and I recall remarking that he looked much better with it than without. Viv got furious with me, as if she were defending some wayward relative. She hardly talked to me the rest of the night. That's when I realized how she felt about him. And Larry, the poor bloke, hadn't the slightest notion."

Olivier would not remain in the dark for long. Not more than a week after their first meeting, Vivien was backstage at the New Theatre late one afternoon to audition for a role in a future Gielgud production of Shakespeare's *Richard II.* Her timing was good—she "happened" to run into Olivier as he came into the theatre for that evening's performance of *Romeo and Juliet.* He expressed surprise at her interest in Shakespeare and invited her to his dressing room for a talk.

No one knows what occurred behind the closed door, but afterward Vivien was more ecstatic than ever about Olivier.

As January progressed into February, though, there were more backstage visits after Gielgud, at Olivier's urging, gave Vivien the role of the Queen in his limited-run production of *Richard II.* Rehearsals for *Richard II* were held in the afternoons at the New Theatre during the last weeks of the run of *Romeo and Juliet.* According to an observer, "Larry took to coming in early almost every day and coaching Vivien Leigh in her lines. His dressing room became her private acting school. Who knows what else?"

In February, Olivier and Jill Esmond took a country house near the Thames Valley town of Maidenhead so that Jill would be able to spend most of her pregnancy outside the city. "It was Larry's idea after he met Viv," says the observer. "I don't think they'd started an affair yet, but I'm sure Larry got the idea from Viv that she was open to one. And I'm sure that, after some soul-searching, he felt ready. But if there was going to be an affair, it was going to have to be top secret as far as Larry was concerned. The first thing he had to do was get Jill out of town. Her pregnancy provided the perfect excuse."[13]

Olivier stayed in London during the week and visited his wife at weekends during the spring. Late in February, Vivien Leigh started her first film for Alexander Korda at his Denham Studio—not *Cyrano,* which had been permanently scrubbed, but a spy tale set in Sweden called *Dark Journey.* When she first saw the rough footage, she was roundly depressed by the way Korda's editing had cut up her performance. She sought out Olivier for solace. He was only too glad to commiserate with her about the frustrations of film acting.

"Viv was still dying to get romantically involved with Larry," says a woman who, with her husband, got to know both of them well at the time. "But Larry, except for flirting, was all caution. He was aware of how Vivien felt, and he was awfully tempted to plunge in. But he kept holding off. Later he told my husband that the reason was Vivien's husband, Mr. Holman. Larry hadn't met him, he'd only heard about him from Vivien. Nevertheless, he felt awful about the idea of cuckolding another man. He fought it for a long time. Larry was, after all, a very honorable man, and he wasn't used to sexual intrigue. Vivien, on the other hand, although she was only twenty-two, was. In fact she delighted in it."

In April, Vivien undertook another co-starring role in the West End, this time performing with the celebrated actor-playwright Ivor Novello in his play *The Happy Hypocrite.* Olivier, meanwhile, threw himself into rehearsals for a play he and Ralph Richardson had decided to co-present and act in, a J. B. Priestley farce called *Bees on the Boatdeck.*

"Larry and Viv didn't see much of each other during that period," says their friend, "although it was by Larry's choice, not Vivien's. If anything, that only made Vivien more determined to get Larry. She resented his unavailability to a degree, but she was also overawed by his capacity for work and by the attention to detail he brought to everything he did. Larry's part in the Priestley play was a showy one, much like Tony Cavendish. But everything he did was different. Vivien was enthralled as she watched him formulate the character, watched how he observed other people and adopted their traits and idiosyncracies until they became his own. Vivien had very little in the way of acting training. She wanted, more fervently than ever, to learn from Larry. When you come right down to it, that was what attracted Larry to Vivien. More than her beauty, more than her vivacity, more than her directness—he was attracted by her innocence as an actress. In a way, Vivien became for Larry the child he was supposed to be having with Jill."[14]

Laurence Olivier at the Samuel Goldwyn Studio in 1938. (*United Press International Photo*)

Olivier with his first wife, Jill Esmond, arriving at the Newark, New Jersey, airport from Hollywood. They were enroute to England where Olivier would act in a movie made by Gloria Swanson. (*United Press International Photo*)

Vivien Leigh and Olivia de
Havilland with Olivier, arriving
at the First Annual Academy
Awards Banquet in Hollywood
on March 14, 1940. (*United
Press International Photo*)

Olivier, Vivien Leigh and Cecil
Tennant checking their baggage
after their forced landing in
Willimantic, Connecticut, on
June 18, 1946. (*United Press
International Photo*)

Laurence Olivier in 1946.
(*United Press International
Photo*)

Olivier and Vivien Leigh arriving in England, after touring with the Old Vic in Australia and New Zealand in 1948. (*United Press International*)

Laurence Olivier in 1951 when he was starring on Broadway with Vivien Leigh in *Antony and Cleopatra. (United Press International Photo)*

Olivier saying goodbye to David Niven before he and Vivien Leigh, who was suffering from a breakdown, left Los Angeles for England in 1953. (*United Press International Photo*)

Olivier with Marilyn Monroe in New York in 1956, announcing that they had agreed to star in a film version of the London stage hit, *The Sleeping Prince,* to be filmed in England. (*United Press International Photo*)

Helen Hayes and Olivier aboard the sightseeing steamer *Knickerbocker VII*, in 1958, for a midnight cruise around New York. He was host to a large group of show people. (*Wide World Photos*)

Sir Laurence Olivier, fifty-four, and Joan Plowright, thirty-two, were married in Wilton, Connecticut, on March 17, 1961. He was appearing in the Broadway production of *Becket* while she performed in *A Taste of Honey*. (*United Press International Photo*)

Carol Channing visiting Olivier backstage. He was playing Shylock in the National Theatre production of *The Merchant of Venice* in 1970. (*United Press International Photo*)

Cary Grant presenting Olivier with an Academy Award in Hollywood in 1979.

Sir Laurence Olivier in 1976.
(*United Press International Photo*)

15

A Hamlet in Life

"I never saw such a transformation in a man as the one Larry Olivier went through after he became involved with Vivien Leigh," said an actor friend. "His entire personality changed. He went from a rather somber, pessimistic chap to an upbeat, gay bon vivant and raconteur. Oh, with his close friends—fellows like Ralph Richardson and Jack Hawkins—I suppose he had been always like that. But with people he didn't know well, he was usually aloof and humorless. Suddenly he was gregarious with everyone, not exactly backslapping, but expressive and talkative and full of quips. No one knew, of course, that he was so deeply caught up with Vivien, so we all wondered what had happened. We assumed that Larry had simply decided to become an actor in real life as well as on the stage. We laughed at him a bit, I'm afraid—I mean, it all seemed such artifice at first. . . . There was a bit of Korda in his sudden flashiness, a bit of Gielgud in his voice, a bit of Ivor Novello in his swagger, a bit of Noel in his feyness. We figured that Larry must have decided to do an overhaul of his personality and present a new Olivier to the world, consisting of all the characteristics he admired in others. For such a good actor he seemed to be doing rather a bit of a hammy job of it. But then, later, we realized it was Vivien's influence.

"Vivien overflowed with girlish enthusiasm and good cheer, and Larry was very affected by it. Jill was a no-nonsense girl, sharp as a pin mentally, direct and explicit in her approach to people, always in charge of everything, the type of woman who wouldn't say anything unless she had something to say. Vivien, on the other hand, would talk about anything, and she'd do it with great style and charm, but without any naiveté. Her most singular asset, I suppose, was her ability to focus all her attention on whomever she happened to be with. This was an immensely endearing trait and was what made her so popular with everyone. And it was very sexual where men were concerned—this great beauty running her hand up your arm, laughing at your jokes, seeming to be immersed entirely in you—all so natural and without any sort of guile.

"Well—she got Larry under her spell, obviously, and he responded with this huge personality change."[1]

•

Jill was among the first to notice the change, and she didn't know what to make of it.

The initial evidence of it came one weekend in the spring of 1936 when Olivier invited Vivien Leigh and her husband to visit Jill and him at their country house near Maidenhead. Vivien, despite the separate life she was leading, still resided with Leigh Holman and maintained the pretense of a happy, settled marriage. For his part, Olivier wanted to meet Holman and take his measure of the man before getting any deeper into his relationship with Vivien.

"Vivien did a perfect acting job," said a friend of Jill's who was invited by that weekend. "She was attentive to her husband, charming to Jill, and totally natural with Larry—not sneaking glances at him or exchanging meaningful looks when she thought no one else was observing. She almost overdevoted herself to Jill, in fact, peppering her with questions about her acting, about Hollywood, and so on. Jill was thoroughly charmed by her.

"It was Larry who was the puzzle. He was like I'd never seen him before—effusive, grandiose, excessively talkative, full of jokes, reciting speeches from this or that play, gadding about as though he were giving a performance. Jill and I talked about it the next day. She couldn't understand what had gotten into Larry. She said that when she questioned him about it, after Vivien and her husband left, he told her he had carried on so because he was bored—that he had gotten tired of listening to Jill and Vivien chatter away about having babies and because Vivien's husband was so dull and straight-laced. He said he was putting on an act to shock Vivien's husband, to show him how ridiculous theatre people really were, to confirm what he was sure were Leigh Holman's suspicions. Jill thought it was grossly rude of Larry. Of course, she hadn't the slightest inkling, nor did I, that Larry was probably showing off for Vivien."[2]

Olivier's *Bees on the Boatdeck* had opened in mid-May to indifferent reviews. By early June he and Ralph Richardson were forced to face the fact that they had another financial failure on their hands. They closed the play and set out to recover by going back into movie work for the Korda organization. For Olivier, Korda scheduled an historical costume drama, based on the popular novel by A. E. W. Mason, *Fire Over England.* Korda decided to sweeten the book's historical theme by adding a love-story subplot to the film.

In June, having closed in the Ivor Novello play, Vivien Leigh was rehearsing for an appearance as Anne Bullen in an outdoor production of Shakespeare's *Henry VIII,* to be mounted in Regents Park by Sidney Carroll. She was experiencing great difficulty with her voice, however —the same difficulty in projection she had experienced a few months before when she'd played the Queen in *Richard II.* She sought Olivier's help.

Some time that summer, Olivier evidently decided that he was no longer bound by his ethical considerations from fully responding to Vivien Leigh.

"Larry worked with Viv almost every day," said her friend Oswald Frewen. "He'd go up to her house in Shepherd Market in the mornings and they'd work on her voice and line delivery. Then, often, they'd go out to lunch. Leigh knew about it but he didn't pay it any attention. He assumed that it was just another of those theatrical relationships. Jill Esmond knew about it too. She was fat with child by then, which I suppose made Vivien that much more attractive to Larry. But I don't think Jill ever had the whisper of an idea that Larry had more on his mind than helping out a young actress friend of both of them."[3]

At one of their lunches, in July, Olivier told Vivien about his coming movie role in *Fire Over England.* "Alex has put in a part for a girl to play my love interest," Olivier said. "He's been wondering who to cast. I recommended you. In fact I told him I won't work in the picture unless he has you as the girl."

Vivien replied by saying that she'd sell her soul to get the part, if only because it would enable her finally to kiss Olivier. She had been aching to do so for months, she added coyly, but had been afraid to try.

Here an assistant in Alexander Korda's office entered the picture. "I was in the office at Denham," he recalls today. "A phone call from Olivier came in. There were several people in the office. Alex took the call. Then he told all of us: 'It looks like Larry has something going. He wants to use my house this afternoon. He won't tell me who he's bringing with him.' Alex had servants at the house. He told me to go into London in his car and get rid of them for the rest of the day, then to let Olivier into the house and return to the studio.

"Well, I drove in and got rid of the servants. Then I waited. Soon a taxi arrived. Olivier got out. He was alone. I let him into the house —he didn't know who I was, only that I was someone who worked for Alex. He nodded, I left. I got back into Alex's car. But instead of leaving right away, I waited. In a few minutes another taxi arrived, this time with a woman. She was let into the house by Olivier. I recognized her, of course. I was under orders from Alex to try to find who she was.

"I went back to Denham. Alex said, 'Well?' I was reluctant to say anything. I knew Alex had been . . . engaged with the woman at one point. I thought there might be trouble. Finally I said, 'Everything's all right.' He said, 'So? So? Who did he bring?' and I said, 'It's that actress you've got under contract. Vivien Leigh.' Alex roared with laughter. 'Ring up each of them in the morning,' he said. 'Tell them I want to see both of them here tomorrow afternoon.'

"They arrived the next day. Alex had them in his office alone for an hour. Then they came out, and Alex said to his secretaries, 'Make a release for the newspapers. Say that we've completed casting *Fire Over England*. Vivien Leigh to star with Laurence Olivier and Flora Robson. Make a special paragraph—Larry and Vivien in their first film together, a vibrant love story.'

"And that's how it happened. Later, listening to Alex talk, I received the very distinct impression that in their meeting he told Olivier about his affair with Vivien Leigh and that she acknowledged it, and that they all had a friendly chat about it to set the record straight. Evidently Olivier took it all with equanimity. I don't doubt that that's what happened, because afterward Alex conspired with them to keep their affair going. For the filming of *Fire Over England,* he had special accommodations made up at the studio where they could be alone when they weren't on the set."[5]

Fire Over England took more than two months to film. Olivier's swashbuckling role as an Elizabethan seafarer, for which he insisted on doing most of his own stunts, exhausted him to the point that he, as one observer has said, "seemed barely aware of it" when on August 21, 1936, Jill Esmond gave birth to their child.

Olivier had earlier insisted that if Jill had a boy, he should be called Tarquin—a name that showed up in the ancient Olivier family ancestry and was also prominent in Shakespearean literature. Since he had made his greatest mark acting in Shakespeare and was eager to play more classic roles, it would be the actor's way of celebrating the happy congruence between himself and the Bard. The child was a boy, and Simon Tarquin Olivier he became. The Simon was at Jill's insistence, but Tarquin was the name by which he would thereafter be called.

Although the impact of the birth of his son took a while to register on Olivier, when it did it had a sobering effect. During the first few weeks of filming *Fire Over England* at Denham, he and Vivien Leigh conducted their affair in passionate bits and snatches, and it was made all the more feverish by the secrecy it entailed. Soon, however, it was no secret, at least at the studio. "Everyone involved with the picture knew about them," said an actor who played a role in the epic. "One morning Larry and I shared a car out to the studio. I tried to hint in a subtle way that what he was doing mightn't be such a good idea, considering he'd just had a child. He looked at me and said, 'So you know.' I said, 'Larry, old boy, everyone knows. They're all talking about it.' He cursed and said, 'So much for secrecy. Well, I've got to do something, haven't I?'

"Then we got to talking about his work in the picture. He was doing some terribly demanding stunts and looked beaten up and exhausted. I said, 'Jesus, why don't you use a double? You'll be all done in before you're finished.' And he answered, 'I'm done in already. But it's not the stunts. It's Vivien. It's every day, two, three times. She's bloody wearing me out.' "[6]

Olivier's friend wasn't the only one worried about the affair. Korda grew concerned too. According to his former assistant, "Alex heard the talk. He began to worry about a scandal. The film was an expensive project, and he knew the only way he'd get his money back would be through its acceptance in America. He thought American audiences would reject the picture if it ever got out that its two stars—both married, both with children—were having an affair. Finally he called them in and pleaded with them to put an end to it, at least until production was finished. By that time Olivier and Leigh knew that it was no longer a secret, that everyone at Denham knew about it. They too became concerned. So they stopped. At least they stayed pretty well apart during their spare time for the rest of the picture. The accommodations Alex had arranged for them—they were hardly used anymore."[7]

Raymond Massey had a small role in the movie. He later said, "I knew what was going on. I felt sad for Jill, because I knew her and I knew she was ignorant of the whole business. In a way I was happy for Larry, for I could see that Vivien was making a new man out of him. On balance, though, I had a feeling of foreboding for all of them, a dread that everything would end in a mess. But then I talked with Larry. It was about a month after his son was born. He was consumed with guilt. He was putting an end to it, he said. He loved Jill and he'd been a fool. With Vivien—well, it was just a wild infatuation, but it was to Jill he owed his loyalty, and the child. He had talked to Vivien about it. She had agreed to a cooling-off period. And that, I thought, would be the end of it."[8]

As, perhaps, did Olivier. But not Vivien Leigh. As Eve Phillips later recalled, "Viv said that Larry Olivier was in love with her, that he had told her so over and over again during *Fire Over England.* She couldn't understand his sudden withdrawal. But she was not going to let him get away."[9]

James Wong Howe, the cameraman on *Fire Over England,* said: "Toward the end of the picture Olivier was in a melancholy state of mind. Earlier, his love scenes with Vivien had come across with tremendous vitality because of the way he felt about her. But later he seemed less intense. I asked him: 'Has something happened with you and Vivien, Larry?' And he said: 'I've got to give her up, Jimmy. I don't want to, God knows. But I must. And I can't.' "[10]

What occurred next was symptomatic of Olivier's dilemma. The Old Vic Theatre, once a lowlife music hall south of the Thames across Waterloo Bridge, had been turned in 1914 into an acting company specializing in Shakespearean productions by Lilian Baylis, an eccentric spinster who devoted her life to bringing culture to the masses. Since its transformation, the Old Vic had become a popular institution in London. Shakespeare was the national playwright of England and people came from all over the country to see his works performed there. Its appeal was not only Shakespeare, however; it was also the actors who performed in the plays. The Old Vic had evolved into a mecca for actors and actresses who wished to be taken seriously by the public and critics. A season or two spent performing at the Old Vic had become almost obligatory for any actor worth his or her salt. The pay was low, but the prestige was high.

Olivier had already gotten a taste of the Old Vic during his portrayal of Romeo, since most of the people connected with John Gielgud's production had been Old Vic regulars. His announced desire to do more Shakespeare had not gone unnoticed. In September of 1936, toward the end of his stint in *Fire Over England,* Tyrone Guthrie, one of the Old Vic's most celebrated producer-directors, proposed that Olivier spend the forthcoming season with the company. Olivier at first declined on the ground that the pay would be too low. But when he learned that Guthrie planned to do another revival of *Hamlet* as the Old Vic's major production of the winter, and that he could play the legendary title role, he changed his mind.

Some say that he agreed because, at twenty-nine, he felt that he was ready to take on the role that was the ultimate goal of every ambitious young English actor. Others say that his motivation was not so much to play Hamlet as to topple John Gielgud from his throne as England's champion classical actor—Gielgud had been awarded the crown by the press as a result of his cerebral but lyrical interpretation of the tragic Danish prince the year before.

Both contentions are no doubt partly correct. But as Tyrone Guthrie later said, "For a young man who had everything going for him in his career, Larry was profoundly unhappy at the time. It all had to do with the conflict between his violent, immature love for Vivien Leigh and his more mature, subdued attachment to Jill Esmond. He was literally in a quandary as to what to do. When I first talked to him about *Hamlet,* he said, 'Oh no, how I'd love to do it, I already know what it feels to be a Hamlet in real life.' But he was afraid, he said, that he'd suffer dreadfully by comparison to Johnny Gielgud's version. He wanted to do it because he believed he had a great deal of personal Hamletlike anguish and spiritual paralysis to bring to the part. What I had to do was convince him that he was ready for it, and that he had a chance to outshine Gielgud."[11]

Olivier agreed to spend the 1936–37 season at the Old Vic at about the same time he ended—he thought—his affair with Vivien Leigh. In

October, when he completed work on *Fire Over England,* he took Jill on a three-week holiday to Capri. "It was a reconciliatory move on Larry's part," said a friend. "He didn't confess his affair to her, but he did concede that he'd drifted from her. The purpose of the trip was to revitalize their marriage, and he tried to put Viv out of his mind. Later he said it didn't work. All he could think about was Viv."[12]

And all Vivien Leigh could think about was Olivier, according to Oswald Frewen. He has said that when she learned Olivier and Jill would be staying at the Hotel Quisisana in Capri, she quickly arranged her own trip to the Mediterranean—with a two-day stopover at the Quisisana. Since she didn't want her husband with her, she asked Frewen along as her "chaperon."

Frewen claimed not to have known that Vivien had planned the trip in order to encounter Olivier in Capri. But when, on their arrival at the Quisisana, they ran immediately into Olivier and his wife, he began to put two and two together. That it was no coincidence was soon confirmed when Vivien told him that she was hopelessly in love with Olivier and couldn't bear his three-week absence from London. The fifty-year-old Frewen was shocked, for now he was a collaborator in Vivien's deception of his friend Holman.

He was not the only one to be shocked. Vivien was unable to maintain the simulated indifference to Olivier with which she had masked herself the previous spring when she and her husband had visited the Oliviers. Now she cast openly adoring glances at Olivier, repeatedly touched him in familiar, almost intimate ways, and visibly shivered at his casual touch—all in open view of Jill. At first Jill excused the behavior as a hangover from the love scenes they had done together for *Fire Over England.* But soon she grew annoyed by Vivien's actions, and more so by Olivier's responses.

The moment Vivien and Oswald Frewen left for Rome, Jill complained about Vivien's behavior. During Vivien's visit, Olivier had struggled silently but furiously with himself over his feelings. He had contrasted Jill's familiar reserve to Vivien's free-spirited vivacity. He had measured the difference between Vivien's youthful, almost ethereal beauty and Jill's more mature, somber attractiveness. But most of all he had succumbed once again to Vivien's outgoing sensuality, against which Jill's reserved demeanor suffered in comparison. His desire for Vivian was reignited, and was made all the more painful by his inability to give expression to it because of Jill's presence.

When Jill complained about Vivien, Olivier could no longer suppress his frustration. He defended her, in the process demeaning Jill for her "Victorian" attitude. A violent argument followed, bringing their holiday to an abrupt end. Jill and Olivier left for Naples in bitter silence on the first leg of their journey back to London. While waiting for the train in Naples, Olivier phoned Vivien in Rome.

"He told Viv he was finished with Jill," Frewen later recalled. "He was all set to send Jill back to London on her own, and he wanted Viv to go back to Capri with him."

Frewen felt constrained to intervene. Vivien was willing to do anything Olivier wanted. But Frewen cautioned her urgently against it, then got on the phone and repeated his warnings to Olivier. Wait, he urged both of them. Vivien had a child, and there was no telling what Leigh Holman would do if he discovered that they were alone together. And Olivier had just become a father—what would it do to his career if the public learned that he had left his wife just a few months after she had given birth?

The two heeded Frewen. Olivier and Jill went back to London together. Vivien arrived quietly with Frewen a few days later. Life returned to normal, if only barely, for each.[13]

16

Hamlet on Stage

O<small>N</small> his troubled return from Capri in the fall of 1936, Olivier went immediately into rehearsals for Tyrone Guthrie's Old Vic production of *Hamlet.* Guthrie had become enamored of recent psychoanalytic critiques of Shakespeare's most celebrated character—critiques that viewed Hamlet, a man of action, as having been driven into hesitation over avenging his father's murder by confusion about his real motives. Was Hamlet's urge to kill Claudius, the man suspected of having slain his father, motivated by natural love for his father? Or was it motivated by jealousy over the fact that Claudius had become the husband of his mother, whom Hamlet loved in an unnatural way?

The tale of Hamlet's paralyzing dilemma had begun to be used as a case study to illustrate Sigmund Freud's doctrine of the Oedipus Complex as the prime source of human psychological disturbance. Tyrone Guthrie wanted Olivier to formulate his characterization of the Danish prince in this light. Olivier, anxious to succeed in the role in which so many other fine actors had failed, and even more anxious to etch Hamlet in sharp contrast to John Gielgud's celebrated interpretation of the year before, agreed. The result was a mixed-bag performance that perplexed critics and audiences alike but stamped Olivier as a Shakespearean actor to be taken seriously, if only for his audacity.

•

Hamlet opened at the Old Vic on January 5, 1937, for a month's run. Olivier played the title role in a style that was in every way the opposite of Gielgud's elegant, detached prince. Rather than a passive man caught up in melancholic self-doubt, Olivier performed Hamlet as a lusty, athletic, impulsive young royal whose moments of introspection were more reflections of an impatient, petulant nature than a nature beset by philosophical agony. Although daring in its conception, it ultimately failed to satisfy most of the critics. "Mr. Olivier does not speak poetry badly," said James Agate. "He simply does not speak it at all. . . . His performance is entirely without melancholy. . . . To sum up . . . it is not Hamlet, but a brilliant performance of the part such as Stanhope of *Journey's End* might have put up on some rest-interval behind the lines."

For Agate's "brilliant," other critics used such adjectives as "flashy" and "pretentious," with one adding, "Mr. Olivier seems to divert our attention from his paucity of intellectual substance with a goodly amount of physical dashing about. He has failed in this goal. It's about time someone told him that there is more to acting than gymnastics. . . . If gymnastics were the sole criterion for good acting, Britain un-doubtedly would have done better for herself in the recent Olympic Games with Mr. Olivier's participation."

Despite the critics, Olivier's Old Vic *Hamlet* was a resounding suc-cess with the public. Said Jack Hawkins, "It's true, Larry by that time had settled on a style of acting that included a great deal of physical surprise and daring. It was his way, some thought, of hiding his acting deficiencies. Because he was such a dashing fellow, he knew the audi-ences were more likely to love it than not. And they did. That was unfortunate in a way, because he got caught up in this mystique of his physical power and neglected other vital aspects of the craft. There's no doubt that he's since turned out to be a great actor. But he might have been greater yet had he not spent so much of his earlier career emphasiz-ing the physical side of himself. Other actors resented all the attention he got because they felt he was conning the public into a wrong percep-tion of what good acting is."[1]

Some of those who resented Olivier were Alec Guinness and Michael Redgrave, both young members of the Old Vic. Guinness was Olivier's understudy in *Hamlet*. In 1973 he described himself as "outraged at the gymnastic leaps and falls required by [Olivier's] example. I never liked the performance or Guthrie's production."

Redgrave, who played Laertes, said: "The truth is that I thought he was a bad Hamlet—too assertive and too resolute. He lacked the . . . subtleties the part demands."[2]

And even Tyrone Guthrie had misgivings about Olivier's acting style. In his 1972 autobiography, *A Life in the Theatre,* Guthrie wrote: "Offstage [Larry] was not notably handsome or striking, but with makeup he could achieve a flashing Italianate, rather saturnine, but fascinating appearance. . . . He had, if anything, too strong an instinct for the sort of theatrical effect which is striking and memorable."[3]

"Guthrie's assessment was on the mark," Kenneth Tynan told me. "Larry was interested in being an entertainer above all things, an actor-entertainer rather than just an actor, a showman. And that's what elevated him over all the others eventually. He felt a responsibility to his audiences. He felt audiences should never be disappointed, even when the material is second rate. When he and I were at the National Theatre [in the 1960s], he used to say to me, 'God, went to see so-and-so in such-and-such play last night. The play was awful, but the actor'—and he'd name the name—'did nothing to improve on it. He just went with the material. He could at least have made it entertaining.' That was Larry. In a way he was contemptuous of audiences' ability to appreciate a play. He always believed that it was his job to seize their attention, to entertain them even in a bad play. Which is why he tended so often to overplay a role. He wanted audiences to remember at least something of their night at the theatre. That's why he became so popular. Audiences, even critics, often forgave his overacting because they sensed he was doing it in service to them."

Was that the reason he broke all the rules with Hamlet? "No," said Tynan. "It was more a case of his own personal concerns at the time. He was in love with Vivien Leigh. For reasons of marital politics, plus simply the time-consuming and energy-exhausting factors that went into preparing his Hamlet, he was unable to see much of her. He admitted to me once that his Hamlet was done primarily for Vivien. With all its physical virility and acrobatic flash, it was his way of wooing her. And she confirmed it. She told me later on that she went to see at least half the performances, just so that she could be near Larry during a time when she was supposed to be staying away from him. Larry's performance was his long-distance valentine to her."[4]

Olivier followed Hamlet by playing Sir Toby Belch in the Old Vic's February production of Shakespeare's comedy of errors, *Twelfth Night.* Again he delighted audiences, this time stealing the play with a roundly slapstick interpretation of the bawdy part. Yet again, the critics were not amused. "Mr. Olivier," wrote one, "shows more and more a tendency to distrust Shakespeare's intentions and to impose his own views upon the Bard's characters and text. Admittedly, this can sometimes produce an interesting performance. But here he has gone too far. We tend to laugh at Mr. Olivier rather than at Sir Toby. Which is tantamount to laughing not out of appreciation but of pity."

"Larry's idea in going from Hamlet to Toby Belch had been to demonstrate versatility," said Jack Hawkins. "He had great fun with Sir Toby, of course, but I'm afraid it didn't do a hell of a lot for the versatility question. Everyone knew by then that he could play just about any part he wanted to and make it at least different and, for that reason, interesting. But at bottom there was not a great deal of difference between his Hamlet and his Toby Belch. I mean, both were basically Larry showing off his physical virtuosity at the expense of anything else. . . . The Old Vic was supposed to be the ultimate in ensemble playing, but Larry simply made that impossible. He just stood out so much with his pyrotechnics that he seemed to be playing for himself all the time. He succumbed to the old ego business—he had discovered that audiences liked his rambunctious kind of acting and he kept trying to give them more and more of it. There's nothing to an actor like an audience wildly cheering you at the curtain, even if the cheers are for all the wrong reasons. Larry was being cheered for all the wrong reasons, and although he was mature enough to realize it, he wasn't mature enough yet to do anything to correct it. It was only when he became mature enough for that, that he began to be a genuine actor."[5]

According to Tyrone Guthrie, the maturing process started with the Old Vic's next production of the season, Shakespeare's *Henry V.* Olivier had been stung not only by the critics but by several actors in the company who publicly complained of his excessive histrionics. Given the title role in *Henry V,* he sought out his backstage critics and resolved to play the part in a more subdued fashion. But this may have been due to factors other than his concern about the criticism he had been receiving.

The spring of 1937 was a strangely emotional time in the life of England. King George V had died the year before, to be succeeded by his eldest son, Edward VIII. The new king, however, deeply involved in his affair with the American divorcee Wallis Simpson—an affair that had caused great consternation in Britain—renounced the throne and passed it on to his younger brother, the Duke of York, who became George VI. George VI was about to be crowned, but the mood in Britain was by no means improved. The rapid rise of Hitler in Germany, after the Allies' defeat of that country less than twenty years before, had put Britain on an increasingly nervous edge in 1937.

As Olivier himself described it later, "It was a time when it was unfashionable to be patriotic. We had already had one great patriotic war, the so-called war to end all wars, and suddenly we could see another, greater war looming on the horizon in the person of this Hitler. We thought, well, maybe if we don't get caught up in all this old-fashioned patriotism, we'll avoid another war. People became apolitical, then cynical—all of which led to the mood of appeasement that Chamberlain later personified at Munich.

"But here at the same time we had *Henry V* to put on at the Vic, an old-fashioned, rousingly patriotic drama. Even I was caught up in the country's cynical mood, and I had little interest in portraying the traditional Henry, all full of warrior speeches and battle cries in defense of the England of old."[6]

Indeed, Olivier and Tyrone Guthrie objected to the selection of *Henry V* by the Old Vic's board of directors, who had chosen it to celebrate George VI's coronation. After their objections were overruled, they set out to soften as much of its blatant nationalism as they could. The result was a performance from Olivier that was at once subdued and eerily right for the time. Olivier would later contend that he didn't so much underplay Henry V as walk through the part out of his personal distaste for the character. But for perhaps the first time in his career he learned firsthand that, in acting, "Less can be more."

At least that's how the critics viewed his interpretation. "What he could have done with Hamlet, Mr. Olivier *has* done with Henry Five," wrote one. "It is by far his best handling of a major character in Shakespeare."

Audiences reacted with similar appreciation. Says one veteran theatre-goer who was present on opening night, "Olivier was at his most brilliant. He played young Harry throughout most of it at what you might call three-quarter speed, which served to give his climactic moments that much more power and astonishment. I heard later that he said he never really got into the character, that he was just playing it to fulfill his contract. If that's so, then—by God!—he should have taken the same attitude to all his roles. He was so natural, and out of that naturalness came his stunning power."

If Olivier was befuddled by the acclaim he received for *Henry V,* he did not betray it. "But he *was* perplexed," said Denys Blakelok. "Here he had been expecting to be condemned for an indifferent portrayal, and he was glorified for his clever genius. He truly didn't know what to make of it at first. But then he understood, and I think it was Jill, his wife, who helped him on that score. She'd appeared with him in *Twelfth Night.* 'There, you see?' she said. 'I've always told you that you don't have to be bizarre to captivate an audience.' It was a lesson Larry finally took to heart, I think. Thereafter, most of the time, he became a much more subtle actor. It was not *Hamlet* that completed his acting education, but *Henry V.* Hamlet marked the end of his immaturity as an actor, Henry the beginning of his maturity."

If *Hamlet* marked the end of a stage in Olivier's professional life, it represented both an end and a beginning in his personal life. After the Old Vic production closed and Olivier was engaged in *Twelfth Night,* an invitation came from the Danish government for the company to take its *Hamlet* production to Denmark—the locale of the play—for a special week of commemorative performances at Kronborg Castle in late May, 1937. Because it was a signal addition to the Old Vic's prestige, the directors accepted the invitation. But Cherry Cottrell, the actress who had played Ophelia to Olivier's Hamlet, could not make the trip. A search was begun by Tyrone Guthrie for someone else to perform the role for the week in Denmark.

Olivier had seen little of Vivien Leigh during the two months of *Hamlet* and *Twelfth Night*—since Capri their romance had been quiescent, although their feelings for each other remained at fever pitch. In April, however, Alexander Korda had come to them with another film proposal, this one based on the John Galsworthy play *The First and the Last,* retitled *Twenty-one Days* by Korda. He intended to co-star Olivier and Leigh as lovers in Galsworthy's tale of murder and suspense. Filming was scheduled for Denham during May and June. At a meeting in Korda's office one afternoon in April, according to Korda's onetime assistant, "It was the same old thing. Larry and Vivien were all over each other. Alex looked on with amusement. Then he sent them back to his house in London."[7]

The affair resumed. In the days that followed, the two lovers abandoned their secrecy, meeting for lunch at prominent restaurants around town and then disappearing together in the afternoons. Word soon reached Jill Esmond. What she had suspected was now confirmed. When she challenged her husband, he confessed his love for Vivien. What was perhaps even crueler news was Olivier's announcement that he wanted Vivien to play Ophelia in Denmark the following month. Just a few days before, Tyrone Guthrie had privately invited Jill to take the role. She had agreed, provided Olivier approved.

Guthrie had a temporary falling out with Olivier over the matter. Although he didn't think Jill was the best type to play Ophelia, it was only for a week, she was both competent and available, and in his view it would make a pleasant symmetry for the Danes to watch a real-life husband-wife team in the roles of Hamlet and Ophelia. When Olivier went to him in late April and demanded that Vivien Leigh be given the part, he was outraged. Vivien was suitable from the point of view of her looks, Guthrie thought, but her voice—she had no voice for Ophelia, her voice was too thin, too diaphanous.

"Not to worry," said Olivier, "I'll work with her. Her voice will be all right."

"But I've already asked Jill."

"I don't care. Look, Vivien plays it or I don't go. It's no skin off my nose. I have a movie to make for Korda. You can find yourself another Hamlet."

Guthrie was tempted. But the only actor available who knew the part was Alec Guinness, Olivier's understudy in the original production. And Guinness was not the actor the Danes expected to see. To find another star and rehearse him in the few weeks left would be an impossible task. So Guthrie gave in.

"But you must do it correctly," Olivier said. "I don't want Viv to know I'm behind it. You must contact her separately and invite her to do the part."

"But what if she declines?" Guthrie said.

"Oh, she won't decline, old boy. She wants it more than I do."[8]

Vivien Leigh thus joined the Old Vic's Danish production of *Hamlet*. She and Olivier started filming during daylight hours in May on *Twenty-one Days,* while at night they rehearsed *Hamlet.* Late in the month, with a break in filming granted by Korda, they left with the rest of the Old Vic troupe for Denmark.

Just before their departure, Jill Esmond paid an unannounced visit to Vivien Leigh at her house in Shepherd Market. She told Vivien that she knew what was going on; she asked her to give up Olivier and not

148

to go to Denmark with him. She got nowhere. Rather than the penitent Vivien Leigh she had hoped to find, she encountered a twenty-four-year-old who seemed without a care or concern in the world.

"Do you mean to marry Larry?" Jill asked at one point.

"I do. And he intends to marry me. Perhaps not immediately. We know the difficulties. But one day, when all the hatred and resentment is finished and we are forgiven our mistakes—at least in the eyes of the law—we will marry."[9]

According to several friends of Jill Esmond, she came away from her encounter with Vivien Leigh more fascinated than angry. Said one, "Jill was astonished by Vivien's directness, particularly when Vivien started asking her intimate questions about Larry. I mean, questions like how did he like his eggs cooked, how did he like his shirts ironed—that sort of thing. Jill felt as though Vivien was some kind of housemaid who was taking over from her. She was fascinated by Vivien's gall. It was Vivien's matter-of-fact way of letting her know that she, Vivien, was succeeding to the throne. Jill found it amazing, even amusing, while at the same time resenting it. It was almost impossible for her to be angry with Vivien."[10]

Said another, "Jill was astonished, of course. But she still had Tarquin and that fact softened her anger. She wasn't ready to give Larry up, certainly, but she knew if eventually she had to, she would always have Tarquin.

"She *did* worry about what would happen when Leigh Holman found out about it, though. What if he instituted adultery proceedings against Vivien and named Larry as corespondent? That would put her in the midst of a scandal. What's more, what would it do to Tarquin, later on, to learn that his father had left him and his mother for another woman? Jill's first impulse, despite her anger, was to protect Tarquin. So, after her pride had a chance to recover, she gave Larry implicit permission to carry on in the hope that the affair would run its course and he'd return."[11]

Jill did not have to wait long to learn what Leigh Holman would do when he found out about his wife and her husband. While in Denmark, Olivier and Vivien resolved to leave their respective homes and begin living together on their return to London. Vivien wrote to Holman from Denmark and informed him, confessing her love for Olivier and rationalizing her inability to return to Shepherd Market. Holman, once over his initial shock, reacted resignedly to the news, according to Oswald Frewen. He too would wait.

But all was not well in Denmark, either. Heavy rains had marred the rehearsals of *Hamlet* and forced its opening night performance out of the Kronborg Castle courtyard into a nearby banquet hall. Vivien, having gotten drenched in rehearsal, came down with a severe cold. A member of the troupe recalled, "Vivien was really trying her hardest to be good in the part, for Larry. But in addition to being a bundle of nerves, she also got sick. Tyrone Guthrie was impatient with her, Larry was impatient with Tyrone, and everyone fell into a foul mood. Amazingly, the first performance came off with few hitches despite the suddenly unfamiliar surroundings. But later, once the weather abated and we started playing outdoors at the castle, everything collapsed. The performances for the rest of the week were perfunctory at best, and everybody was counting off the days before they could get out. Somewhere in there, about midway through the engagement, Larry and Vivien had an enormous scrap. It was about her drinking and smoking so much, if I remember correctly."[12]

It wasn't about drinking and smoking. Vivien had become a heavy smoker the year before as well as a regular drinker—according to friends, because of her anxiety over her personal life. These habits did not particularly bother Olivier, since he was also fond of smoking and drinking. What did bother him was something in Vivien that he had never seen before.

The two had gone to Denmark not only to work but to celebrate their love and their decision to live together. Just before leaving London, they had secretly picked out a house for themselves in Christchurch Street, Chelsea, just a few blocks from the Oliviers' Whistler residence in Cheyne Walk. It was called Durham Cottage. Olivier bought it with an advance on his salary for *Twenty-one Days,* and Vivien planned to furnish it with her earnings from the same film.

With Vivien's dispatch of her letter to her husband from Denmark, their pact seemed complete. They even took Tyrone Guthrie, his wife and actor Anthony Quayle—who had replaced Michael Redgrave as Laertes for the Danish presentation of *Hamlet*—out to dinner to commemorate the occasion.

Toward the end of their stay at Elsinore, however, Vivien, evidently worn down by a combination of flu and tension, went through a brief—and to Olivier, disturbing—metamorphosis. "It was some sort of spell," recalls the cast member. "At first no one paid it much mind, not even Larry—we all thought it was something to do with Viv's fragile constitution, a bit of female hysteria brought about by the monthlies.

She sort of disappeared inside herself, at first wouldn't talk to anyone, then wouldn't stop talking—yelling, really. It was all very strange, and Larry hustled her off to their rooms in the hotel. Then we didn't see Larry for a while. When he reappeared that night before the performance, he was chalk-white. Said something about Viv having gone bonkers, having attacked him, having had a fit of some kind. He didn't think she'd be able to go on.

"Just then Viv appeared. Not a word to anyone, just staring blankly into space. She got her makeup on, got into her costume and did the performance. Then she disappeared back into their rooms without a word. At first Larry was afraid to follow her. But he did, after arming himself with a lot of aquavit. He was totally at a loss to explain what was bothering Viv. You see, that's what we all thought—something was bothering her. Had Larry done or said something? A lover's spat? No, he said, he had no idea what it was all about, but Viv definitely wasn't right. But next morning Viv and Larry appeared and all was right with the world again. Viv was her familiar old charming self, there was no mention of the day before, no apologies to those she'd screamed at, just as if it hadn't happened. As for Larry, well, he was still puzzled. But he was greatly relieved."[13]

Olivier had no way of knowing it, but he had witnessed for the first time an aspect of Vivien Leigh's personality over which she had no control. The incident was a harbinger of things to come.

17

The Dream Couple

"YOU see it so often," said actress Margaret Leighton, once a close friend of Vivien Leigh's. "A woman gets her man and then quickly settles into smug contentment, as though the battle is over and the time has come to enjoy the spoils of victory. This, I think, is what makes men become bored with their women so quickly. The women lose their air of seductresses and turn into ordinary people.

"This is just the opposite of what happened with Viv. Probably it had to do with the fact that they could not get married right away. She had taken a great gamble in leaving her husband and child to be with Larry. . . . Although she gave the appearance of being gloriously elated about her new life with Larry, deep down there was a terrible anxiety that it wouldn't last, that there was nothing that bound Larry to her except for the attraction he had for her. So she never let up for a minute. I mean, she never became matter-of-fact about him or for a moment allowed him to think she took him for granted.

"That had been Larry's problem with Jill—Jill had ceased to adore Larry and had turned into a normal wife given to challenging and contradicting him. Viv perceived this early on and resolved never to fall into that trap. So she was constantly adoring of Larry, constantly deferring to him, constantly flattering him and making him feel like the greatest, most attractive and brilliant man under the sun. She always made herself look perfect to him, she worked hard to make their surroundings perfect—there was no end to what she did to try to create a perfect fantasy life for them. . . . There was a joke that went round—that even when they made love Viv would have every hair and eyelash in place, and would never sweat. . . . Of course, that wasn't true. Everyone knew that Viv was a sexual dervish, especially with Larry, and she probably put all the rest of us to shame in the bedroom.

"But that was Viv. Once she had Larry, she was always 'up' for him. When he wasn't around she was forever talking about him. When he was around she showered him with attention and affection. Of course, Larry basked in it at first—Viv was such a change from Jill. But after a while it began to irk him. . . . Viv invested everything she had in Larry emotionally, and she became tremendously dependent on him for her own sense of self-worth—both as an actress and as a woman. Larry began to feel put upon by Viv's dependence. Outwardly she was a very free-spirited, lusty young woman. But inside she had a terrible anxiety going on all the time about keeping Larry attracted to her the way he was attracted in the beginning. The harder she tried as the years went by, the less attractive Larry found her and the more troublesome she became to him."[1]

●

On their return from Denmark, Olivier and Vivien Leigh settled immediately into the elegant Durham Cottage in Chelsea. Their intention was to obtain divorces and marry as soon as they could, despite the fact that, under English law, divorces would mean putting their adulterous affair on the public record.

Oswald Frewen was among the first to see Vivien at Durham Cottage. He tried to talk her out of any thought of divorce. "It will kill your career," he said.

"So be it," she answered defiantly.

"But it will kill Larry's too," Frewen went on. "You'll both be outcasts. How will you live if you're unable to work? You know how the public are about these things."

Vivien already had considered that, and she had an answer. "We'll go to America if they don't want us here. We've talked to Alex Korda about it. He thinks I can become a star in American pictures. Larry's already known there. If worse comes to worse, we'll go to Hollywood."

"From what I hear about America," said Frewen, "you'll have even more trouble there than here. Americans are even more prudish than we are. A man and woman leaving their spouses and children and running off together—well, it strikes me that Americans wouldn't take very kindly to that either."

"Alex says that would be true if we were Americans, but because we're British the Americans will be fascinated," said Vivien.[2]

It was a moot issue, however, at least for the time being. When Vivien asked Leigh Holman to start divorce proceedings, he refused. As a rising figure in London's stiffly moral legal establishment, he could afford the public limelight surrounding an adultery-tinged divorce even less than Vivien could. And being perceived as the "victim" would only compound his embarrassment—he could imagine the ribald gossip at his clubs.

Olivier and Vivien finished their film work on *Twenty-one Days* during the week after their return from Denmark. Soon thereafter they learned that Leigh Holman and Jill Esmond had teamed up to deny them both divorces. Given the situation, they decided to continue to keep their relationship, if not secret, at least as quiet as possible for the sake of their careers and children. There was no point in sharing their love with the world if the world demanded that marriage be the sole vehicle in which love and the desire to live together could travel. They began their life at Durham Cottage circumspectly, then, sharing it with only a few close friends, swearing those friends to secrecy, and trying to make sure that the newspapers and public did not get wind of their relationship.

Alexander Korda, however, had been preparing for what he expected would be the imminent scandalous public divorces of two of his leading contract players and the subsequent negative effect on their reputations in England. Accordingly, as soon as they finished *Twenty-one Days,* he tried to get them immediate work in American films by offering to loan them out to several Hollywood studios. He got hold of the studios' schedules of forthcoming movies and scanned them for parts Olivier and Vivien Leigh could play—even secondary parts. Then he dispatched a blizzard of cables to Los Angeles, suggesting Leigh for this part, Olivier for that.

Korda knew that the prospect of getting Hollywood interested in

Olivier again was dim—the older studio bosses had already made up their minds that he was not screen-star material. He was more optimistic about Vivien's chances, though. She was barely known in the United States, with only two of her films—*Fire Over England* and *Dark Journey*—having recently been released in New York. He was certain that once Hollywood noticed her screen beauty and acting ability, it would be anxious to use her. Not the least to benefit from such a development would be Korda, who had Vivien under exclusive contract for three more years, with an option to renew for an additional five years.

He was right—Hollywood's first reactions to his cables were expressions of interest in Vivien, but not Olivier. M-G-M had decided to make its first movie in England and had engaged producer Michael Balcon to put together a romantic vehicle for one of its top young male stars, Robert Taylor. The vehicle was a screenplay called *A Yank at Oxford.* To play the female lead opposite Taylor, M-G-M had cast Vivien's old school chum, Maureen O'Sullivan. The studio asked Korda if Vivien Leigh was available for a supporting role as an English bookseller's flirtatious wife.

At first Vivien balked at the idea of accepting a secondary role. With a potentially explosive divorce no longer looming on the horizon for either herself or Olivier, they could be more choosy in the handling of their careers. Besides, Olivier had already more than once expressed his displeasure at the idea of having to go back to Hollywood to make his living.

A friend said, "I think Larry was relieved that Leigh Holman and Jill had decided to withhold divorces. Frankly, he was not as keen to marry Viv as she was to marry him. This stemmed from Alex Korda's telling them that the divorces necessary to enable them to marry might force them to leave England and pursue their careers in California. Viv had never been to the States. Larry was repulsed by the idea of having to go back to Hollywood—not just to work, but to live! To him, staying unmarried in London and keeping their romance quiet was much the better alternative."[3]

Korda finally prevailed with Vivien by giving her a copy of America's most recent book phenomenon, the dizzyingly successful novel by Margaret Mitchell called *Gone With the Wind.* Hollywood producer David Selznick had acquired the screen rights to the book and had just launched a "worldwide search" to find an actress to play the heroine, Scarlett O'Hara.

"They're looking for a newcomer," Korda told Vivien. "Whoever gets the part will become an instant international star, believe me. I think it can be you."

"But Alex," Vivien laughed, "this Scarlett O'Hara, she's American, from the South. I couldn't possibly play a Southern belle. The accent!"

"Forget the accent," said Korda. "They teach accent. Anybody can learn accent. What they're looking for is a face. And you have the face. And Larry. They're also looking for someone to play Rhett Butler. Larry could do it. You two—it would be fantastic."

"But we're British. Americans wouldn't accept British actors in these parts—even if we got the accents right. Alex, you're mad!"

"Darling," said Korda, "don't sell me short. I know Hollywood. I know how these idiots think. Selznick's in trouble with this picture. He's short of money. He needs terrific actors, but he's got to get them cheap. That's where you come in. And Larry."

"Larry would never do it. He hates Hollywood."

"Maybe not. But you—would you pass up the chance?"

"I've always wanted to see Hollywood," said Vivien.

"You'll see it, my darling. But you must trust me. I am going to get you *Gone With the Wind,* you watch. But before I can do that, they've got to see you. That's why you must do *A Yank at Oxford.* Forget that it's not the lead part. I want them to see you in Hollywood."[4]

On the basis of Korda's argument, Vivien agreed to take the part. Then she went back to Durham Cottage and read *Gone With the Wind.* When she finished, she was even more convinced than Korda that the role of Scarlett was made for her.

Said Eve Phillips, "From the moment Viv read it, she never stopped pestering Korda about what he was doing to get her the part. Her entire characterization in *A Yank at Oxford* was worked out as a kind of screen test for Scarlett O'Hara. Larry helped her some, but it was Korda who really coached her. Her part was that of an Englishwoman, yes, but really an atypical Englishwoman. She played her as saucy and sexual, like an imperious modern-day Cleopatra. It was out of character for the film, and it brought a lot of arguments on the set between her and the director. It even caused her old friend Maureen O'Sullivan to get mad at her. But Viv wouldn't budge. She had this vision that she had to do an English version of Scarlett O'Hara."[5]

What *was* Korda doing to get Vivien the role of Scarlett O'Hara? Not a great deal. He knew that Selznick's celebrated "worldwide search" was merely a publicity ploy mounted to maintain interest in the picture until he could get enough financing to put it on the screen. He knew also that Selznick was quietly screen-testing a number of established Hollywood actresses and actors for the Scarlett and Rhett roles. He decided to wait until the initial furor died down. Then he would make his move. In the meantime, he had seen a rough print of Vivien and Olivier in their recently finished *Twenty-one Days.* It was dreadful, and for the sake of his long-term strategy he decided not to release it. If he did, he feared, it would destroy any chances Vivien and Larry had for *Gone With the Wind.*

While Vivien worked on *A Yank at Oxford* during August and September of 1937, Olivier was busy with his own movie project at Denham—a co-starring role opposite Korda's soon-to-be wife, Merle Oberon, in *The Divorce of Lady X,* with Ralph Richardson in a featured part. Playing trifling roles in a trifle of a story, Olivier and Richardson gave less than their all.

"They horsed around a lot," Timothy Wheelan, the movie's director, said later. "They were generally more intent on showing their contempt for film acting than trying to advance their art. They'd both signed up for another year of Shakespeare at the Old Vic, and they lorded their superiority on the set. Merle Oberon was furious with both of them and complained to Korda. It was her film, after all. She held a grudge against Larry and Ralph for a long time."[6]

Olivier's decision to spend another season at the Old Vic was prompted in part by his desire to expand his professional reputation before any unfavorable publicity about his private life reached the public.

"It was mostly on the advice of Richardson," says a friend of both. "Ralphie had agreed to spend the season with the Old Vic. Larry was looking around for a big commercial play to do after he finished the Oberon picture. Ralphie knew all about Larry and Vivien and their fears for their careers. He urged Larry to go back to the Vic because he thought that if a scandal broke, the public would be much less liable to condemn Larry if he was playing Shakespeare. 'Put a little more money in your reputation bank,' was the way he put it. That way, Larry would be in a better position to withstand any storm. A famous, highly admired and respected Shakespearean actor would incite the public less than a West Ender. Then Ralphie had the same idea for Vivien, and he and Larry got her into the Vic that same season. It was to be their safe refuge in case the public learned of their affair and there was an outcry."[7]

Olivier and Vivien Leigh were by then genuine stars throughout England. *Fire Over England,* released earlier in 1937, had established them as the country's top romantic screen team. The press's interest in them became much more intense than it had been when they were known merely as stage performers. Both had managed to protect their privacy, but at some effort and expense. After completing *Twenty-one Days* in the spring, they left London for a month in Italy so that they could carry on their affair in relative anonymity. When they returned and started work on their respective pictures at Denham, they established a routine whereby Vivien's presence in Christchurch Street would go undetected. Vivien decorated the quaint eighteenth-century house by buying furniture and other appointments under a fictitious name and having them installed when she wasn't there. In the fall, she and Olivier started to give parties at the house for their friends, almost all of whom were from the local theatre and movie world.

One frequent visitor later said, "Larry found an entirely new dimension in himself once he took up with Vivien. She was absolutely infectious in her charm. She made everyone feel good, but particularly Larry. Having been exposed to the rather coarse chaps at Denham for a year or so, she had learned to utter the most vile obscenities. She delighted in startling her friends with profanity, yet coming from her lips it was like music. She was always gay and companionable and full of stories. She delighted in gossip, but never in the malicious sense. Underlying it all one sensed a tremendous nervous energy—almost an hysteria. I often wondered what she was like when she was alone. I imagined this enormous sense of deflation, of panic at being alone.

"Anyway, Larry absorbed much of Vivien's style. He became a raconteur, a great story-teller, a performer in private as well as public. He and Ralph Richardson would do the most humorously bizarre turns at parties. Everything was intensely gay, intensely high-pitched, intensely outgoing whenever one was around Larry and Vivien. Great style, great sophistication. Yet underneath it all, one felt a great sadness on Larry's part. As though, somehow, he was not being true to himself, as though he was living outside himself. For all their apparent happiness, he and Vivien struck me as two exquisite pieces of china teetering on the edge of a shelf. I was fascinated to watch them, yet frightened lest they slip off the edge and shatter into pieces."[8]

Olivier started his second season at the Old Vic in the title role of *Macbeth,* which was staged by the French director Michel Saint-Denis, a proponent of the naturalistic school of acting pioneered in Russia by

Constantin Stanislavski and the Moscow Art Theatre. Saint-Denis and Olivier were at odds from the very first rehearsal of one of Shakespeare's most violent tragedies, with the Frenchman trying to bridle Olivier's natural stage exuberance and Olivier resisting on the ground that Saint-Denis, because he was French, had no understanding of how the ancient Scottish warrior king should be played. The result was an uneven performance by Olivier, and again his delivery of Shakespeare's verse was singled out for harsh criticism. Yet his physical magnetism and star quality overrode the nitpicking of the purists, and the production was a commercial success.

Olivier brought Vivien Leigh back with him to the Old Vic. She was featured with Ralph Richardson in the company's second production, *A Midsummer Night's Dream*, in December of 1937, while Olivier continued in *Macbeth*, which had been moved to the New Theatre in the West End. "Viv went into the Vic under a bit of a cloud," says a friend today. "She was somewhat embarrassed about it because previously the critics had made her feel insecure about her ability to do Shakespeare. She expected resentment on the part of other members of the company on the theory of favoritism—that she was Larry Olivier's mistress, or whatever one chose to call it. But Viv had a backbone made of steel, and she pressed on gamely. She knew, though, that she'd have to be good, that she'd have to make her own mark as a Shakespearean actress to be accepted. And she was. She got lots of coaching from Larry for her part in *A Midsummer Night's Dream* and she played it well, although she was never happy with herself in Shakespeare. It was Larry who wanted her to do as much Shakespeare as possible because he had become so immersed in it. He was trying to invent a new way to play Shakespeare, different from the traditional style of the Edmund Keans and the Irvings and the Forbes-Robertsons, and different too from the abstract, stylized method that Gielgud had made so popular. He was going for earthiness and a certain kind of romantic, lyrical naturalism, but he was having a devil of a time getting it across. He became obsessed with Shakespeare. And of course his obsession became Vivien's, since she was so mad about him."[9]

Olivier's efforts to imprint his own acting views on Shakespeare came to a climax in February of 1938 when he agreed to play Iago in the Old Vic's next production, *Othello*. To be directed by Tyrone Guthrie, with Ralph Richardson as Othello, the play had long been hailed as Shakespeare's finest illumination of the tragic consequences of jealousy. With the character of the devious Iago as the story's linchpin, it had always been played in that fashion. Following their failure the year before to get across the modern-day Freudian overlay of their *Hamlet,* Olivier and Guthrie decided to try again. This time they treated Iago as a man motivated not by conventional envy of Othello but by homosexual jealousy: Iago poisons Othello's mind against Desdemona not because he lusts after Desdemona, but because unconsciously he lusts after Othello himself.

The traditionalist Richardson, who had played Iago five years before, was appalled to learn of their plans. He was particularly shocked one day early in rehearsals when Olivier, experimenting with how far he could go to personify Iago's "queerness," planted a soulful kiss on his mouth. Richardson reeled away in sputtering embarrassment and refused to continue. Guthrie and Olivier apologized by saying it was just a joke and that Olivier had no intention of including the kiss in the ultimate performance. Richardson was mollified, but only barely. Thenceforth he played Othello warily and without enthusiasm, on his guard for any further expression of what he later called Olivier's "perversity."

Nevertheless, when *Othello* opened at the Old Vic in March, the intended perversity of Olivier's Iago was all too apparent to the critics. Although some admired the chance he had taken in his unorthodox interpretation, all adjudged the performance a failure. "Mr. Olivier," wrote one, "gives us Iago as a man driven to evil by an unusual compulsion. Unfortunately, all we get is puckish, prancing Iago who is far more cheery than churlish and glaringly without the malevolence with which Shakespeare invested him. Absent that malevolence, what is the point of putting *Othello* on?"

"By then," said Jack Hawkins, "Larry was very discouraged. His career at the Old Vic seemed to be regressing rather than progressing. He was ready to chuck it in and start looking for something else to do. He began to believe that his style of acting would never be accepted as suitable for Shakespeare."[10]

What Olivier didn't know was that he was on the verge of his greatest acting achievement, thanks to his old benefactor Lewis Casson, the husband of Sybil Thorndike. For its last production of the 1938 spring season, the Old Vic had chosen the relatively minor and seldom mounted Shakespearean drama *Coriolanus.* While still playing Iago, Olivier, who had been assigned the title role, decided to drop out. Sybil Thorndike was recruited by Lilian Baylis to dissuade him. She brought in Casson, whose authority she knew Olivier respected. Olivier finally agreed to finish out the season on the condition that Casson himself direct *Coriolanus.*

"Larry was beginning to realize that many of his problems at the Vic stemmed from the fact that he was working under weak directors," Sybil Thorndike later said. "Not that Tyrone Guthrie and the others were weak directors per se, but they tended to be overwhelmed by Larry and indulged him awfully. Larry's great difficulty as an actor was in editing himself. He was so naturally powerful onstage that he didn't need to do all his tricks to hold the audience. Yet he did them all the same, thereby diluting his natural power. It was an insecurity on his part. Lewis used to comment on it frequently, every time we saw Larry in something. He consented to direct *Coriolanus,* but only on the understanding that Larry would agree to follow his orders. His orders were that Larry was to get rid of all of his experimental ideas and tricks and act *Coriolanus* in a natural, straightforward way, with an emphasis on the text."[11]

Coriolanus had its premiere in May of 1938 to extravagant notices, particularly for Olivier. The critics rated the performance as his best yet and even complimented him on finally mastering Shakespeare's verse. Everyone involved in the production agreed that Lewis Casson's direction was largely responsible.

"Lewis," said one, "directed with a tight rein and got a calm, quiet but riveting performance out of Larry. Of course, Larry wasn't happy with it. It was like someone used to drinking champagne having to switch to ale. He overdid the makeup to a certain extent—a common thing with Larry—but Casson overlooked it since he himself was of the old school that used a lot of makeup. What he was interested in was toning down Larry, in getting a more or less orthodox interpretation of Coriolanus and letting Larry's inner power elevate it to something extraordinary."[12]

Olivier marked his thirty-first birthday at the end of the month's run of *Coriolanus* with a gala party at Durham Cottage, put together by Vivien Leigh. The two had gradually relaxed their vigilance with regard to living together; to those in London who cared about such things, including newspaper people, their affair was no longer a secret. Yet because the newspapers, abetted by Korda, were still in the process of promoting Olivier and Leigh as England's motion-picture dream couple, they remained silent about their status. As a veteran Fleet Street journalist told me, "It would not have done for the papers to puff up Olivier and Leigh for the public's panting consumption only to have it revealed that they had left their respective spouses and children to live together. It would have been an embarrassment to the papers, which always liked to give the public the impression that nothing scandalous ever escaped their notice.

"I remember interviewing Vivien Leigh at about that time. She had me over to that house in Chelsea where she was living with Olivier. She was no longer intent on keeping the whole business a secret. In fact, she complained to me about the fact that none of the papers had told the story. She wondered if it might not be a good idea to get the story out, in the hope that it would put pressure on her husband to start divorce proceedings. The only reason she and Olivier were living 'in sin,' she said, was because her husband and his wife were in cahoots to prevent divorces. They were the villains, not she and Olivier. The real scandal was not that she and Olivier were living together in a state of adultery. The scandal was that they were being forced to do so—otherwise they'd have been married a long time before. When I asked her if she wasn't worried about the effect of the story on their children, she got very upset. It was a worse effect on the children, she said, for the mother of one and the father of the other to be prevented from having normal lives together. I got the very clear impression that she did not like questions about their children being inserted into discussions about what they were doing. She got very defensive. She seemed to suffer from enormous guilt."[13]

At his birthday party, Olivier, fresh from his critical and public acclaim as Coriolanus, announced to the forty guests—most of them theatre friends—that after a summer of "delicious idleness with Vivien, she and I will do a season of the four great tragedies"—*Hamlet, Othello, Macbeth* and *King Lear.* Of the four, the last named was the only one that he had not acted in before. He planned to play Lear to Leigh's Regan, one of the aged king's treacherous daughters. He wanted to play Hamlet again, this time in a different style from before, with Leigh once again as Ophelia. He intended to perform Othello rather than Iago, with Leigh as Desdemona. And he would have another go at Macbeth. All four productions would be produced and directed by him in one of the West End's smaller houses, starting in October, and would be done in repertory style—a different play each night.

It was a gargantuan plan, but Olivier had no doubt that he was up to it. He had finally captured the essence of Shakespearean acting in *Coriolanus,* he thought, and he felt that he could bring that essence to the four greatest characters in Shakespearean literature with compelling finality.

Most of the party-goers were suitably impressed and many instantly volunteered for other parts in the dramas. But one, an actress, was not so impressed. "It was to be the Laurence Olivier–Vivien Leigh Repertory Theatre," she said. "It was a cockeyed idea. No one doubted for a minute that the real motive behind it was Larry's desire to turn Viv into an important Shakespearean actress in her own right, which she very dearly wanted to become. Well, I wasn't about to get involved in a proving ground for Vivien Leigh—as much as I adored her. Nor was I going to help Larry publicly enshrine his love for Viv. You see, although Larry was devoted to Viv, one never got the feeling that he was comfortable with his devotion. He was always trying to improve her. One couldn't help but feel that he'd never be comfortable with her until she measured up to his expectations. She was very affectionate and loving in a little-girl way, but he soon grew bored with that. She had to be more to him than a doting young lovebird; she had to be an actress of stature and accomplishment. He was then very much engaged by the idea of their becoming a team like Lunt-Fontanne. The reason it hadn't worked with Jill Esmond was because in many ways Jill was the dominant mind in that relationship. But now Larry was dominant—just as Alfred Lunt dominated Lynn—and he wanted it to happen . . . his way.

"Viv wasn't all that interested in the idea. In the first place, she felt she could never measure up, and in failing to do so would lose Larry's devotion to her. Second, she didn't cotton to having to work so bloody hard. She was really more interested in movie work, which was less wearing and where the financial rewards were greater. She wanted still to go to Hollywood. And that was a bone of contention between the two of them, because Larry's last thought was of Hollywood. He was very happy to do an occasional picture for Korda for a lot of money by English standards. But he intended to devote most of his energy to the stage."[14]

Olivier's plans for another season of Shakespeare on the stage never came to pass. In fact, he would not set foot on a stage in England for another six years.

18

Hollywood Redux

ACTRESS Ruth Gordon first got to know Laurence Olivier and Jill Esmond when she appeared in a production of *The Country Wife* at the Old Vic during the 1935–36 season. She quickly became aware of the tension between Olivier and his wife, and a year later she met the reason for it—Vivien Leigh. A year after that, she was in Hollywood to make a movie. In her memoir *An Open Book,* she writes of encountering Olivier and Leigh there and of later being invited to lunch at the house the two secretly shared. "Sunday I arrived on time, a maid opened the door and looked surprised. I said I was expected and she disappeared. From above I heard a knock on a door, muffled voices, then the sound of two people jumping out of bed. . . . In no time both beautiful people were apologizing. They offered something, then led the way to the sausage and mash, two beautiful and adorable people."[1]

•

Olivier and Leigh spent much of the early summer of 1938 on holiday in the south of France while Olivier tried to firm up his plans to present the four Shakespeare tragedies. To get financial backing, he had gone to Hugh "Binkie" Beaumont, at the time the most successful theatrical impresario in London and the manager of several leading British actors, including John Gielgud. Beaumont, a showman who had little interest in the cultural aspects of Shakespeare, was enthusiastic about the idea, but only on the condition that Olivier include Gielgud in the project. "Just think," he said to Olivier, "you and Johnny, the two greatest stars of the theatre, appearing together in the West End in Shakespeare's most important dramas. It would be the event of the decade!"

Beaumont's idea was for Olivier and Gielgud to alternate between Othello and Iago in *Othello,* Lear and Gloucester in *King Lear,* Hamlet and Laertes in *Hamlet,* and Macbeth and Macduff in *Macbeth,* with Vivien Leigh to play the leading female roles in each. Each of the eight versions of the plays would be performed once a week so that audiences would feel compelled to return to see each version.

Olivier had arranged his and Vivien's trip to the south of France so that he could work on the Shakespeare project with Beaumont and Gielgud, who had rented a villa together for the summer near the town of Vence. Olivier had serious misgivings about Beaumont's conditions, particularly since the producer had also insisted that Gielgud direct one version of each play as well. Although he acknowledged Gielgud's skill as an actor, Olivier thought his directing ideas too cautious and conventional. The notion of another *mano a mano* appealed to him. But he was not sure that he wanted to give Gielgud any directorial authority.

In the meantime, the efforts of Alexander Korda to sell Olivier once again to Hollywood unexpectedly bore fruit. Korda had already arranged to loan Merle Oberon to the Goldwyn Studio and United Artists for the female starring role in Goldwyn's projected movie version of Emily Brontë's famous nineteenth-century English novel *Wuthering Heights,* to be filmed in California. When Korda learned that Goldwyn was having difficulty casting the part of the leading male character, Heathcliff, he urged him to consider Olivier and sent him a print of *The Divorce of Lady X,* which Olivier and Oberon had done for Korda the year before. That picture was hardly a good sample of either performer's screen-acting ability, but William Wyler, who was to be the director of *Wuthering Heights,* didn't care. Wyler, an autocratic perfectionist as a director, had seen Olivier act on stage and discounted his awkwardness in *The Divorce of Lady X.* As far as he was concerned, Olivier was the perfect type for the fiery, sensuous Heathcliff. That was his primary interest in screen actors: type. He believed that under his method of directing, he could draw a brilliant performance from any actor so long as he fit the part physically and vocally.

Wyler overcame the strong objections to Olivier among the executives at United Artists and received tentative approval to cast him as Heathcliff. All that remained was to get Olivier to California. He shot off a cable to Korda: OLIVIER OKAY HEATHCLIFF. ARRANGE.

But it was not to be that simple. Korda knew that Olivier was against returning to Hollywood. He also knew how anxious Vivien Leigh was to go—she still nursed her dream of getting the part of Scarlett in *Gone With the Wind,* as did Korda. There was a secondary role in *Wuthering Heights* for a young English actress. If he could get her cast in that part, it would make her better known in Hollywood and improve her chances for *Gone With the Wind.* He was being kept up to date about the Scarlett O'Hara casting problems David Selznick was having by Selznick's agent brother, Myron.

Korda also knew of the Olivier-Leigh plans for the coming theatrical season—plans that would make him no money whatever. He therefore felt that he had to approach them about *Wuthering Heights* circumspectly. At the beginning of July, he had Myron Selznick's London co-agent send Olivier a cable in the South of France: ARE YOU INTERESTED GOLDWYN IDEA FOR SEPTEMBER FIRST FOR VIVIEN YOURSELF AND OBERON IN WUTHERING HEIGHTS? ANSWER AS SOON AS POSSIBLE.

Olivier received the wire on a day when his negotiations with Beaumont and Gielgud had just collapsed. Without Beaumont's backing, Olivier could not realistically hope to put his Shakespeare project on stage by fall. Moreover, Vivien Leigh was excited by the cable. Unaware that Korda had already sold Merle Oberon to M-G-M for the lead role of Cathy Earnshaw—an omission Korda had deliberately woven into the message—she immediately envisioned herself in the part, playing opposite Olivier as Heathcliff.

"It was," said Angela Baddeley, who saw them in Vence shortly after the cable arrived, "their chance to play together in a big Hollywood film. Larry was inclined to reject the proposal out of hand. But Vivien pestered him into considering further."[2]

Olivier cabled back to London asking to see the script. It was delivered a week later. When he and Vivien read it, she was more enthusiastic than ever. Olivier had realized by then, however, that Korda would not have included Merle Oberon in the deal unless she was to play Cathy. Which meant that Vivien would be offered only the supporting role of Isabella Linton. He suspected that the inclusion of Vivien, then, was merely bait to get him to accept the offer. He was not only angry about that but was intent on not acting again with Merle Oberon, who had made his life so difficult during *The Divorce of Lady X*.

Olivier sent back his answer: NO TO WUTHERING HEIGHTS UNLESS VIVIEN PLAYS CATHY.

The two returned to London at the end of July. There they found William Wyler waiting for them. He had been told by Korda why Olivier had turned down *Wuthering Heights* and had decided to journey from Hollywood to try to get him to change his mind.

Wyler visited Durham Cottage where he met with Olivier and Vivien. A forceful salesman, he managed to persuade Olivier to reconsider by offering him a flat fee of seventy-five thousand dollars for the picture and an all-expenses-paid stay in Hollywood for the duration of the filming. Although he admitted that he could not give Vivien the part of Cathy, he urged her to take Isabella.

Vivien was torn. She realized that it was she who stood in the way of Olivier's taking an important movie role—a role that Wyler promised would make him finally a full-fledged star in America. And she herself had just been offered a good part in an upcoming play, *Serena Blandish*, by S. N. Behrman. Having co-starred with Robert Taylor in *A Yank at Oxford*, she could not bring herself to accept a lesser role in *Wuthering Heights*.

Then there was the matter of her four-year-old daughter, Suzanne. "Viv had been away from Suzanne more or less regularly since Denmark," says a friend. "Suzanne still lived with her father in the Shepherd Market house with a nanny, and Viv was going over there to see her only once every few weeks. She said she was beginning to feel like a great-aunt to Suzanne, rather than a mother. Viv's own mother, Gertrude, was constantly on Viv's back about that. Viv was beginning to pick up hints of disapproval from her friends, too, which bothered her more. She started to feel guilty. She told me that she was the one who made Larry accept *Wuthering Heights*. She knew that so long as she was with Larry in London, she would go on seeing hardly anything of Suzanne. But if Larry and she were apart for a while, she could spend the time making up for her neglect.

"She and Larry had a furious row about it. Larry had broken off completely with Jill and there was no chance of their ever reconciling. And Larry saw very little of Tarquin, who was only a year or so old. But Viv was still, if not friendly with Leigh, at least in frequent communication with him about Suzanne. Larry began to feel that Viv wanted him out of town because she might try to get back together with Leigh. Of course, she had no intention of that. She was motivated solely by her desire to do right by Suzanne and see more of her."[3]

It was partly their argument that prodded Olivier into accepting the *Wuthering Heights* role. But even more influential was some advice he received from Ralph Richardson. He and Richardson were cast by Korda in co-starring roles in a quick mystery movie called *Q Planes.* During the filming, in October of 1938, Olivier confided his dilemma to Richardson. Richardson was also a good friend of John Gielgud's and had acted as an intermediary between Olivier and Gielgud during their discussions of the Shakespeare project. He had failed to bring about a meeting of minds but still was anxious to help the scheme work, since he wanted to be part of it himself. All it needed was time, he said. Meanwhile, it would be a good idea for Olivier to go back to Hollywood for *Wuthering Heights.* "Bit of fame," he muttered in his typically cryptic way to Olivier. "Can't hurt you a bit, old boy."[4]

Olivier left for the United States from Southampton at the beginning of November on the French liner *Normandie.* Filming on *Wuthering Heights,* he'd been told, would take three to four months. He planned to use part of his seventy-five-thousand-dollar salary to finance his Shakespeare project the following fall, and he expected to bring Richardson in on it without Gielgud. Vivien Leigh, having left the unsuccessful *Serena Blandish,* saw him off on her twenty-fifth birthday. She had agreed to repeat her role of the year before in a revival of *A Midsummer Night's Dream* at the Old Vic, in December.

Olivier arrived in Hollywood in mid-November, was put up by United Artists at the Beverly Hills Hotel, and plunged immediately into preproduction costuming and rehearsals with Wyler, Merle Oberon, David Niven and the other members of the cast, most of them British. Any thoughts he had of being able to breeze through the film were dashed by Niven, with whom he soon became good friends. Niven, an Englishman who had trained in the army before stumbling into Hollywood acting, had previously worked for William Wyler in *Dodsworth.* Under contract to Sam Goldwyn, he had gone on suspension for two months in protest against his having been cast in *Wuthering Heights* and having to work for Wyler again. Only the news that Olivier had agreed to star in the movie had changed his mind. When they first met, he warned Olivier of Wyler: "The man's an absolute tyrant."

"What do you mean?" said Olivier. "I saw him several times in London and he struck me as perfectly charming."

"Of course. Off the set he *is* perfectly charming. But once shooting gets under way—well, consider yourself warned. You're in for the experience of your life."

Olivier experienced Niven's prophecy all too soon. As Niven later described it in his autobiography, *The Moon's a Balloon,* "No one was spared by Willie. The girls were reduced to tears on several occasions and even Olivier was brought up all standing."

Wyler's directorial technique was to insist on take after take of every shot, every scene, without suggesting to the actors any improvements or changes. Yet changes, and at some point improvements, would occur, if only through the performers' fatigue or exasperation.

"The most talented and most reasonable of performers," Niven went on, "after being told twenty or thirty times to play some long scene once again, without any specific instructions as to how to alter it —he finally confronted Wyler. 'Willie, look—I've done it thirty times— I've done it differently thirty times—just tell me, that's all. *What do you want me to do?'*

"Wyler considered this for a long moment—'Just be *better.'* "[5]

Olivier revealed his own feelings about working for Wyler in *Wuthering Heights* in an interview with London's *Observer* in 1969. "Looking back at it, I was snobbish about films. Then I had the good luck—but what hell it seemed at the time—to be directed in a film by William Wyler, *Wuthering Heights.* He was a brute. He was tough. I'd do my damnedest in a really exacting and complicated scene. 'That's lousy,' he'd say, 'we'll do it again.' At first we fought. Then, when we had hit each other till we were senseless, we became friends. Gradually I came to see that film was a different medium, and that if one treated it as such, and tried to learn it, humbly, and with an open mind, one could work in it."[6]

Wyler has described the difficulties he had with Olivier as deriving from the fact that the actor had not yet learned to cross over from stage to screen acting. "He started out using much too much makeup," Wyler said, "and he was much too broad. Heathcliff was the central character, of course, and he had to express a panoply of powerful emotions and personality traits. Larry's idea of revealing these traits was to exaggerate them. Finally I wore him down by making him repeat and repeat until he got tired and almost indifferent. After a few weeks of that, he began to get the idea. You can show as much rage on screen with the flicker of an eyelid as you can on stage by roaring at the top of your voice. He only had to learn that to become an accomplished screen actor, and he did."[7]

In *Wuthering Heights*, the character of Heathcliff began as an unkempt stable hand and ended as a sophisticated but satanic lord-of-the-manor type. Once he got a feel for the role, Olivier attacked it with sincerity and subtle inventiveness. But his problems were not only with Wyler. After seeing the initial rushes, the acerbic Samuel Goldwyn campaigned openly to get rid of him. "He's a mess, he's stagey, he's hammy, he's awful!" exclaimed Goldwyn to anyone who would listen. "He's gonna ruin me with this picture!"

Another firing from a Hollywood picture would be fatal to Olivier's film career, not to mention the effect it would have on his morale. Although he didn't possess the authority to do so, Wyler overruled Goldwyn, using the threat to walk off the picture himself as his leverage to keep Olivier. Olivier was indebted to Wyler. At the same time he remained exasperated by his directing methods. His indebtedness persuaded him, finally, to give up resisting Wyler and do what the director wanted with a minimum of protest.

Then there were his problems with Merle Oberon. Oberon was in Hollywood without her mentor and the man who wanted to marry her, Alexander Korda. Olivier had long suspected that she had no real feelings for Korda and had been using him solely to advance her career. Ordinarily he would not have thought this worth his concern, since there was an amusing irony in it. Korda was in many ways a con man —an elegant, sophisticated con man, but a con man nevertheless. It was a necessary facet of any movie mogul's nature to be a con man, Olivier conceded. Hadn't Korda tried to con Olivier into *Wuthering Heights* with his misleading cables the summer before?

Notwithstanding that, Olivier remained fond of Korda and felt keenly protective of his interests. He was considerably less fond of the ambitious Oberon. He saw her as a young woman engaged in conning a con man. For her part, Oberon resented Olivier's presence in *Wuthering Heights.* She believed that Korda had arranged it so that he would have a faithful retainer in Hollywood to report on her activities.

Jerry Dale was a young press agent working at United Artists in the late 1930s. He was assigned the task of handling Olivier's relations with the Hollywood press during the actor's stay at the Goldwyn studio, and

Olivier quickly befriended him. In becoming his friend, the unobtrusive Dale also became Olivier's confidant.

"The thing was," Dale says today, "that Merle Oberon wanted to have a romance with Larry and he refused. It stemmed back from several years before, Larry told me, when they first met through Alexander Korda. Korda was in love with Merle. She was his protégée and he wanted to marry her. She kept putting him off, saying that she couldn't think of marrying him until she became the star he'd promised to make her.

"Evidently at some point back in England, Merle had let Larry know that she was available to him if he wanted her. It was just before Larry began his relationship with Vivien Leigh. Larry disliked Merle from the start for having suggested that he double-cross Korda. Then he opted for Vivien, and that made Merle mad. She was jealous of Vivien too, for there was Vivien with the handsome Larry Olivier while Merle was stuck with this rich but aging, not very good-looking Hungarian—Korda.

"Anyway, Merle and Larry came to Hollywood—each of them alone—for *Wuthering Heights.* Merle decided to make another try for Larry. At some point during the preproduction on *Heights,* she made a pass at him. She used the excuse that since they were both alone in L.A. and were both close to Korda, it would be all right, that Korda wouldn't mind if he found out, that she knew Korda had been to bed with Vivien —all that sort of thing.

"Any other man might have been sorely tempted, because Merle *was* a beauty. But not Larry. He gave her a dressing down, I think. In any event, they ended up as enemies on *Wuthering Heights.* And they never really became friends, not even after Merle married Korda. I understand that Larry tried to talk Korda out of marrying her, but he wouldn't listen."[8]

The enmity between Olivier and Merle Oberon during the making of *Wuthering Heights,* much of which was filmed at a mock Victorian-era English estate constructed especially for the movie in the mountains fifty miles from Los Angeles, had a curious result on the finished product. Despite the fact that Olivier and Oberon came across with little of the tragic grandeur of the characters in the Brontë novel, their love scenes contained an eroticism seldom caught on the screen before. The worldwide release of the picture in 1939 would make both bona fide international movie stars, if only for a short while.

When Olivier arrived in Hollywood to start *Wuthering Heights,* most of the talk in the movie industry was about David O. Selznick and his problems with *Gone With the Wind*. Selznick was way behind schedule in starting the expensive production; even though he had most of the cast ready, including Clark Gable as Rhett Butler, and planned to begin shooting the following month, he still had not chosen an actress for Scarlett O'Hara. Several stars, older and upcoming, were still in the running in what appeared to be the continuing campaign to keep the public's interest at a fever pitch. But Selznick seemed no closer to making a final decision about who should play Scarlett than he had been a year before.

Olivier, intrigued by the publicity machinations of Hollywood, asked his agent, Myron Selznick, about it. Was David Selznick's procrastination just a publicity scheme, or was he really in a quandary about whom to cast? Myron, several of whose female clients were among those being considered by his brother, said, "Hell, no, he's stuck. It started out as publicity, but it got out of hand. David has seen so many screen tests in the last year that he can no longer visualize what Scarlett should be like. Every time he sees a test of one actress, he'll see something missing that he saw in another one. What he needs is a completely fresh, new face. And he can't find one."

"What about Vivien?" Olivier said.

"He passed on Vivien months ago. Saw her in that picture with Robert Taylor. I pushed her, but he didn't think she was right."

"But that was a terrible film on which to make a judgment," Olivier said. "She didn't look anything like she really looks."

"What can I tell you?" said Myron Selznick. "That's David. He knows what he wants, he knows what he doesn't want. Nobody can tell him anything."[9]

Olivier mentioned his conversation with Myron in a letter to Vivien a day or so later. It was too bad she couldn't have gotten Scarlett O'Hara, he added by way of telling her how much he missed her. Otherwise they would be in Hollywood together rather than separated for four months.

Vivien received the letter at the end of November. Two days later, after cabling Olivier, she was on her way to New York by ship, her ultimate destination Hollywood. She was committed to start rehearsals at the Old Vic for *A Midsummer Night's Dream* in three weeks; thus she would have less than a week to spend in Los Angeles.

But, as she told Alexander Korda and John Gliddon, her agent, "I've got to let this David Selznick see me."

"He's already turned you down, my darling," said Korda.

"I know, I know. But Larry says his turndown was based on *Yank at Oxford*. All I ask is that he look at me. Maybe it's a silly lark. But maybe not. Anyway, even if it doesn't work out, I'll be with Larry for a few days."

"That's a frightful amount of traveling just to spend a few days with Larry," said Gliddon.

"Oh, John, darling, don't be such a disapproving old fart."[10]

After a rough six-day voyage across the wintry Atlantic and an all-day airplane flight from New York, Vivien Leigh arrived in Hollywood on December 8, 1938. "They literally disappeared into the bowels of the Beverly Hills Hotel for two days," says Jerry Dale, who was with Olivier at the Burbank airport to greet Vivien. "I was captivated by her the moment I met her. Not only was she exquisitely beautiful after a long, exhausting trip, but she was kind and thoughtful. There is nothing I could ever say about Vivien Leigh that would be in any way negative. Here she was, an important star, and I was just a press man. But because I was with Larry and he seemed to trust me, she treated me like an equal. He was the same way. They were both that way, not at all like most of the stars I was used to dealing with. She had never seen Los Angeles before, and on the ride in from the airport she was full of questions and curiosity. And when I dropped them at the hotel she was effusive in her thanks. All the way in, though, you could cut the sexual tension in that car with a knife. They were both smoldering with a desire to get at each other."[11]

When Myron Selznick had learned that Vivien was on her way, he called Olivier and said, "I've got an idea." His brother David had scheduled *Gone With the Wind* to start the night of December 10, 1938, with the shooting of the story's climactic sequence—the burning of Atlanta. The filming was to take place on the back lot of the Selznick studio in Culver City. Old sets from previous movies were being given false fronts and new profiles in order to recreate Civil War Atlanta. Seven Technicolor cameras were to photograph doubles for the characters of Rhett Butler and Scarlett O'Hara from long distances against the background of the fire. Selznick had decided to shoot the sequence first as a convenient way to clear the lot for the construction of the various interior and exterior sets to be used in the making of the rest of the movie.

December 10 was a Saturday. "Keep Saturday night open," Myron Selznick told Olivier. "David wants me to come see the burning. I'll take you and Vivien to dinner beforehand. Then you can both come with me to watch the fire. I'll introduce Vivien to David. Who knows?"

The reason Myron wanted to have dinner beforehand was to establish his agent's rights in the event what he hoped would ensue actually did. "I don't know if my brother'll consider you or not," he told Vivien Leigh over cocktails at Chasen's restaurant. "But he's in a bind, and he can't start production until he makes up his fuckin' mind about who the fuck's going to play Scarlett."

Vivien winked at Larry. She'd decided that she liked their foul-mouthed host, although Olivier still found him distasteful. She'd made that decision the day before, when Myron had come to the Beverly Hills Hotel to meet her for the first time. "Jesus," he had exclaimed, "you *are* fuckin' Scarlett."

"Like I said," he now went on, "if I was him I'd hire you immediately. And I say that despite the fact that he's still considering three of my top clients. But I'm not him. And it's a bitter fact that anytime I try to push somebody on him for a movie, he resists. So I can't promise anything. All I want to do is take you over to meet him and then let nature take its course. I think he'll go for you, but a lot's up to you. Don't come on like some shitty two-bit actress dying to play the part, don't start talking in any fuckin' Southern accent. Just be your natural self and see what happens."

Vivien promised to follow Myron's advice.

"Okay. Now, there's one more thing."

"Shit!" exclaimed Vivien. "How fuckin' much d'you expect me to remember?"

Olivier roared with laughter as Selznick blinked in surprise, then laughed himself.

"Not bad," he said. "Now, here it is. You got an agent in London, I understand."

"Yes," said Vivien. "John Gliddon."

"All well and good," Selznick said. "But here you're represented by me. I'm your agent here. I do all your negotiating for you. And I get ten percent of whatever you make. Agreed?"

"If it's all right with Larry," said Vivien.

"It's all right with Larry. We already talked about it."

Olivier nodded.

"Then I agree," said Vivien. "Now, let's eat so we can go out and see the fire."

"Whoa," Selznick said. "We'll take our time. We're not going to see the fuckin' fire—David'll be too preoccupied to pay you any notice. We go when the fire's over. I already got a guy out there to call me when it's nearly finished."[12]

The phone call came two hours later. The three piled into Selznick's car and headed for Culver City, fifteen minutes away. As they approached the studio, they could see the glow of the conflagration fading against the night sky. When they arrived, all but a few pockets of flame were out. The replica of Atlanta was a charred, steaming skeleton.

Myron Selznick led Olivier and Vivien through a mass of production assistants and firemen to the raised platform from which David Selznick had supervised the filming. David was exhilarated, but when he saw his older brother coming he turned sour and shouted, "Schmuck! Where were you? You're late. You missed it all."

Myron resisted an urge to shout an insult back. Instead he calmly led Vivien Leigh to his brother and introduced her.

Two days later, in a letter to his wife in New York, David Selznick wrote, "Myron rolled in just exactly too late, arriving about a minute and a half after the last building had fallen and burned and after the shots were completed. With him were Larry Olivier and Vivien Leigh. Shhhhh: she's the Scarlett dark horse, and looks damned good. (Not for anybody's ears but your own. . . .)"

Still later he said: "Before my brother Myron . . . brought Laurence Olivier and Miss Leigh over to the set to see the shooting of the burning of Atlanta, I had never seen her. When he introduced me to her, the flames were lighting up her face and Myron said: 'I want you to meet Scarlett O'Hara.' I took one look and knew that she was right—at least right as far as her appearance went—at least as far as my conception of how Scarlett O'Hara looked. Later on, her tests, made under George Cukor's brilliant direction, showed that she could act the part right down to the ground. But I'll never recover from that first look."[13]

Within two weeks of meeting Selznick, Vivien Leigh was offered the role of Scarlett O'Hara. As a result, her life and career would change radically. So would Laurence Olivier's.

19

Keeping the Secret

ANNE EDWARDS wrote in her popular 1977 biography of Vivien Leigh: "As soon as she had signed her contract, David Selznick met with her and Olivier. He explained to them that one of the reasons Paulette Goddard's casting had been held up (she was very close to being signed for [*Gone With the Wind*] before Vivien entered the contest) was her ambiguous relationship with Charles Chaplin (no one knew if they were or were not married) and that the American public was sensitive to such unorthodox arrangements. He went on endlessly, stressing that the reason he had taken so long to notify her that she had been chosen . . . was the company's fear that her love affair with Olivier could present a difficult problem if the public learned about it. He recognized that theirs was a deep and genuine love, but they were still married to other mates, and there was a child involved on each side. Both of them were famous now, he reminded them, and though their liaison was common knowledge in England, it was not in the United States. He impressed upon her that scandal at this time—particularly a sensational divorce suit on either side—would ruin him, her career in the States, and the chances of a grand success with the film.

"To bring the point home to them he added that Gable and Lombard were having an affair and Gable was married, though they did not share a house. But before he announced that Gable would portray Rhett Butler, he [Selznick] and his father-in-law, Louis B. Mayer, had made an arrangement with [Gable's wife] to file suit for divorce of an amicable nature against Clark.

"Then, before they left his office, he begged them not to be seen alone together in public and to use discretion at all times."[1]

•

Olivier and Leigh were back at square one. But keeping their relationship a secret from the American public was not all that difficult for the moment. When principal photography began on *Gone With the Wind* in mid-January of 1939, Olivier was still deep in his work on *Wuthering Heights* and would not finish that picture for at least two more months. Off to their respective studios early in the morning and back to the Beverly Hills Hotel late at night, they hardly saw each other except on weekends. In order to cooperate with Selznick's dictum about appearances, Olivier officially checked out of the Beverly Hills Hotel and took a room at the Beverly Wilshire in the center of Beverly Hills, which would become his official address for the remainder of their stay in Los Angeles.

The fact that Olivier was working in *Wuthering Heights* had created no great stir in Hollywood. The movie capital was, after all, a company town, and it was accustomed to the presence of famous performers. But the announcement of Vivien Leigh as Scarlett O'Hara *had* created a stir. She was a relative unknown who was destined for first-order celebrity as a result of having been chosen to star in what was then being billed as the most important American movie ever. All of Hollywood, naturally, wanted to know more about her and, if possible, get close to her. Suddenly, invitations to parties and other social events poured into the Selznick studio for Vivien. Hollywood journalists clamored for interviews. People wanted to see and be seen with her.

She was able to plead the press of work to maintain a low profile. Her pleas were genuine. Problems with *Gone With the Wind* cropped up almost immediately once filming began in January. Vivien couldn't stand Clark Gable, whom she accused of having bad breath as well as repulsive manners. Then George Cukor, the picture's original director, was fired by Selznick, and Victor Fleming, a close friend of Gable's, was brought in to replace him. Vivien had become immensely fond of the sensitive Cukor—known in the industry as a woman's director—and was profoundly depressed when he was sacked. Soon she just wanted to get the job over with.

Olivier, in the meantime, was going through similar struggles on *Wuthering Heights.* "Toward the end of the picture," says Jerry Dale, "Larry lost all interest. He was so fed up with Wyler that he just did whatever he was asked and spent the rest of his time joking around with the cast—all except Merle Oberon, of course. He became especially pals with David Niven, and the two of them concocted elaborate jokes to play on the set. I remember once Merle had to leave the set in the middle of a scene—she had been caught unprepared by her period. Everything stopped until she could get herself together. Larry and David got their hands on several boxes of Tampaxes, and while they were waiting for Merle they constructed a kind of daisy chain of Tampaxes which they wrapped around their necks like Hawaiian leis. When Merle finally came back to finish the take, she saw these adornments. Not recognizing what they were, she said to Willie Wyler, 'Have you made a change in their costumes?' And before Willie could answer, Larry piped up: 'No, Merle, darling, these are just to mop up the blood the next time.' Not those exact words, but something funnier. The crew collapsed with laughter. Had it been Vivien playing the part, she would have enjoyed the joke. But Merle was horrified, and she stalked off the set in tears."[2]

David Niven was one of the few British actors who had broken out of the insular English colony in Hollywood and learned to socialize with the natives. Since most Americans in the movie business were avid Anglophiles, he was accepted with open arms and was on practically everyone's party list. He began to bring Olivier and Vivien Leigh around to weekend parties, where at first they made an effort to appear to be nothing more than casual friends. It soon became clear to everyone that they were more than that, however, and as winter turned to spring in Southern California they abandoned their charade in the presence of those with whom they were becoming friendly.

"They were still fairly discreet, though," recalls Jerry Dale. "I mean, they wouldn't show any open affection for each other when they were out in public-public, like at a restaurant or a theatre. But when they were in private-public, they no longer hid their relationship. This was much to the consternation of people like Selznick and Goldwyn and the executives at United Artists, which was financing *Wuthering Heights.* Part of my job was to keep the truth of their relationship out of the papers. I was getting so many memos every day from upstairs that it soon turned into a full-time job.

"Finally I went to Larry and Vivien one day and said, 'Look, folks, everybody's worried that it's going to get out, and I'm getting the brunt of it. Couldn't you cool it for a couple of more months, at least until Larry's finished with *Heights*?' Vivien giggled. 'I have an idea,' she said. 'Jerry, from now on you appear with me in public wherever we go. We'll give Larry a pad and pencil and let him follow us around taking notes. He can become our press agent.'

"One night we actually did that. We went to an opening, and Vivien arrived with me and Larry tagged along after—without pencil and pad, I might add. It was one of the most enjoyable nights of my life."[3]

Nonetheless, the Hollywood gossip columnists began to speculate about the Olivier-Leigh relationship. David Selznick grew increasingly worried and hounded them about it incessantly. They assured him that they were still trying to get divorces so that they could marry, but that their spouses back in England continued to resist. Selznick came up with a solution to quash the rumors. His solution was to separate them, at least until the filming of *Gone With the Wind* was completed. To accomplish it, he had to offer them two strong inducements.

One was an offer to star them together in another expensive movie he was planning to begin in the fall of 1939, based on Daphne du Maurier's brilliant novel *Rebecca*. Selznick had seen a rough print of *Wuthering Heights* and was convinced that its release a few months hence would turn Olivier into a major star. The same happy fate was almost guaranteed Vivien Leigh once *Gone With the Wind* was finished and released. Selznick knew that they yearned to work together. Casting them opposite each other in *Rebecca* would not only enhance their individual stardom but would give them the added image of a torrid romantic team—an image that would prepare the public to accept the inevitable disclosure of their real-life love affair. Once the secret of their romance was out and accepted, Selznick said, Leigh Holman and Jill Esmond would have no further reasons for withholding divorces. Olivier and Leigh could finally marry and live happily ever after.

The other inducement was that of a play in New York for Olivier. The play was S. N. Behrman's *No Time for Comedy*, which producer-director Guthrie McClintic was preparing to mount on Broadway in April with his wife, Katharine Cornell, as the female lead. Selznick had contacted McClintic and suggested Olivier for the male lead, sweetening the suggestion by offering to finance much of the play himself.

When a deal was struck, all that remained was for Selznick to persuade Olivier to take the part. With the help of Vivien, he succeeded. Olivier had finished his work on *Wuthering Heights* and had nothing to do in Hollywood until the fall. Vivien would be working on *Gone With the Wind* well into the summer. It made sense for Olivier to go to New York, Vivien told him, rather than remain in Hollywood for her sake. The opportunity to act on stage with Katharine Cornell was too good to pass up and she, Vivien, would be too busy with *Gone With the Wind* to give him her full attention.

In April, when Olivier first strode onto the stage of New York's Ethel Barrymore Theatre as Gaylord Eastbrook in *No Time for Comedy,* he was already the talk of the city. *Wuthering Heights* had been released a few days before in a whirlwind of publicity and received lavish acclaim. Advertising posters of the hauntingly wild-looking and sensuous Olivier as young Heathcliff were everywhere. Selznick was right: Olivier had become a genuine movie star. Audiences flocked to see him in *No Time for Comedy,* turning a modestly accomplished play into a smash hit.

Olivier used the occasion to cap his reputation as an actor. The Broadway critics were unanimous in their appreciation of his performance, Brooks Atkinson in *The New York Times* saying, "Laurence Olivier, a most remarkable young actor, knows how to play a part from the inside. He has a hundred ways to express as an actor what the author has put into the lines."

Olivier was bemused at first by his sudden fame in New York, writing to a friend in England that "these American women have made me their idol of the moment, and it seems there's nothing they won't do to have a moment with me. It's all totally insane, I tell you, nothing like the ladies in London who keep a respectful distance."

His bemusement quickly turned to annoyance, though, when he learned that he couldn't go anywhere in New York without being recognized and mobbed by autograph-seekers. He made some caustic comments to a newspaper reporter about the "bad manners" of New Yorkers. After the remarks were published, the local press answered with its own volley of reports about, as one paper put it, "Olivier's uppitiness."

At the urging of Katharine Cornell, Olivier sought to make amends by giving an interview to a reporter from the paper. "Life is very dull for Laurence Olivier," went the printed story. "Being a matinee idol is very dull. Having a couple of dozen adoring women waiting in the alley of the Ethel Barrymore Theatre is very dull. Giving interviews is ditto, and playing opposite Katharine Cornell in the hit *No Time for Comedy* is very dull. . . . 'Really I'm just a dull fellow,' Mr. Olivier repeated. 'Really, I am. I don't ever know what to say to you reporter fellows. I suppose it's because I don't have a viewpoint about anything. One should have viewpoints about things, I suppose, but I just don't. I just sit here and realize I am becoming more and more boring, and then I try to say something dangerous just to be interesting. Or else you take one little thing I've said and pull it way out to make headlines. . . .' "[4]

Olivier felt betrayed and angry when he read the story, particularly because it made him seem bored to be playing opposite Katharine Cornell. It was true that after just a few weeks in the role of Gaylord Eastbrook he felt restless. But that was due to the prospect of his continued separation from Vivien Leigh—something he couldn't tell the reporter—and had nothing to do with Cornell. What's more, he had just received word that his father had died in England. Unable to return for Gerard Olivier's funeral because of his commitment to *No Time for Comedy*, he was taking out his melancholy on his stage character.

It was a time when neither his theatre nor movie work seemed very important to Olivier. Although he had never managed to get close to his father after leaving home, the elder Olivier's death at seventy was a stark reminder of his own mortality. It also provoked in him a sense of sadness and guilt over his self-imposed estrangement from his own son. His mood was darkened even further by his separation from the woman for whom he had given up Tarquin, and by reports from Hollywood that Vivien was embroiled in a series of frustrating disputes over her performance in *Gone With the Wind*. A few weeks before, he had flown out to Hollywood for a one-day visit. He had been shocked to find Vivien worn down and sickly.

Thus worldwide fame, when it came at last to Olivier at the age of thirty-two, seemed hollow and meaningless. Its meaninglessness was punctuated by the destruction of his privacy and by the tendency of the press—the American press, at least—to misrepresent him. He vowed never to talk to newspaper people again. He did not realize that such a vow would only make the press more curious about him, and more vindictive.

Late June brought an end to Vivien Leigh's toil in *Gone With the Wind* and she joined Olivier in New York for her first visit to the city. Their secret reunion was not a happy one, though, for Vivien arrived angry after having learned that David Selznick had second thoughts about starring her with Olivier in *Rebecca*. In order to get the role of Scarlett O'Hara, she had had to sign a seven-year contract with Selznick that gave him the right to use her in the future as he saw fit, whereas Olivier was under contract only for *Rebecca*. The possibility now existed that Olivier would have to do the picture without Vivien.

The news distressed Olivier, but he was disturbed even more by another matter concerning Selznick. As Vivien was preparing to leave Hollywood for New York, the producer had written to Olivier to warn him that the release of *Gone With the Wind* was still at least six months away and that, for the sake of the picture, he and Leigh must maintain the secrecy of their relationship. Olivier concluded that Selznick's second thoughts about using Vivien in *Rebecca* had more to do with his concern over their relationship than with Vivien's suitability for the leading female role.

When Olivier voiced his suspicion to Vivien, she said, "We've got to do something, Puss [their term of endearment for each other]."

"But what?" said Olivier.

She suggested they return immediately to England for another try at persuading their respective mates to divorce them. If they could go back to Hollywood with divorces in hand, Selznick would have no excuse for keeping her out of *Rebecca*.

Olivier made immediate arrangements to be released from *No Time for Comedy* and, on July 11, the two sailed for England on the liner *Ile de France*. When they arrived in London, they were astonished by what they saw. During the previous two years the British government had avoided facing the threats posed by the increasingly bellicose Nazi Germany by following a policy of appeasement. But by mid-1939 it was apparent that appeasement had been a vain pursuit—Germany had made clear its intention to expand the idea of Nazism through Europe. England had reacted by warning the Germans that any expansionary move would bring immediate British countermeasures.

Consequently, at the time of Olivier's and Leigh's return, London was girding itself for war. Citizens were being issued gas masks, barrage balloons hung high over the eastern edge of the city, air raid drills were conducted daily, and practice blackouts were announced. Yet the mood of appeasement still lingered, and few people took the preparations seriously. The general belief was that they had been organized solely for Germany's benefit.

Olivier and Leigh stayed at their house in Chelsea, entertained friends and joked about the war preparations. Vivien saw her daughter on a few occasions during the remainder of July and early August, and she made a concerted attempt to convince her husband to start divorce proceedings. But Leigh Holman was one of the few in London who took the war preparations seriously. Despite his realization by then that his marriage was beyond saving, he had little interest in discussing divorce. "When I get around to it," was as much as he would promise Vivien.

Olivier had no better luck with Jill Esmond. *Wuthering Heights* had just been released in London and had given every indication that Olivier was on his way to becoming a movie star of vast future wealth. Jill intended to have a generous portion of that wealth for herself and Tarquin.

"That's what really held things up for so long," an Olivier friend said. "Larry had always been on the parsimonious side by nature. He was perfectly willing to support Tarquin, but he did not relish the idea of paying huge sums of alimony to Jill—particularly because the life he and Vivien were leading was so expensive. He saw alimony as punitive, and he didn't care for being penalized financially for his mistake in marrying Jill.

"It's my understanding that he kept this from Vivien. She thought it was Jill's vindictiveness toward her rather than Larry's stubbornness over money that was preventing their divorce. When she finally learned that Jill had come round to the idea of divorce but that Larry was throwing up the obstacle by not wanting to pay her what she was asking for, Vivien got terribly exercised with Larry. They had quite a few arguments over it. Vivien used to say, 'For Christ's sake, Larry, pay her what she wants. I'll be making enough money for both of us.' But the idea of being supported by Vivien did not appeal to Larry one whit."[5]

Olivier and Leigh sailed back to the United States in mid-August, their marital situations unchanged. With them came Gertrude Hartley, Vivien's mother, whom Vivien had decided to treat to a stay in California during the filming of *Rebecca*. Midway across the Atlantic, on the *Ile de France*, Vivien received a cable from Selznick in Hollywood announcing that she was out of *Rebecca*. Joan Fontaine had been cast in her stead.

20

The Star-cross'd Lovers

JERRY DALE told me: "I saw them when they got back to Beverly Hills with Vivien's mother—they had me to lunch one day. Vivien had to do some retakes on *Gone With the Wind* and she was furious with David Selznick about not being allowed to do *Rebecca.* Even when Vivien was furious, though, she was charming. Larry more or less accepted the whole thing. In fact, I think he was secretly pleased Vivien hadn't gotten *Rebecca.* For all her charm with others, she had a way of clinging to Larry that I think sometimes made him feel uncomfortable. There was no question that they were both deeply in love, but at times Larry would get annoyed with Vivien, impatient. He was not an openly affectionate man, and Vivien's constant affection toward him embarrassed him. The fact that her mother was there made it even harder for him. Her mother had a slightly disapproving air about the entire relationship, and Larry was uneasy with her around.

"We talked about the situation in Europe, I remember. The Nazis had made their pact with Russia, and somebody present—Nigel Bruce, I think it was—said, 'Well, that means war for sure.' Everyone else jumped on him, saying, 'No war, no war, Hitler would never dare, he doesn't have the resources,' and so on. Larry and Vivien were particularly vehement about it. They'd just gotten back from England, and they were confident there'd be no war."[1]

•

That was at the end of August 1939. On September 1, Germany invaded Poland. The invasion came at the beginning of the Labor Day weekend in California. Douglas Fairbanks had hired a motor yacht and invited Olivier, Vivien, her mother and several other English guests to spend the weekend cruising the coastal waters of Southern California. On Saturday evening Fairbanks put the boat in at the Catalina Island Yacht Club, twenty miles off the coast. The party, which also included Fairbanks's wife Mary Lee and actors David Niven, Robert Coote and Nigel Bruce, awoke late Sunday morning to the news, broadcast over the yacht's radio, that England was at war with Germany.

After they recovered from their shock, Fairbanks the Anglophile broke out several bottles of champagne and said, "Here's to old England." The men on board began to plot their future courses. Niven, a former British army officer, intended to head back to England immediately to rejoin his old regiment. Nigel Bruce, seriously wounded in World War I, doubted that he'd be allowed back in the service, but he would volunteer anyway. Robert Coote talked of going to Canada and joining the Royal Canadian Air Force—if England was at war, so was Canada. Fairbanks would go to England and become an American volunteer. And what about Olivier?

Olivier had quietly finished off a bottle of champagne while the others were discussing their futures. When the question came around to him, Fairbanks later recounted, he was roaring drunk. He clambered into the boat's dinghy and, pointing at the nearby yacht of Ronald Colman, moored among dozens of others, shouted, "I must go tell Ronnie!"

Olivier paddled off and disappeared behind a row of yachts. Soon his voice could be heard booming over the harbor as he drunkenly roared warnings about the war at each boat he passed. Presently he found his way back to the Fairbanks yacht, threw up and passed out cold on the sun-splashed deck.[2]

The following day was Labor Day, and as the Fairbanks craft sailed back to Los Angeles, Olivier, sober now, considered his options. The first was to report to the British Consulate in downtown Los Angeles the following morning to learn what was happening. He arrived at the Consulate to find it swarming with Britons trying to arrange transport back to England. Many of them, notable actors, writers and directors who had settled in Hollywood during the previous decade, were now eager to rush to the defense of their homeland. Their patriotic fervor was doused by the diplomats in charge of the Consulate. Unless someone had an emergency in England requiring his presence there, no one could go back at that time; indeed, no one would be permitted to return until the Consulate received instructions from the Foreign Office in London. It might, after all, turn out to be a short war.

Olivier and Vivien knew from what they had seen on their recent trip to London that it would not be a short war—the extent of the government's preparations was evidence of its expectation of a long struggle. They were content, nevertheless, to follow the Consulate's wishes for the moment. But they did have an emergency. Word came from London a few days later that Leigh Holman had been called up for navy service. It was imperative that Vivien's mother get back to England to take over the care of Suzanne. After pulling strings at the British Embassy in Washington, Olivier got permission for her to return.

Gertrude Hartley left California with several commissions from Olivier and her daughter. The first was to get Leigh Holman's permission to bring Suzanne back to the United States for the duration if it seemed that the war was going to pose a threat of violence to England itself. The second was to encourage Holman to start divorce proceedings before he went to sea. The third was to get in touch with Jill Esmond and persuade her to do the same; Olivier would drop his objections to her financial demands.

Once Vivien's mother was gone, life for Olivier and Vivien settled into a quiet but anxious routine. Checking almost daily with the Consulate, Olivier learned in early October that at thirty-two he would have a long wait before he was called up for service. Besides, the war seemed to be settling into a stalemate; so far the Germans, after their initial brutal excursion into Poland, were playing a waiting game. "Stay in California and continue your film work," Olivier was told. "You can do more good here right now than at home." Nonetheless, he arranged to take flying lessons at a small airport in the San Fernando Valley. When the time came for him to return, he would try to go into the RAF as a pilot rather than the army as a soldier.

Olivier spent most of the fall working on Selznick's *Rebecca,* which was directed by Alfred Hitchcock. Going from William Wyler to Hitchcock did little to improve his actor's temperament, since Hitchcock, although not the loud martinet that Wyler was, worked in a similarly detached and uncommunicative fashion. Playing the role of Max de Winter, Olivier would later be amazed by the positive reception his portrayal would have. "Hitchcock treated us like pawns in his own personal chess game," he was to say in a later interview.

"I had no idea whether my performance was any good or not. But then I learned that it didn't really matter. I literally walked through the part—it had nothing to do with the real work of acting. But then the picture was released and most people thought I was excellent in it. It was a strange feeling for someone who was utterly convinced that he had done far from his best. That, of course, was the bloody exasperating thing about film acting. The less acting one did, the better one came across. . . . I didn't like it because it all seemed so hollow and unethical, as though I was cheating the public."[3]

December brought the release of *Gone With the Wind*, which was given its premiere in Atlanta during a gala publicity festival arranged by David Selznick. Olivier accompanied Vivien to the opening but was forced to remain discreetly in the background as she and Clark Gable became the focus of everyone's attention.

Olivia de Havilland, who played the featured role of Melanie Wilkes in the movie, said that "Vivien was having problems. I was fairly close to her but I didn't know what they were, although they seemed definitely problems having to do with her nervous system. She was worried about what was going on in England, she was fighting with the Selznick brothers about doing a picture with Larry, she had any number of things making her unhappy. As a result she was very unpredictable —up one day, down the next. Larry sort of hovered over her, watching her every minute as though looking for some sign that she was about to fall apart or break. Of course, I didn't know that she had a history of these . . . episodes. I thought she was just your normal neurotic actress at first. But then, as I got to know her, I saw that there was more to it than that. She was always living on an emotional edge."[4]

According to Jerry Dale, Vivien evidently had one of her "episodes" shortly before going to Atlanta. He tells of encountering her one day at M-G-M, where she had gone apparently to discuss the starring role in a film for which she was being loaned to that studio by Selznick. The movie was *Waterloo Bridge,* the story of a ballet dancer who becomes a prostitute and decides to commit suicide by leaping from London's

Waterloo Bridge. She had been angling with M-G-M's L. B. Mayer to get Olivier cast in the male co-starring role, but to no avail. Mayer had chosen Robert Taylor, then almost as big a box-office draw as Clark Gable.

Dale says that Vivien "was in some kind of state." He had never seen her "behave so strangely," and when he went up to her to greet her, "she looked right through me as though she had never seen me before." Dale later learned that throughout this time in Los Angeles, Vivien went through two or three episodes of what "for a better term I'd call manic-depressiveness." He adds that Olivier was probably the only person to have fully witnessed them. "Larry was certainly confused and mystified, but he was very protective and would keep her incommunicado whenever they occurred. He thought it was just plain old depression over the fact that they still couldn't get married, and nobody knew any more than he did."[5]

After its Atlanta premiere, *Gone With the Wind* was released nationally in a torrent of further publicity, and Vivien Leigh, as anticipated, immediately became a full-fledged star. Simultaneously, as the year 1940 began, word came from Gertrude Hartley in London that Leigh Holman and Jill Esmond had finally agreed to proceed with divorce actions.

"That was it," said Gladys Cooper, who was then filming *Rebecca* with Olivier. "Vivien had never stopped talking about how the studio bosses were cheating her and Larry out of playing together. But now, she figured, they no longer had any excuses."[6]

On to a successful formula, M-G-M was planning to film another classic nineteenth-century novel, *Pride and Prejudice* by Jane Austen. They wanted Clark Gable to play the male lead, Mr. Darcy, and discussed with Selznick the idea of teaming Gable again with Vivien Leigh in the role of the heroine, Elizabeth Bennett, in order to borrow on the success of *Gone With the Wind.* But Gable, who had never had much confidence in his acting ability, shied away from the challenge of portraying the icily haughty, priggish Darcy. The company's next choice, Robert Taylor, was going to be busy with *Waterloo Bridge,* so L. B. Mayer offered the part to Olivier. He accepted on the condition that Vivien be taken off *Waterloo Bridge* and be given the co-starring role of Elizabeth Bennett. Mayer, not a man given to being on the receiving end of conditions, said he'd consider it. On that basis, Olivier agreed to play Darcy.

"Larry knew, though," says Dale, "that the likelihood of L. B. keeping his word was remote. With Clark Gable out as Darcy, L. B. lost all interest in Vivien for the Elizabeth part. He now claimed that Vivien was too powerful and earthy in *Gone With the Wind* to convincingly play the refined, delicate Elizabeth Bennett. But the real reason he dropped her was because he had been convinced by David Selznick, who was his son-in-law, that putting Larry and Vivien in the same movie was still too risky commercially, given the chance of their affair coming to light.

"Larry knew all this, and although he made a show of wanting Vivien in the picture, it was mostly for her benefit. Actually, Mayer had decided to use Greer Garson for *Pride and Prejudice* and keep Vivien in *Waterloo Bridge,* and this suited Larry fine. Garson had just been signed by M-G-M, and it was to be her big debut picture. The reason it suited Larry was, I understood, because he and Garson had had some kind of relationship a few years before in London, before Larry met Vivien."[7]

According to others, the entire roundelay of casting on the two movies turned Vivien Leigh into a different person. "She was bitterly disappointed not to be with Larry in *Pride and Prejudice,"* says one, "and she became insanely jealous of Greer Garson, whom she began to imagine stealing Larry away from her. Larry unwittingly fed her jealousy by expressing his fondness for Greer in public. I don't think anything in the way of a romance went on between them, but they were very affectionate with each other and this drove Vivien up the wall. She became alternatingly more loving toward Larry and more catty with him. One never knew how one would find her with him, adoring or frosty. She became agonizingly insecure. I think a lot of it had to do with the fact that after becoming a top star with *Gone With the Wind,* she expected to get her way in anything she chose to do in Hollywood. She just couldn't understand why the studio bosses kept her from acting with Larry."[8]

Vivien's mystification intensified in January and February when, in London, Leigh Holman and Jill Esmond filed for and were granted divorces on grounds of the adultery of their respective spouses. The divorces were given back-page treatment in the American press and raised barely a ripple of interest. "Whether Selznick, Mayer and the others influenced the general press to downplay the divorces I don't know," says Jerry Dale. "But I do know they got the trade papers here in L.A. to go easy."[9]

Laurence Olivier and Vivien Leigh were now free to marry after the obligatory six-month waiting period required by English law. And no longer needing to hide their relationship for the sake of Selznick, they moved together into a rented house on San Ysidro Drive, just off Benedict Canyon above the Beverly Hills Hotel. The house had been recommended to them by Danny Kaye and his wife Sylvia, who lived next door. A few doors up the hill lived Fred Astaire, and across the way nestled the legendary estate of Mary Pickford and Douglas Fairbanks, Sr.—Pickfair.

Soon after moving in, Olivier and Leigh began work at M-G-M, on *Pride and Prejudice* and *Waterloo Bridge,* respectively. Vivien set about immediately to use their new status as a tool to force David Selznick and other studio heads to find a movie that she and Olivier could star in together. But now she encountered new objections. As Myron Selznick said, "Before, it was no picture together because they were having a love affair while they were still married to others. After their divorces, when they said they were going to get married, it became: no picture together because the public would be bored watching a married couple romancing on the screen. You figure it."[10]

"It was true," says Jerry Dale. "But then Larry had an idea. It was more to calm Vivien down than anything else, but he thought it might also force Hollywood to take notice of the fact that they would be a terrific box-office draw together."[11]

Olivier's idea was for him and Vivien to co-star in a play and take it on a tour of the United States. The play Olivier had in mind was *Romeo and Juliet,* produced and directed by himself so that he would have complete control over it. To finance it, he and Vivien would pool their cash resources, which amounted to about fifty thousand dollars.

Dale recalls, "Larry started working on it while still shooting *Pride and Prejudice.* He consulted me a couple of times at the beginning on the publicity angle. Vivien was in seventh heaven once preparations got underway. They would rehearse and discuss the play every night up on San Ysidro Drive and would have friends over to hear a scene or two once in a while. The whole preparation seemed to unite them. She became her enthusiastic self again, and he was all attention to her. She used to say, 'My God, I'm so thrilled and scared all at once. Larry's teaching me so much about acting, and yet I'm afraid I'll never be a proper Juliet to his Romeo.'

"The whole idea had tremendous publicity potential. They were going to play a week in San Francisco, then two weeks in Chicago, then on to New York for the really big test. Larry and Vivien playing Romeo and Juliet—it was a publicity man's dream. But Larry immediately put the kibosh on any big publicity push. He wanted the whole thing to be presented in a dignified way. That's when I began to worry for him."[12]

The Star-cross'd Lovers

Olivier and Vivien made their first public appearance together following their divorces at the 1940 Academy Awards ceremonies at the end of February. *Gone With the Wind* swept most of the important awards and Vivien won an Oscar as the best actress of 1939. "I tried to convince Larry," says Dale, "that Vivien's best-actress award was a tremendous publicity bonanza for *Romeo and Juliet,* and that he should use it for all it was worth on the tour. But he wouldn't hear of it. His initial impulse in doing the play was to promote himself and Vivien as a box-office acting team for the movies. But once he got into it, some instinctive devotion he had to the dignified tradition of the theatre took over. He got so wrapped up in every phase of the production that he forgot all about Hollywood. In fact, I think getting back into a theatrical experience turned him against everything he'd been doing in Hollywood. He realized how much he missed the theatre."[13]

As for emphasizing the publicity value of Vivien's Oscar, Olivier was right, the production didn't need it—at least at the beginning. Opening in San Francisco in April, *Romeo and Juliet* was a nightly sellout and its two stars were followed everywhere by adoring fans. Little noticed were the reviews, most of which adjudged Vivien excellent as Juliet but criticized Olivier's Romeo as lacking credibility.

Vivien's reception in Chicago was even more glowing, while mystification over Olivier's portrayal deepened. He seemed to be tossing off his lines with indifference, and one critic suggested that he deliberately gave a dull performance so as not to steal the spotlight from his co-star; or conversely, to ensure that she would steal it from him.

There was truth to this, as actor Edmond O'Brien, who played Mercutio, would later attest. "I was mystified myself. It was the thrill of my life to get the part. I thought, Jesus, playing with Olivier, I'm going to learn so much. But Larry really did give a lifeless performance. There was none of the electricity I expected. Part of it, I suppose, was because he'd done the thing before in England. Part of it was that he was weighed down by so many other things—everything from getting the sets mounted to box-office details, as well as directing. But most of it was—well, I think he thought the whole thing should be Viv's show. It was a major exposure for her, playing Juliet, whereas for him it was like brushing his teeth every morning. He wanted to make sure she wasn't disappointed. He believed the pure power of his stage presence would carry him through, and that American audiences wouldn't know the difference between a great portrayal of Romeo and a lackluster one. There was a lot of that familiar English arrogance and superiority in his attitude, and he eventually paid for it."[14]

Cornel Wilde, who played Tybalt, had this to say many years later: "Something happened in Chicago and it was a mystery to all of us. Larry and Vivien had been lovey-dovey all through rehearsals in Los Angeles and during our stay in San Francisco. But when we got to Chicago things changed. Larry was clearly upset by his reviews and was trying to do something to improve his playing. Vivien kept saying, 'No, no, you're perfect, pay no attention to the critics, what do they know, they wouldn't recognize dog shit if they stepped in it, so how can you expect them to recognize brilliance?' I vividly recall her using that phrase 'dog shit,' trying to cheer Larry up. But he wouldn't be cheered up. He got gloomier and gloomier. Then Vivien got gloomy. She was a fish out of water without Larry. She was really dependent on him, and once he began to panic, she did too. She went through a sudden change over a period of a day or so that was almost like catatonia. She froze up or something. She thought Larry had lost confidence in her, that maybe he was blaming her for the fact that she'd gotten good notices and he'd gotten lousy ones. Anyway, she went through this strange thing, a series of irrational tantrums, and we had to cancel one or two performances. Vivien refused to go on, and we had no understudy for her."[15]

The situation grew worse when the troupe moved to New York. The production was soundly spanked by most of the Broadway critics when it opened at the Fifty-first Street Theatre early in May, with Vivien faring only a little better than Olivier in the unanimously negative reviews.

Also in the cast as a supporting player was the twenty-three-year-old actor Jack Merivale, stepson of English actress Gladys Cooper and stepbrother of John Buckmaster, who had first introduced Vivien to Olivier at the Savoy Grill in London five years before. Merivale had become a student at the Old Vic's drama school in 1937 and had played a minor role in the Olivier–Old Vic production of *Macbeth*. When Vivien discovered in the early spring of 1940 that Merivale was in Hollywood, she persuaded Olivier to hire him for the *Romeo and Juliet* tour.

Merivale had made no secret since then of his awe for Olivier or his adoration of Vivien Leigh. "Indeed," said Dame May Whitty, also in the cast of *Romeo and Juliet,* "Vivien rather adopted Jack as a kind of surrogate brother, or son, during the tour. He was a gorgeous boy, but timid. He was a few years younger than Vivien, but he was madly in love with her from the start. Of course he had to keep his love to himself, but everyone knew it just from watching him with her. He didn't quite know how to deal with it, especially when Vivien was affectionate with him. One could see him just melt in confusion and embarrassment."[16]

Merivale has often told the story of an incident among himself, Vivien Leigh and Olivier during the New York run of *Romeo and Juliet.* After the play's opening in New York, Olivier and Vivien took up residence at Katharine Cornell's comfortable country house in Snedens Landing, about thirty miles up river from Manhattan. Vivien invited Merivale to the house for a weekend. After a Sunday night dinner, he and Vivien became involved in a card game while Olivier perused the Sunday newspapers, catching up on events in Europe. Merivale noticed that Vivien had grown increasingly edgy during the previous few days. He had blamed it on her concern over the financial losses she and Olivier were bound to suffer as a result of the play's poor reception and dwindling audiences in New York.

After winning a hand and preparing to deal another, Merivale was stunned to hear Vivien angrily accuse him of cheating. Was this a joke on Vivien's part? At first he thought it must be. But Vivien repeated her charge, this time throwing in some obscenities that left him with no doubt that her anger was real.

But it was also irrational—Merivale hadn't cheated. He tried to defend himself, but that only heightened Vivien's hysteria. Merivale appealed to Olivier, who just shrugged helplessly. "Had a bit too much to drink, she has," he said, himself a bit drunk.

Merivale's turning to Olivier for help brought another round of invective from Vivien. She accused him of wanting to steal her away from Olivier. Although it was something Merivale might have wanted, he would not have known how to go about trying. He was at the same time astonished that she knew how he felt about her, and embarrassed that she should reveal it in front of Olivier.

Merivale started to sputter a denial but was cut short by Vivien, who ordered him to leave first thing in the morning. The next morning he was gone before she was up. Yet when he saw her that night at the theatre, it was as if the whole contretemps had not happened. Vivien treated him as she always had. When he asked Olivier about it later, all he would say was, "When she's had too much to drink, she occasionally behaves like that. Not to worry, old chap, she doesn't even remember it."[17]

As the audiences for *Romeo and Juliet* grew sparser throughout the rest of May, Olivier decided that he had no choice but to close the production. His decision was hastened by the sudden renewal of the war by Germany the month before. Within a period of a few weeks the Germans had overrun Western Europe, and it was obvious that they planned to invade England before long. Olivier announced that he intended to return to Great Britain as soon as possible. In the meantime he stepped up his flying lessons at a seaplane base on the Hudson River, opposite Snedens Landing.

Olivier's announcement soon reached the newspapers of London, and one replied with an editorial entitled "Thanks, But No Thanks." The gist of the piece was that the people of England were disgusted with the privileged show business personalities who had remained in America after the outbreak of the war nine months before. It ended with the declaration that "We have gotten along very well without the Mr. Oliviers so far, and we can do without them now, thank you very much."

Other papers sounded similar themes. If the British public had been indifferent about the matter up to then, it no longer was. Olivier was outraged when he learned of the editorial. He demanded that the British Embassy in Washington release a statement that he, and others like him, had been urged by the government to stay in the United States to help advance the British cause in an isolationist America that had been, and still was, decidedly cool toward England's plight. At the same time he redoubled his efforts to get back to his homeland, first to arrange the evacuation of Vivien's mother and daughter, and possibly his son Tarquin, and second to enlist in the armed forces.

His efforts were unavailing, for the new British government under Winston Churchill had other plans for Olivier. He received a cable from Duff Cooper, the government's minister of information, instructing him to stay put in the United States and promising to assist in the evacuation of the children. A follow-up letter told Olivier in cryptic terms to look for the arrival in America soon of Alexander Korda, who was being sent on a special mission by none other than Churchill himself.

21

Mr. and Mrs. Laurence Olivier

"**Y**OU WOULD have thought Alex produced Pearl Harbor personally, the way he boasted after the war about getting the United States into it," says a longtime friend of Alexander Korda's. "Well, he gave a little of the credit to the Japanese. But he assured everyone that because of himself and Churchill, Roosevelt was persuaded to bring the U.S. in, and that FDR precipitated the attack on Pearl Harbor so as to give the U.S. an excuse to go in as quickly as possible."[1]

•

In 1940, the mass of public opinion in America was heavily—and in many sectors passionately—against the country's involvement in the intensifying war in Europe. Roosevelt was campaigning for an unprecedented third presidential term on a platform that promised that no American blood would be spilled in Europe—a promise designed to quell the fears of the powerful isolationist movement in the country. By late summer of 1940, Germany was in firm control of Western Europe, and Great Britain was considered by many to be all but defeated. Isolationist sentiment was keenly on guard against any official expressions of pro-British sympathy, lest they presage an American commitment to go to the active aid of England.

At the same time, the British government was trying just as diligently to provoke sympathy for England in America. With Roosevelt's secret permission, the British already had established a secret undercover intelligence operation in New York and Washington, designed to enable them to conduct espionage against Germany and lobby for American aid.

British operatives reported back to the Churchill government that American public opinion remained mired in indifference, and they recommended a concerted propaganda push to reverse the situation. Britain responded in several ways, one of which was to send Alexander Korda to the United States. Korda's mission was to stir up sympathy for Britain in Hollywood and to produce movies himself that would create a more sympathetic attitude toward England and ultimately create a demand in America for the U.S. to help its English cousin.

Korda arrived in New York in midsummer of 1940 carrying his secret commission directly from Churchill, with the recommendation from the new prime minister that he make as his first film a stirring historical romance-adventure based on the life of Lord Nelson, one of England's foremost naval heroes, and Lady Emma Hamilton. Churchill even suggested the casting: since they were both in America, Laurence Olivier and Vivien Leigh as Lord Nelson and Lady Hamilton.

Korda contacted Olivier on his arrival and explained the plan. "Churchill wants this done," he said, "and he wants you and Vivien in it."

Olivier agreed. But then he learned from Korda that it would take two more months before they could begin production—sets had to be built, a script had to be written, a cast had to be assembled, American distribution had to be arranged, a myriad of other details had to be worked out.

"What are we to do in the meantime?" Olivier asked. "We're out of money."

"Not to worry," said Korda. "I'll give you half your salaries in advance. In the meanwhile, you and Vivien spend your time reading all you can about Nelson and Hamilton." He went on to explain that although it was to be a propaganda film and would climax with the spectacle of Lord Nelson's victory against Napoleon in the Battle of

Trafalgar, the propaganda value could not be too blatant. He would sugar-coat it with the story of the love affair between Nelson and Emma Hamilton, both of whom were married to others. "That should give you and Vivien something to work on," Korda added.[2]

While waiting for the Nelson picture to start, Olivier and Vivien remained in the East, where Olivier continued his flying lessons. He was still intent on returning to England after the film was completed. He had received a letter from Ralph Richardson telling him that his only chance of getting into the air force was if he arrived with a pilot's license. The air force was no longer accepting untrained pilots over the age of twenty-five, and Olivier was thirty-three.

He and Vivien returned to Hollywood in late August, by way of Canada. The detour was made so that they could meet Vivien's mother, who had just arrived with Suzanne on the same boat as Jill Esmond and Tarquin. Gertrude Hartley planned to take Suzanne on to Vancouver and put her in a boarding school before returning to England. Jill had arranged to stay in New York with the four-year-old Tarquin, who was recovering from a bout of spinal meningitis.

It was an awkward meeting. Jill had refused to talk to Vivien's mother during the dangerous voyage across the Atlantic. The feeble Tarquin barely recognized his father, and Suzanne, then almost seven, demonstrated little interest in her mother. The meeting was made more discomfiting by the fact that Olivier and Vivien's six-month waiting period was about to come to an end. They announced to Vivien's mother and Jill that they intended to marry once they got back to Hollywood.

Their marriage took place on August 31, 1940, a few days after their return to Los Angeles.

Olivier had wanted a simple civil ceremony in Los Angeles with a few friends around afterward for champagne at the new house they had rented in Beverly Hills' Cedarbrook Drive. But according to Jerry Dale, when Alexander Korda heard of the plans, he said, "Larry, no, that is not the way to do it. We must make your marriage an event."

"What kind of an event?" Olivier asked suspiciously.

"A publicity event for *Lady Hamilton* [the title Korda had decided to give the Nelson movie to draw attention away from its propaganda function]. You owe it to your country as a duty."

"And how do you propose to make it an event?" said Olivier. "Would you have us get married in our costumes?"

"No, no, dear boy. You get married secretly."

"Secretly! Alex, old horse, you mystify me. How does that constitute a publicity event?"

"Larry, the press here speculates daily about whether you and Vivien will marry. You get married in secret and then dash away for a secret honeymoon. In the meantime we drop hints to selected reporters about it. It will make the front pages. 'Where are Olivier and Leigh? Is it true they are married and are off on a secret honeymoon? They are nowhere to be seen around Hollywood.' Do you get my point?"

"I get your point," Olivier laughed, "but are you sure anyone will care?"

"You wait and see. Then, after you return and confirm your marriage, we announce that you and Vivien are about to co-star in *Lady Hamilton.* Scarlett O'Hara and Heathcliff on the screen together for the very first time in a pulsating tale of illicit romance amidst the Napoleonic Wars!"

"I've heard of hyperbole before, Alex, but isn't that a bit much? Aren't you forgetting *Fire Over England?*"

"Ah, but when you made *Fire Over England* you were not yet Heathcliff. And Vivien was not yet—"

"All right, Alex, all right. We'll get married in secret. Are you going to be there?"

"Of course not, dear boy. When the newspapers call me for comment on the rumor, I must be able to say: 'Really? Secretly married? Why, they never told me a thing.' "[3]

Living in the guest house of the property Olivier and Vivien Leigh had rented on Cedarbrook Drive was writer-director Garson Kanin. Kanin was then romancing Katharine Hepburn, who had gotten her spectacular start in movies as a result of Jill Esmond's decision eight years before not to accept the starring role in *A Bill of Divorcement.* Kanin would later marry Ruth Gordon, Olivier and Vivien's friend from the 1936 Old Vic season who was at that time living with Olivier's New York directing nemesis, Jed Harris. Olivier and Vivien, now committed to a secret marriage, enlisted Kanin and Hepburn to be best man and maid of honor.

To complete the secret plan, Korda brought in Ronald Colman and his wife, Benita, who arranged to make the ranch of a friend in Santa Barbara available for the ceremony. Afterward, the newly married Oliviers would board the Colman's fully staffed yacht *Dragoon* for their secret honeymoon—another Labor Day weekend cruise to Catalina. The irony was not lost on the two. It would be one year to the very same weekend that they were last in Catalina and heard the news of the outbreak of the war.

Colman said, "If you don't mind, old chap, I'd be grateful if you stayed out of the *Dragoon*'s dinghy. The last time you dinghied about the harbor, everyone thought it was me. I received a rather stern visit from the commodore of the yacht club, who accused me of making a drunken commotion."

"Not to worry, Ronnie," said Vivien. "I'll make Larry shave off his moustache. No one will be able to mistake him for you this time. If he goes out in the dinghy, I'll tell everyone it's David Selznick."

"Ah, but, darling," Colman replied, "they don't allow Jews in Catalina." Everyone laughed but Garson Kanin, whose forebears came from the ghettoes of Russia.[4]

With one exception, Korda's elaborate plan for the secret wedding and honeymoon went without a hitch. The exception was that when he had one of his aides spread the "rumor" to the press during the weekend, there was no reaction. Thus, when the Oliviers returned from Catalina the morning after Labor Day, no one was the wiser. For Vivien Leigh it mattered little. She had achieved the two dreams of her life. She was finally Mrs. Laurence Olivier. And she was about to star in a Hollywood movie with Olivier.

Yet it really wasn't a Hollywood movie in the true sense of the term. Korda, directing the Nelson film himself to save money, shot it on a shoestring budget. He left the Oliviers alone to create their own characterizations and concentrated his energies on the battle scenes, which were woven into the hastily assembled script as a celebration of British heroism in an earlier war.

Olivier portrayed Lord Nelson with, for much of the movie, one arm, an eye patch and a prominent scar, looking for all the world like a flamboyant Caribbean pirate. Yet his characterization was straightforwardly English and totally at odds with his physical image.

For her part, Vivien played Emma Hamilton as an English Scarlett O'Hara—feisty and high-spirited, at turns sullen and seductive. Although she put no real effort into her performance, her portrayal came out in the end as considerably more complex, sophisticated and rounded than Olivier's. Indeed, she stole the picture from him, a fact that he immediately recognized and that left him not a little annoyed. He might have subdued his stage portrayal of Romeo in order not to dominate Vivien's Juliet, but in *Lady Hamilton* (released in the United States in 1941 as *That Hamilton Woman*) he made no such concessions. The plain and simple truth was that as a screen actor, he still lacked the natural accomplishment of Vivien Leigh. Not only that, but as a screen team they failed to generate the electricity they had expected to, and it was his fault.

The filming of *That Hamilton Woman* had lasted until early December of 1940. When it was hurriedly released early the following spring, according to people close to Korda, it had a desired and an undesired effect. It aroused a certain amount of sympathy in America for the current plight of England, which had just endured a furious and protracted German bombing siege. But it also aroused the ire of the isolationists in Congress who launched an investigation of British "fifth-column" activities in America and summoned Alexander Korda as a witness. The investigation would come to naught, however, for midway through it, Pearl Harbor occurred.

By the time the picture was released, the Oliviers were back in England. They left at the end of December 1940, voyaging by sea from New York to Lisbon and then by air to home soil. The contrast between sybaritic Beverly Hills and bomb-ravaged London staggered them, not the least because they found their house in Chelsea heavily damaged and the Holman house in Shepherd Market a pile of rubble.

Olivier, having finally gotten his pilot's license in Los Angeles during the filming of *That Hamilton Woman,* was quick to present himself for service in the RAF. A physical exam disclosed a damaged nerve in his inner ear, however, and he was rejected for combat duty. That left him with two choices: he could allow himself to be drafted into a troop-entertainment unit, or he could try for the Fleet Air Arm, whose principal mission was coastal air patrol. Since Ralph Richardson was already in the FAA, he decided to try for that. With considerable help from Richardson, he was accepted as a training pilot.

Despite widespread destruction, London had survived the worst of the blitz by the time the Oliviers arrived early in 1941. And although much of the city was without heat and light, spirits rose as the populace began to realize that the once imminent German invasion was no longer so. England was now mobilizing to strike back. Aware of the public anger over the entertainment figures who had stayed away during the worst of the country's tribulations, the Oliviers expected to be pilloried in the press when news of their return became known. Consequently, while awaiting his assignment to the FAA, Olivier accepted a featured role in an anti-German movie then being made for morale purposes at Denham.

Mr. and Mrs. Laurence Olivier

Called *The Forty-ninth Parallel,* and later released in the United States as *The Invaders,* it told the story of a group of survivors from a sunken German U-boat trying to escape through Canada into neutral prewar America; encountering a happy-go-lucky French-Canadian fur trapper (played by Olivier), they brutally kill him when he becomes an obstacle to their progress.

Olivier took the assignment solely in the hope that his appearance in the patriotic film would forestall further public criticism—the picture was due to be rushed into release immediately upon its completion. He needn't have worried. Soon after his and Vivien's return to London, *Lady Hamilton* was released and drew appreciative throngs throughout England. Once it was generally known that they were back in the country, the public became more fascinated by the fact that Olivier and Leigh were married than by the memory of their absence the year before. And not much later, after America got into the war, Winston Churchill would quash any lingering resentment by nominating Alexander Korda for a coveted knighthood. Korda had been among those most bitterly raked over the coals for having "fled" London for America in 1940. Churchill let it be known that Korda, as well as other entertainment personalities such as Olivier, had been working in England's interest in the United States at the government's behest.

It was not until April of 1941 that Olivier finally received orders to report to the FAA base at Lee-on-Solent, near Portsmouth, for basic flying training as a sub-lieutenant in the Royal Navy Volunteer Reserve. Vivien went with him, and there they joined up with Ralph and Muriel Richardson.

Rob Walker, the well-known English racing driver, had been posted to Lee-on-Solent for advanced pilot training just before Olivier's arrival. "We'd heard he was coming with his new wife," he said not long ago. "We were all of us curious to see what they were going to be like. Well, they weren't bad at all. Larry turned out to be a terrible pilot— taxiing into other planes on the runways and that sort of thing—but he was a wholly engaging chap with a great sense of humor. He didn't give much of a hoot for the military drill, nor did his pal Richardson, but they kept us properly entertained. Richardson was an even more inept pilot, and at the end of a day's training it would be Larry saying in a rather loud voice, 'Well, how many aircraft did you crack up today, Lieutenant Falstaff?' And Ralph would shoot back in some upcountry accent, 'Waal, I dah say one less than yer tally fer the day, *Acting* Sub-Lieutenant Hotspur.' That was another joke between them. Richardson had been in service longer and he'd moved up to a full-lieutenant rating, while Larry had just come in as acting sub-lieutenant.

"Larry was fun, and God knows we needed some fun in those days. But beyond the mirth, he was eager to go to war. But it's just as well he didn't—at least not as a pilot. He used to excuse his ineptitude by saying, 'Gar, I learned to fly out in California, where you can see where you're going. Who can expect anyone to fly here? It's all thick soup every day.'

"But he just outright had a way of getting in trouble with machines, flying machines, road-running machines, you name it. For example, when he and Vivien arrived at the base they had a beat-up jalopy of a car. A lot of us so-called veterans got about on motorbikes—I mean really good, solid prewar bikes, not the things that pass for motorbikes today. It was part of our pilot mystique, you see. One drove up to one's plane on a smashing 1000-c.c. Rudge or Norton, or even a German BMW, scarf flowing in the wind, and then jumped into the plane and took off. You could look at the empty tarmac after the squadron took off and it would look like a motorbike salesroom.

"Well, Larry decided that he had to have a bike. Now Ralph Richardson, he had a beautiful drophead twelve-cylinder Lagonda touring car, and he turned his nose up at the idea of getting about on a mere motorbike.* But Larry—he simply had to have one. So he came to me and I found him an old BMW and he bought it. I got him a lesson on the machine and then sent him out on it, watched him wobble down the road out of the air base. He disappeared from sight and didn't come back. After a while I went out on my own bike looking for him. I found him about two miles away with his brakes burned out. He'd run on his brakes the whole way."[5]

From Lee-on-Solent, Olivier was transferred to another FAA base at Worthy Down, near Winchester, ninety miles southwest of London. There he encountered Robert Douglas, the actor who had replaced him in *Theatre Royal* after he broke his ankle. "Larry was sent to us, I think, to get him out of Lee-on-Solent. He was an absolute disaster there as a pilot, and the commander couldn't wait to get rid of him. On his first day at Worthy Down he messed up three planes on the runway, so he was living up to his reputation. Finally it was decided that he was unfit

---

*After the war, Richardson changed his mind about motorbikes and became an aficionado of them.

to become a full-fledged pilot—I mean, he was causing more damage than the Germans had—and he was switched to gunnery school so that he could eventually instruct in air-to-air and air-to-ground shooting. Frankly, try as he did, he had no better success at that than he did piloting. It was ludicrous, really. Here was this handsome chap who looked the epitome of the gallant English air warrior in his dress uniform—and he couldn't get a plane off the ground without something going wrong! What they really should have done with Larry was used him for recruiting posters. Of course, in those days there was no need to recruit."[6]

The war, Olivier would say later, was not kind to him. Not in the sense that he suffered any physical harm, but because it thrust him into a dismal backwater for several years with nothing meaningful to do. Aside from occasionally entertaining the forces on the home front—if readings from Shakespeare could be called entertainment—and appearing in another propaganda movie, he remained trapped in the stranglehold of the military bureaucracy at Worthy Down. His repeated requests for transfer to the battle zones—if not as a pilot, at least as a support officer—went ignored.

And yet Olivier would also credit the war with providing a crucial turning point in both his and Vivien Leigh's lives. They had returned to England as major movie stars. Had there been no war, undoubtedly they would have remained in America to build upon their celluloid celebrity—particularly in light of Vivien's seven-year contract with Selznick. And once the war was over, they could easily return to reclaim their star status.

But, Olivier told *The New York Times* many years later, "The war stopped us from being sucked into Hollywood." Forced to remain in England for five years, back among the company of theatrical friends with whom he'd practically grown up as an actor, witness to the way in which the native theatre valiantly carried on during the hardest of times, discovering a new sense of pride in the character of his country, and perhaps struck by guilt at having remained in Hollywood during the first and most terrible year of the war—all these things conspired to convince him, to convince them, to remain in England once the war was over.

"I did not see Larry from the time he left to go back until a year after the end of the war," says Jerry Dale. "The change in him was profound. When he was here in Hollywood at the start of the war, he was still—well, I guess you could say a free-wheeling, youthful soul. But then, when I saw him five years later, he was a completely different man.

"He had made the film of *Henry V,* and United Artists was distributing it in this country. A big opening was planned in Boston in 1946. Larry came over for it, and I was sent East to work on the publicity and accompany him around to other cities. When I first saw him I was struck by how much more mature and serious he was. And when we talked he said that he and Vivien had agreed to stay in England and concentrate on stage work, rather than go back to Hollywood to pick up where they'd left off as movie stars. The war had definitely changed his outlook, he said, and he realized that his place was in England and on the stage. And because he felt that way, Vivien did too."[7]

Another friend gives another reason for Olivier's decision. "I've heard all the things attributed to Larry's refusal to return to Hollywood," she says, "and none of them was correct. The fact of the matter was that Selznick had Vivien still under contract and was pressuring and clamoring for her to go back. When Larry did the movie of *Henry V* he wanted to use Vivien in the role of Katherine, but Selznick wouldn't allow it. He said Vivien could only make the pictures he wanted her to make, and that if she appeared in *Henry V* he would get an injunction against it on the ground that she was in violation of her contract. Vivien was furious about that. She never forgave Selznick for preventing her from appearing with Larry. She said, 'I'll show him. I'll never go back to Hollywood, I'll never work for Selznick again.' It was Vivien who refused to go back, which made Larry say, 'Oh, well, might as well stay here and work on the stage.' "[8]

If the war was unkind to Olivier, as he claimed, it was only so because of his inability to do battle against the enemy. But in 1944, after the danger to England had passed, he found a way to do battle in another way—on the screen.

Filippo del Giudice was an Italian immigrant who had followed such other foreigners as Korda, Gabriel Pascal and Anatole de Grunewald in becoming prime molders of the British film industry. Del Giudice had joined forces with flour millionaire J. Arthur Rank to challenge Korda's London Films as Britain's preeminent producing organization. Interned at the beginning of the war because he was still an Italian citizen, del Giudice was later released on the condition that he devote his energies, talents and financial resources to making wartime propaganda and morale-boosting feature films. He pursued the task with a singular devotion and produced one movie, *In Which We Serve,* which won critical honors and a special 1943 Academy Award. Noel Coward was its star.

While at Worthy Down in 1942, Olivier was asked to play the title role in *Henry V* in a radio version of the Shakespeare play that was being broadcast for morale purposes. Del Giudice heard the broadcast and decided that *Henry V,* with its stunning pageantry, its patriotic themes and its portrayal of the great English victory over France at Agincourt, would be an ideal vehicle for his next propaganda film.

The Italian producer contacted Olivier and proposed that he star in the movie. Olivier at first rejected the idea—he had seen a number of movie renditions of Shakespeare and was convinced that the Bard was impossible to capture on film. But then he talked it over with Vivien and Ralph Richardson. Vivien, anxious to divert him from his continuing efforts to get transferred to a war zone, urged him to do it. And Richardson, agreeing that Shakespeare had yet to be done well on film, said, "Why don't you be the first, old boy?"

"But del Giudice is thinking of nothing more than filming the play," said Olivier.

"How would you do it?" Richardson asked.

Olivier threw out a few ideas, "literally off the top of his head," as Richardson would later say.

"Capital," Richardson enthused. "Then you *must* do it. But do it on your terms. Total artistic control. Write the script. And direct it yourself."

"Me direct a film?" said Olivier. "You must be joking."

"Better than rotting away in Worthy Down," Richardson retorted.[9]

When Olivier presented his demands to del Giudice, he fully expected the volatile Italian to erupt in a storm of protest: "Entrust a million-pound production to a man who has never directed, never written before?" But del Giudice quietly agreed. "I do whatever you want," he said.

22

Olivier's War

HAVING acquired complete artistic authority, Olivier needed all of his sense of command to carry off the filming of Shakespeare's *Henry V*. It was a monumental task of almost singlehandedly orchestrating what turned out to be a mammoth movie company into producing one of the more memorable motion pictures in history. As Leslie Banks, who was a member of the cast, said, "Larry ended up fighting his war with the making of *Henry V*, and he won a more glorious victory than most of the field marshals of the British army."[1]

•

Although he won the war, Olivier started out on *Henry V* by losing the first battle, that over Vivien Leigh. After getting permission from the military authorities to engage full-time on the production, and after being taken off active duty at Worthy Down, he wrote a rough-draft screenplay of *Henry V* that was a novel stylistic departure from all previous attempts to adapt Shakespeare's works to the motion-picture form. In constructing the screenplay, he shaped the pivotal female character—the French princess Katherine—around Vivien Leigh, fully expecting her to play the role. Then, by cable after threatening cable from Hollywood, came David Selznick's intervention. Olivier finally acceded to del Giudice's pleas that he drop Vivien from the film; the production needed American financing and distribution to succeed, and if Selznick sued he would block the complicated American distribution deal del Giudice was working on.

Olivier eventually cast an unknown young actress, Renee Asherson, in the role of Katherine. She acknowledged that it was a "tremendous break" for her but conceded that the only reason she was chosen was because "all the costumes for Katherine had been made for Vivien Leigh, and they didn't want to have to redo the costumes, and I happened to be the very same size."[2]

The making of *Henry V* at Denham Studios spanned almost a year —from the summer of 1943 to the spring of 1944—with the huge and colorful Battle of Agincourt, ten minutes in the film but six weeks in the filming, mounted at budget-busting expense in Ireland. When the picture finally premiered in London in November 1944, it was acclaimed almost unanimously as a masterpiece of film making, Shakespearean and otherwise.

"Larry didn't realize it at first," Kenneth Tynan said to me, "because he was so close to it and so exhausted, but he had created what was perhaps the first true work of art that had ever been put on film. And he'd had a hand in every bit of it. Although he'd had help on the screenplay, its essence was mostly his. The camera work, the lighting, the sets, the music—all were done under his close supervision. And of course the acting. He'd turned Shakespeare into a vibrant cinematic force all on his own. And yet he was so fed up with film work that he said, 'Christ, never again.' He didn't realize what he had. And he didn't realize what it meant. With the brilliance and originality he showed in *Henry V,* he could have become one of the greatest film figures of all time —acting, directing, producing and so on. But by then he wanted nothing more than to get back to the stage."[3]

There was yet another factor that drove Olivier back to the stage rather than pursue his art in movies, suggests a lawyer who once represented him. "Larry, as I recall, had a provision in his contract for *Henry V* that prevented him from appearing in any other movie for a year and a half, two years—something like that. That's the concession he had to make to get complete artistic control and a piece of the picture's profits.

The idea was that he would not do anything else to compete with *Henry V.* Once having signed on that basis with del Giudice and Rank, he figured that after he finished the picture he would have no choice but to return to the stage for a few years. I think he planned it that way—it was a useful device by which to avoid the temptation to go back to Hollywood."[4]

An additional factor that might have had to do with Olivier's determination to put aside a commercial movie career occurred in July of 1944. According to several friends, Vivien Leigh felt she had lost touch with Olivier during his year of intensive work on *Henry V.* "Viv did a couple of small stage things in London and then went out on an expedition to entertain the troops in North Africa in 1943," recalled an actress friend. "When she got back, she discovered that she couldn't be in *Henry V.* The main reason she'd agreed to go to North Africa was to get some sun so that she'd be rested up and healthy for the film. Then Larry got so deeply involved in it that she felt totally left out of his life. So she decided—'Well, I'll use this time to have a baby.' She had been dying to have a child by Larry.

"Viv finally got pregnant—oh, in the spring of 1944, after some months of trying. She was thrilled. In the meantime she had agreed to do a film of *Caesar and Cleopatra,* and then she got into this awful legal wrangle again with David Selznick over her right to do it. It all became a terrible source of anxiety and depression, and she suffered a miscarriage. The grief! She felt she'd let Larry down—he was keen on having another child—and she blamed it all on Selznick and the horrid troubles he was making for her. She went along and made the film anyway [most of her salary had to be paid to Selznick—au.], but it marked an awful change in her. That's when I first noticed that she was beginning to have mental problems. Also, she wanted to have another try at having a child, immediately. The thing began to feed on itself. Vivien went through increasing depressions because of her failure to become pregnant.

"Actually, had Larry and Vivien gone back to Hollywood, I think it all would have turned out differently for her. She might have become so preoccupied with her own career that she wouldn't have had the time to dwell on her fears and anxieties. But after the war Larry so overwhelmed her with his talents and achievements that she lost her sense of her own worth, and that in my opinion is what led her into madness."[5]

Perhaps more than anything else, what led Olivier to reject a return to Hollywood in favor of staying in England was the influence of Ralph

Richardson. In the spring of 1944, with the Allied invasion of Western Europe about to take place and the war now definitely going in England's favor, Richardson was asked by the National Arts Council, along with stage director John Burrell, to lead the artistic and financial rehabilitation of the Old Vic, whose theatre on the Waterloo Road had been severely damaged during the German bombings. Implicit in the council's request was the promise that if Richardson and Burrell could revive the Old Vic, by then the unofficial national theatre of England, a way would be found for them to establish an official national repertory theatre.

A national repertory theatre, financed and supported by the government, had long been a dream among the more serious actors, directors and playwrights of Great Britain, particularly those who had spent time in the Birmingham and Liverpool reps. The proposal was too inviting for Richardson and Burrell to pass up. But restoring the Old Vic to its former prominence loomed as too difficult a task for just the two of them. Both were well known and respected, but as Richardson with some modesty said later, "I realized that my name alone was not enough to bring people back to the Vic. What we needed was a real crowd-puller. There were only two people who could fill the bill, Johnny Gielgud and Larry."[6]

Richardson went after both to join Burrell and himself in the reconstruction of the Old Vic. Gielgud, although like Olivier a good friend of Richardson's, did not care for Burrell. Nor did he like the prospect of working with Olivier again, especially on a long-term basis. He declined Richardson's invitation, rejecting even his friend's exhortation about patriotic duty. "It would be a disaster," said Gielgud. "You would have to spend all your time as referee between Larry and me."[7]

It was precisely Richardson's appeals to patriotic duty that sold Olivier—plus, perhaps, the knowledge that Gielgud was out of the picture. In June 1944, Olivier agreed to join the Old Vic for five years as co-director with Richardson and Burrell. "There was no question about it," Burrell would say later, "we got Larry because Gielgud refused to come in."[8]

In order to take their assignments, Olivier and Richardson had to be discharged from the Fleet Air Arm. When they applied for their releases, "Larry was rather astonished by the alacrity with which the Navy agreed to let him go," according to John Burrell. "Ralphie too. The war was still well on, D-day had just occurred, and they were still hoping to get in on the action. They applied for discharge as a matter of form. I think they were hoping they could put off the Old Vic business for a while and do some real fighting. But the Navy was happy to see them go. Once out, they had nothing else to do but go to work on the Vic."[9]

Olivier spent the summer with Richardson and Burrell plotting the Old Vic's first season in four years. With the Waterloo Road theatre unusable, they obtained use of the West End's New Theatre and assembled a company that included Sybil Thorndike, Harcourt Williams, Joyce Redman and the young Margaret Leighton. "Because so many actors were still away at war or in the troop-entertainment branches run by Basil Dean," said Burrell, "that first Old Vic company was heavy on actresses. Larry and Ralph consequently had to put together a season of plays that didn't, at the very start, call for many secondary male roles."[10]

The plays they chose were Ibsen's *Peer Gynt,* Shaw's *Arms and the Man* and Shakespeare's *Richard III,* with Olivier to play the title role in the last, Richardson in the first, and the two sharing the leads in the Shaw play.

They opened with *Peer Gynt* on August 31, 1944. Olivier played the Button Moulder, a small part that required him to be on stage only for ten minutes in the last act, while Richardson and Sybil Thorndike, as Peer and his mother, carried the play. The governors of the Old Vic had chosen wisely in commissioning Richardson and Olivier to revive the company. London audiences, starved for great theatre, made the reappearance of the company, with three such idols of the stage, the theatrical event of the war years. Although Olivier, Richardson and Thorndike probably would have been acclaimed had they opted to do nothing more than recite from the London telephone directory, they were inundated with praise for *Peer Gynt,* Richardson especially. The praise was not so much for their performances as for the fact that they had put the Old Vic, a national institution, back in business. It was a sign that times —that England with all its encrusted traditions—were returning to normal.

Olivier approached his role as the priggishly comic Sergius in Shaw's *Arms and the Man,* the Old Vic's next production, with contempt. "It was a part I despised from the very beginning," he later said. "I didn't know how to play him. His humor comes from his obnoxiousness, and I didn't know how to play that quality without being obvious about it. I didn't trust playing him straight and letting Shaw's lines bring out the humor."[11]

He fought with Sergius through rehearsals and a week of tryouts in Manchester and still felt at odds with the character. Then, Olivier related, Tyrone Guthrie came to see a performance in Manchester. "He congratulated me on my Sergius, and I said 'Gawd, it's terrible, I despise it.' And Guthrie said, 'Well, if you despise him, you will never be any good as him, will you?'"

Olivier has since claimed that Guthrie's offhand comment was the most important advice he has ever had as an actor. It brought him back to his experience of acting *Henry V* on stage just before the war, when he'd so disliked reciting Henry's jingoistic speeches at a time when blatant patriotism was out of fashion. During his more recent film version of *Henry V,* given the times, he had found Henry a much easier part to play—indeed, he had enjoyed performing it because by then he sympathized with the patriotic warrior king. And his performance on film, he was convinced, was infinitely better than his stage portrayal years before.

The same prewar dynamic was at work with Sergius, Olivier realized after hearing Guthrie's remark. "One can never be successful in a character unless one gets entirely inside the character and, in effect, learns to love him as one loves oneself," he later said. "It's my first and last piece of advice to actors, and I find it amazing that I took so long to learn it. Even the most despicable character—the actor must first fall in love with him, or her. Only then can the actor truly become the character."

Olivier fully adopted the credo for the Old Vic's next production of *Richard III,* in which he starred as the evil-minded, hunchbacked King Richard. So immersed did he become in learning to love Richard that he had difficulty remembering Shakespeare's lines. He almost literally "became" Richard and found himself driven by a compulsion to speak his own lines instead of Shakespeare's. On opening night he feared his performance would be a travesty as he struggled between Shakespeare's speeches and the ones he imagined Richard should be uttering. His fears went unfounded, however, and he went on to give a performance of unrivaled brilliance. The critics endorsed it with rare superlatives, one calling it "a masterpiece," another "a work of pure genius," still another "the most riveting Richard in the history of the theatre."

Olivier today points to his 1944 Richard III as the signal turning point of his career. Although acclaimed before in other parts, he says that he did not truly learn to act until he confronted the twisted character of Richard. His physical transformation alone was remarkable—he based much of his makeup, voice and movement on the diabolical real-life persona of Jed Harris. But the physical portrayal was only a scratch on the surface of the breathtaking scope of his Richard.

Before Richard, he had always been an "outside-in" actor, applying his own mannerisms, voice and techniques to a character and achieving "at best half the truth." But with Richard he discovered acting as an "inside-out" process. Not the inside-out techniques espoused by the Method, but simply learning to love a character and, as he often said, "thereby wanting literally *to be* that character, or at least to be like him in every way possible. Once one makes that commitment, one can then get at the character's reality and truth. One is no longer acting, one is being. It is the most exhilarating feeling, and when it is achieved it almost guarantees an original and compelling portrayal."

And how does an actor realize his desire to "be" a character? It is all in the preparation once he first encounters the character on the printed page, and it consumes every waking minute of his day. Olivier has often told about how, years later, he developed his memorable characterization of Shylock in *The Merchant of Venice.* "It started in front of the shaving mirror one morning after I knew I was going to play him and had read the play with that in mind. It would take me half an hour or more each day to shave because I would experiment with the way I went about it. I would discard my normal way of shaving and experiment with other ways, finding the way I would do it if I was Shylock. But it is not just the act of shaving—it's everything that goes with it, from how one holds one's hands on the razor to the facial expressions, grunts, sighs, and so on, that are involved in shaving. And how one positions one's head, how one stands and shifts one's weight. All of that, and soon you are shaving completely differently and that's your Shylock shaving.

"And then you go on to other things, the trivial things in your life —how you eat, how you walk down the stairs, how you say 'good morning' in the kitchen. Everything different than your usual way. You accumulate a mass of new mannerisms and ways of doing things and saying things and seeing things. Then, from all of this detail you begin to sort out those things that seem to be true to the character you've been forming as you accumulated them. Things begin to emerge that in their turn help you reinforce and expand the character. And since it is really you, you begin to love this new side of your own character as you have loved the old side. Possibly you love it more, since it is all so new and different, yet still you. This is still working from the outside in, but in a much more substantive way than most actors do it, which is simply to impose their own beings on the characters. This way, you let the character eventually impose himself on your being."[12]

"There was a certain irony in that," Cecil Beaton, who was to become a close friend of Vivien Leigh's, once said. "When Larry started the business of falling in love with his characters, he began to fall out of love with Viv. We often heard him talk about it, and it always struck me, though I said nothing to her, that he used it as a substitute for his flagging love for her. Of course, she never recognized it. Indeed, she was just as enthusiastic about the concept as Larry was, and kept telling everyone how brilliant an acting insight it was."[13]

According to others, if Olivier was falling out of love with Vivien at that time, it had more to do with her behavior than with his acting insights. "The truth is," says a friend, "that during that first Old Vic season, Viv was becoming more and more of a concern to Larry, a burden. She had lost their baby and was in a terrible state about it for the longest time. Then these dreadful fits of melancholy or depression or amnesia she was given to began to increase. And last longer. Larry simply didn't know what to make of them or how to handle them. He tried to get Viv to see a doctor, but when she was in the middle of an attack she was impossible to reason with. And when they were over, she had no recollection of them and of course wouldn't entertain any suggestion that something was wrong with her. Larry tried to keep her hidden whenever they occurred, but I saw one or two of them and I can tell you—he was up against it. She went from the perfectly normal Viv to this unrecognizable, ugly ogre. It put Larry in a quandary at first. Then, out of frustration, his anger began to build. I'm convinced that much of his brilliance in *Richard III* was due to his need to release all of his pent-up frustration and anger."[14]

Says another, "Yes, no doubt there was a connection between Larry's frustration over Vivien and his performances with the Old Vic at war's end. The performances he really excelled at were in the bravura parts that demanded great energy and breadth. Larry was overflowing with repressed emotion in his personal life, and he used these roles as escape valves. Perhaps too, finding it increasingly difficult to love Vivien in the way that he had, he diverted his passions to his characters and then called it falling in love. He was saying that he had to be in love with someone. If it couldn't be Vivien, it would then be Richard, Hotspur, Oedipus—all these characters he played to such stunning effect."[15]

If his portrayal of Richard III elevated Olivier to startling new heights as an actor, his performance a year later of Oedipus in the famous Greek tragedy by Sophocles, *Oedipus Rex,* would propel him into the rarified atmosphere of the immortals.

At the end of his first season at the Old Vic, in the spring of 1945, Olivier directed Vivien as Sabina in the first London production of Thornton Wilder's American hit, *The Skin of Our Teeth.* Then, with the war over, he and Richardson took the Old Vic on a summer tour of British army bases in Occupied Germany, performing *Richard III* and the other plays of the previous season. Olivier had to make an emergency journey back to London in July when he learned that Vivien was diagnosed as suffering from a long-standing case of tuberculosis. His alarm was mixed with relief, for he assumed that the tuberculosis had been responsible for her mystifying mental dysfunction. Vivien was put into a hospital for six weeks and Olivier returned to the continent to finish out the tour. He was confident that her recovery from the TB would put an end to her mental episodes—confident because her doctors had assured him, when he told them about her periodic attacks, that such behavior was common among TB victims.

The film of *Henry V* had been released the previous fall, had received a unanimous ovation from the critics and had drawn crowds daily all over Britain during the winter and spring. Early in the spring of 1945, anticipating considerable profits from the movie, Olivier decided to buy an ancient former monastery building on seventy-five acres of land along the River Thame in the countryside west of London.

"It was after Larry made his decision that he would stay in England rather than return to America once the war was over," said Ralph Richardson. "He had always been an out-of-town boy and had never enjoyed living in London all that much. He had an affinity for plants and the soil, fresh air and tranquil surroundings. And the prospect of living in London after the war, living through the cleanup and rebuilding, did not excite him at all. So he began to talk about living in the country, and eventually he and Viv discovered this marvelous old abbey."[16]

Called Notley Abbey, the twelfth-century stone structure was a ruin when Olivier found it. But the fact that it had been subsidized by the real King Henry V barred any objections Vivien had to his buying it. Workmen were put to work to refurbish it during the summer of 1945. When he returned from the military tour in August, it was almost ready for habitation.

Vivien was ready to leave the hospital at the end of August, and her doctors wanted to send her to a TB sanitorium in Switzerland for at least six months—her disease was far from cured. She refused, persuading them to allow her to go through her long recuperation at Notley Abbey, attended by a nurse. She took up residence under orders to remain out of the theatre for a year. The only activity she was permitted was the planning of the furnishing and decoration of Notley Abbey. Olivier, in the meantime, began to prepare for his second season at the Old Vic.

The agreement between Olivier and Richardson was that since Richardson had been responsible for bringing Olivier into the revitalized company, he would have first choice on the opening play of each season and Olivier the choice of the final one. Since Richardson had long wanted to play Shakespeare's Falstaff, he chose *Henry IV, Parts I and II* to open the 1945 season. Olivier took the part of Hotspur in *Part I* and Mr. Justice Shallow in *Part II*.

It was a decision that Richardson later called a mistake on his part, for in both plays Olivier, playing smaller roles, thoroughly outshone him. With Olivier's *Richard III,* the West End had become in many theatre-goers' minds a personal battleground for primacy among England's three leading actors—Olivier, Richardson and Gielgud. "It was altogether a friendly rivalry," said Richardson, "at least between Larry and myself and Johnny and myself. Between Johnny and Larry—well, not unfriendly, but guarded. Johnny still thought Larry tended to overact and found it hard to understand his popularity. Larry looked on Johnny as being too much on the cool, remote side. Of course, both influenced each other a great deal, not the least in their constant striving to outdo each other. Alas, I think I rather got lost in the shuffle."

If Olivier's stuttering, vainglorious Hotspur was memorable, it was made even more so by his portrayal on alternate nights of the lecherous old Swallow. Audiences were enthralled by his ability to go from one to the other in such convincing fashion, and "tour de force" was mentioned by more than one critic as he rhapsodized over the two portrayals. As Olivier was again to say later, neither role was an especially attractive one from an actor's point of view. But he enjoyed them hugely because, in working out the contrasting characterizations, he confirmed his theory that it was necessary to "fall in love" with one's characters.

"The only trouble was," he added, "that it was at first difficult to be in love with two characters at the same time. Just as it's difficult to be in love with, say, two women at the same time. But then I discovered the trick to it. I realized that the reason you fall in love with one woman is because you are no longer able to love the woman who came before and yet you still have all this love in you. And that's what I did with Hotspur and Swallow. Once finished with a performance of Swallow, I would put him out of mind. I forced myself not to love him anymore, or at least for the next twenty-four hours. And I turned all my love to Hotspur until I got through him the next night, then dismissed him from my affections and went back to Swallow."[17]

It was a prophetic remark.

23

Pursued by the Furies

"I DON'T THINK I've ever seen a woman more desperately in love with her husband," says one of Vivien Leigh's old friends, "even after five, six years of marriage. We know now, of course, what we didn't know then—that there must have been a link between Vivvy's mental condition and her crazy need for Larry. It *was* abnormal; we all thought so. Vivvy was a woman who had everything going for her—beauty, talent, endless charm. It made no sense that she was so dependent on this one man, no matter how much of a giant he was."[1]

•

No one was more confused by Vivien's increasingly neurotic devotion to Olivier than Olivier himself. And no one was more disappointed when, after several months of quiet confinement at Notley Abbey in the fall of 1945, Vivien's mental blackouts resumed.

According to another friend, "Larry even adjusted himself to this.

The doctors had made Viv give up drinking and smoking, so he could no longer blame her problems on that. Then they said her TB was clearing up nicely, and he was without that to use as an excuse. For a while he said—well, maybe it was the giving up smoking, it made her edgy and nervous. But when she started smoking and drinking again, they continued. The tragic thing was that Larry would think he'd adjusted to Viv's having these bouts and get to the point where he could deal with them, only to have them get worse—they would become more intense and last longer. So he could never really adjust. He began to treat her more as a patient than as a wife and lover. What else could he do? And Viv of course caught on to it and went out of her way to reestablish herself as wife and lover, which only served to increase her neuroticism. They were still terrific together in public, but Larry had to be very careful, always on guard against a sudden change in her."[2]

The saving grace, if it could be called that, was that the onset of Vivien's mental lapses began to take on an identifiable pattern while she was recuperating at Notley Abbey. No longer did she spring her bizarre personality changes on Olivier; rather, she built up to them over several days of increasing edginess and moodiness, lapsing finally into a state of alternating amnesial depression and hysteria—almost mania—that was most frightening in the depths of its irrationality. After a day or two in the snakepit of her sickness, Vivien would emerge thoroughly sane but exhausted.

One day in October of 1945, Olivier read an article about himself in a London newspaper. The article summed up his life as that of a "man who has everything." It provoked an ironic, bitter laugh. "The man who has everything," he said, "really has nothing." His bitterness was fueled by his despair over Vivien, but it was heightened by the fact that he was rehearsing to play the role of Oedipus in the Old Vic's next production, *Oedipus Rex.* Sophocles' ancient drama was the prototype of all the great tragedies in Western stage literature, and Olivier had chosen it—a tale of a man who has everything only to lose it because of a tragic flaw in his character—partly because it reflected his own sense that the fates were cruelly toying with him. "If ever Larry could love a character," said Jack Hawkins, "feeling the way he was feeling then, Oedipus was it."[3]

Olivier's first night as Oedipus shook the British theatre world as no performance by an actor had done before. John Mason Brown, a critic celebrated for his strict standards, later summed up the reaction of critics and audiences alike. "No word spills more infrequently or reluctantly from any critical pen," he wrote. "For everyone's sake, for the well-being of the art involved, in the interests of criticism, out of respect for the language, and in defense of standards, 'great' is an adjective which ought to be kept buried in the deep freeze. . . . But Mr. Olivier's Oedipus, considered along with his Henry V and judged in the light of his earlier contributions to the Old Vic, has left me no other choice. . . . I can only say that in *Henry V* and *Oedipus* I have seen the sun rise. And I refuse to mistake it for the moon or salute it as such, when for me it is the sun. Mr. Olivier's Oedipus is one of those performances in which blood and electricity are somehow mixed. It pulls lightning down from the sky. It is awesome, dwarfing, and appalling as one of nature's angriest displays. Though thrilling, it never loses it majesty. His Theban king is godlike in appearance . . . sullen, willful, august, and imperious. There is something of the young Napoleon in him too, but he is a Napoleon pursued by the furies rather than following the Eagle."

Regarding the climax of the play—the moment when Oedipus realizes that he has murdered his father and married his mother—Brown added: "When the fearful realization at last inundates him . . . Mr. Olivier releases two cries which no one who has heard them can hope to forget. They are the dreadful, hoarse groans of a wounded animal. They well up out of a baby that has been clubbed by fate. They are sounds which speak, as no words could, for a soul torn by horror, for a mind numbed by what it has been forced to comprehend. . . . The subsequent moments when Oedipus appears, self-blinded with the blood trickling down his face, are almost more terrible than audiences can bear."[4]

To most theatre-goers it was Olivier's gory self-mutilation at the climactic moment, with blood cascading suddenly from his eyes, that remains etched in their memory. But to more sophisticated observers, it was the two cries mentioned by critic Brown that elevated Olivier's portrayal to the heaven of theatrical immortality. "In those two agonized, agonizing utterances," Kenneth Tynan said, "were contained three thousand years of mankind's confrontation with the fates, with the gods, with himself. They were the cries of a woman you might imagine discovering the bodies of her children in the rubble of a building in London during the blitz. But they were also the cries you might expect some madman to release upon seeing the product of his evil handiwork. They sounded every tortured emotion ever known to the human race. And though they only lasted for a few moments, they drove through the people who watched the play like swords, disemboweling them of their own emotions. This was because of the way

Larry let them loose. They were totally in character—majestic, monumental roars of grief that cut across the hushed audience like jolts of electricity. Hardly a performance went by when people in the audience didn't cry back at Larry out of some reflexive sympathy."[5]

How did Olivier produce this most memorable moment in theatre? "It was the vowel I used," he says today. "One associated a cry of grief those days with an 'Oooooooh' or an 'Aaaaaagh.' I did these in the first rehearsals, but neither felt right. Then, fooling about with it, I happened on an 'er' sound. 'Eeeerrrgh!' And it somehow sounded right—different, eccentric, what this eccentric king would cry. And the rest of it—well, it was simply a matter of timing, of placing it in exactly the right place so that the audience, having expected something and not gotten it, and therefore having relaxed its guard a little, suddenly gets it, this cry, like a delayed reaction. I'm afraid the effect it had was more due to the audience having let its guard down than any brilliance in the cry itself."[6]

It was not Olivier's portrayal of Oedipus alone that cemented his star in the firmament of theatrical immortality, however. In preparing the play for its Old Vic staging, he and director Burrell had condensed it considerably in order to step up its pace and heighten its emotional impact. This had left them with a shortened bill. Olivier decided to make it a two-play evening by adding, after an intermission, a staging of Richard Brinsley Sheridan's one-act, one-character satire *The Critic,* with himself in the sole role of the foppish Mr. Puff. "After we bring them to their knees in terror with Oedipus," he said to Burrell and Richardson, "we should send them home with a bit of cheer, don't you think?"

"Larry's decision to put on *The Critic* was taken not really out of concern for the audience," Burrell said later. "It was mostly an expression of his actor's ego and his desire to dazzle, and it raised a few hackles around the company. To go from Oedipus to Mr. Puff with only a few minutes' intermission in between seemed a bit much to some, pure showing off. I must say, I was doubtful about it at first—why not Ralph as Puff, if we were going to do it at all? But Larry had the choice of the entire bill, and he insisted on himself. And he did it."[7]

To the delight of audiences, by all accounts. Although it was the Oedipus that remained most firmly in their memory, the fact that he could come back fifteen minutes after his agonizing death as Oedipus and give a rollicking performance as Mr. Puff was also a source of awe. The subdued curtain calls he received at the end of Oedipus—subdued because audiences were still numbed by the spectacle they had just witnessed—were more than made up for when the curtain rang down on *The Critic.*

"Larry positively basked in the adulation," said Jack Hawkins. "One couldn't begrudge him that, though. His life wasn't an otherwise very happy one at the time. He took what happiness he could get from his work."[8]

If Vivien Leigh was the primary source of his discontent, anxiety about money and his son Tarquin also vexed him. Tarquin had returned to England with Jill Esmond soon after the end of the war and now was nine. Having given up on the idea of having a child with Vivien, Olivier had made what he thought were sincere and hearty efforts to express his love for his son. The boy, who strongly resembled his father but felt him an intimidating stranger, was unable to respond with anything but juvenile withdrawal. Olivier mistook this for calculated indifference: each time he viewed himself as having been rebuffed by Tarquin, he grew more unsettled.

Vivien complicated matters by making a concentrated effort to draw Tarquin into their orbit. When the boy began to respond to her in ways that he could not respond to his father, Olivier grew angry at both. Vivien's method of bringing Tarquin out of his remoteness, as Olivier saw it, was to spoil him with effusive, undeserved praise and gifts. He did not approve.

As for his anxiety over money, Olivier's share in the profits of *Henry V* were, up to then, minimal; they helped little, added to the modest salary he was getting from the Old Vic, to cover the costs of keeping two houses going, of Vivien's medical care and of his payments to Jill Esmond. Vivien had not worked since the summer before and was forbidden from doing so for another year. They had each achieved a measure of wealth before the war in Hollywood only to squander it on their elaborate, ill-conceived production of *Romeo and Juliet.* Now, in the early months of 1946, Olivier wondered if he shouldn't go back to Hollywood to make a movie or two in order to solve his money worries for a while. He could do it during the summer, between seasons at the Old Vic, and collect a comfortable nest egg to see them through the next few years.

Many contend that Olivier bravely resisted the temptation to return to Hollywood in 1946, but such wasn't the case. He would have gone gratefully if he could have. He learned to his dismay, however, that Hollywood did not want him. Part of the reason had to do with the fact that the American public's demands on Hollywood for postwar movie entertainment had changed radically—the Western, musical comedy and realistic up-to-date home-grown drama were replacing foreign historical sagas as the profitable "product" of the movie industry. But the more distressing reason for Olivier's rejection by Hollywood took on the dimension of an organized boycott of his services.

He found this out in the spring of 1946 when he asked Myron Selznick to find him a starring role in a Hollywood movie during the coming summer. By the time he received a response from Selznick, Olivier was in New York with the Old Vic company to give a six-week repertory presentation of *Oedipus Rex*, the two parts of *Henry IV* and Chekhov's *Uncle Vanya,* and to promote the American release of his *Henry V* film. It was Myron Selznick who told him about the boycott.

The year before, when Olivier had set out to direct Vivien Leigh in *The Skin of Our Teeth,* he and Vivien had been served with papers by lawyers representing David O. Selznick. The papers, also filed in a London court, sought an injunction preventing Vivien's appearance in the play on the ground that she was in violation of her film contract with Selznick. Selznick had not expected Olivier and Leigh to fight back. But they did, not only hiring an attorney and resisting the injunction in court, but quickly winning the case in the bargain. The court declared that Vivien had not breached the contract because as an English subject she had been entitled to stay in England during the war rather than return to Hollywood to fulfill the contract.

Selznick was livid with anger and humiliation. Blaming Olivier more than Vivien for his setback, he put out word in Hollywood that the British actor should never work in the American movie industry again, and that he would refuse to do business with anyone who hired him. Since Selznick was among the most powerful moguls in Hollywood, the rest of the industry heeded his words.

Selznick's wrath soon cooled, and he eventually recanted his words, but it took his counterparts in the industry more than two years—or until Selznick suddenly closed down his studio—before they got the message that it was all right to consider Olivier again for pictures.

"Larry was in a fury when he heard that Hollywood was reluctant to use him because he had allegedly double-crossed David Selznick," says Jerry Dale, who was with Olivier in Boston and New York at the time, helping to promote *Henry V.* "He was never one to share his problems, but he even said to me, 'God, Jerry, who are these people you work for in Hollywood? Myron says they're out to ruin me. I can't let them do it. I need a picture, I need the money.' I think he went to see a lawyer in New York about it, Arnold Weissberger or Louis Nizer, one of those big entertainment lawyers. . . . He wasn't imagining it, that I'm sure of. I mean, I don't know exactly what Myron Selznick told him— maybe he made it all up, because basically he hated his brother and enjoyed embarrassing David. But I later heard the story around Hollywood and I'm sure it was true—there was a kind of informal boycott against Larry. The strangest thing of all was that *Henry V* was a fabulous movie success. Larry produced, directed and starred in it. Why, anyone else with that kind of movie success would have had Hollywood knocking down his doors to sign him up to a multipicture deal. But they stayed away from Larry for the longest time, even after he and the picture won several Oscars the following year.

"The biggest irony of it all was that when Larry was finally allowed to do another Hollywood movie, it was David Selznick who was largely responsible for getting him the part."[9]

Despite his troubles, Olivier's two-month stay in the United States with the Old Vic was another personal triumph. His double-bill performance on Broadway as Oedipus and Mr. Puff won him what were possibly even more enthusiastic accolades than he'd received in London. *Henry V* was launched in movie theatres in large cities around the country to critical kudos and ever-increasing audiences. To top off the visit, he was awarded an Honorary Doctor of Letters degree in June by Tufts University, near Boston.

Jerry Dale, still working on publicity for *Henry V,* was in Boston with Olivier and Vivien when the actor went to receive his doctorate. He says: "I read Anne Edwards's biography of Vivien, and she has an account of that trip that isn't quite accurate. She has Larry experiencing some premonition of a terrible airplane crash and rushing back to Logan Airport from Tufts and breaking down in tears and panic when he saw the plane taking off without him, with Vivien on it. Well, her story about his missing the plane was correct, but as for Larry collapsing in tears—that was bunk.

"I flew up to Boston with them from New York so Larry could accept the degree at the commencement ceremonies at Tufts on a Sunday afternoon. Larry had to get back to New York Sunday night because he had hurt his ankle the night before while horsing around backstage after his performance and had a doctor's appointment. We were all booked on the five-thirty plane coming back. The commencement exercises went on and on Sunday afternoon, and then there was a reception. Larry was quite enjoying himself, but the time was growing short for us to get back to Logan. He didn't want to be rude to his hosts, so he sent Vivien and me ahead to catch the plane and said he would follow as soon as he could. But in case he missed it, he would get the next plane and we should wait for him at La Guardia in New York.

"Well, Vivien and I made the five-thirty plane, but Larry just missed it. In fact we could see him standing there as we were taking off, laughing. Vivien got in a terrible fret about it, and she clutched my hand all the way down to La Guardia. She kept chattering away about the fact that Larry had been laughing—'I'll kill him,' she said, 'he knows how much I hate to fly without him.' And when Larry arrived in New York on the next plane, she was still furious with him. Larry made light of it, saying, 'But, my darling, you had Jerry with you, you couldn't have been in better hands.' "[10]

It was no small irony, then, that a few days later the Oliviers were involved in a plane crash—or, more exactly, a terrifying forced landing. Shortly after taking off from New York to return to London, the Pan American Airways Constellation they were on suddenly caught fire as it rose over Long Island Sound, losing an engine. The pilot quickly descended over the shore of Connecticut and made an emergency landing at a small airfield near Willimantic. Shaken but unhurt, Olivier and Vivien, along with the thirty-nine other passengers, were put on a relief plane in Hartford and arrived home the next afternoon.

The date of their arrival was June 20, 1946, and they landed in London with less than ten pounds to their name. Olivier expected his first check from the American release of *Henry V*, but that would barely get them through the summer. In the fall his Old Vic salary would resume, but that too would be barely enough to cover their expenses during the following year. The solution to their economic problems was for Vivien to go back to work. She was well enough now, and the stay in New York had given her added vitality. Not only that, but there had been no incidents of depression in several months.

Her depression-free state lasted through the summer as she and Olivier relaxed at Notley Abbey, preparing for the coming theatre season. Olivier, given the choice of selecting the Old Vic's opening production that fall, had chosen *King Lear*, with himself as Lear. So that he would not have to overtax himself, Vivien agreed to Olivier's plan to revive the production of *The Skin of Our Teeth* that had been forced to close when she went into the hospital the year before. She would resume her starring role as Sabina and rehearsals would be minimal.

"It was a marvelous summer for both of them," says a friend who visited Notley Abbey on more than one occasion. "They had made the house habitable—indeed comfortable—and they entertained their pals all summer. Just about everyone who was anyone in the West End went down to spend weekends with Larry and Viv. Once the house was fixed up, Larry got very involved in putting the landscape in order, and for two months he was out every day for hours on end planting and pruning and mowing and having a wonderful time as an ersatz farmer. So far as I know Viv had bounced back completely from all her previous problems. There was no sign all summer that I could tell of any further emotional illness, and she was really looking forward to going back to the West End. They were like the Viv and Larry of old. I never saw Larry more pleased or relaxed. He even had his son down for a while and was learning to get on with him."[11]

Olivier had more reason to be pleased than just by Vivien's apparent recovery from her mental afflictions. In August he had a cable from Myron Selznick. The informal boycott was evidently breaking down, for Selznick asked if he and Vivien would be available early the following spring to co-star in a big-budget Hollywood version of the popular *Cyrano de Bergerac,* with each of them to receive a salary of at least a hundred thousand dollars. CERTAINLY WOULD, Olivier cabled back. *Cyrano* would be the answer to their immediate money problems.

On September 11, 1946, Vivien returned to the stage as Sabina in the revival of *The Skin of Our Teeth.* A few nights later Olivier opened at the New Theatre in a debut performance of *King Lear* that, although questioned by some critics, was overwhelmingly welcomed by the public. For the first time in anyone's memory an Old Vic actor was treated like a modern-day pop star, with hordes of worshipers, male and female alike, chasing him from the stage door every night.

"Larry was really in top form during the run of *Lear, "* said Alec Guinness, who was in the cast. "He had turned into a terribly easygoing chap and a very engaging raconteur. I must say, it was great fun to be with him. His acting had calmed down and his confidence in himself had gone up in direct proportion. He told amusing stories, usually on himself, and had lost that hard edge of aggressiveness and self-importance he'd had before. He was probably the most popular figure in England. Had he chosen to run for Parliament, I daresay he would have been elected in a walkover. He might even have made prime minister."

If Olivier was the most popular figure in England, Vivien Leigh was a close runner-up. Her revival of *The Skin of Our Teeth,* of which Olivier was still billed as director, drew full houses throughout the fall—largely because of Vivien's marriage to him. Said George Devine, who played the role of Mr. Antrobus to her Sabina, "In itself the play wasn't all that popular. Half the people who came to see it did so only because they'd seen *Lear* and then had to see Vivien, or else because they couldn't get tickets to see *Lear* and settled on watching Viv as the next best thing to watching Larry."[12]

Olivier could not have been more pleased with his life at that juncture. Vivien had recovered completely from her TB and had not shown a sign of mental malfunction in half a year—he attributed this to the fact that she was once again working and happy. Second, if he had earlier been considered a prince among players, he was now being called the king of the theatre. Third, with Vivien back at work, their financial problems were easing, and they promised to be solved completely when he and Viv went back to Hollywood in the spring to make *Cyrano de Bergerac.* He even looked forward to the experience: the part of Cyrano would be a refreshing change of pace after such ponderous roles as Richard III, Henry V, Oedipus and Lear, for it called for broad acting, sword-fighting, poetry, romance and, above all, comedy.

Olivier was anxious to show himself in a leading comic role because none other than James Agate, in assessing his performance as Lear for the *Times* of London, had written, "I have the conviction that Mr. Olivier is a comedian by instinct and a tragedian by art. He keeps his sense of fun under control in his tragic parts, but I can see him controlling it." And aside from all the other attractions of *Cyrano,* playing the part would put Olivier on the screen almost full-time throughout the film.

But, as he would later say to Kenneth Tynan, "I sometimes have thought that my life was as cursed as some of the characters I played, for after every success I've had, something has come along to muck things up. . . . I've never been able really to sit back and enjoy anything good that happened to me for a very long time. Something has always interfered."[13]

In this case it was the news from Hollywood that *Cyrano de Bergerac* had been shelved indefinitely. Whether this was because of the Selznick-inspired boycott or not, Olivier could not determine. But he would never again get an opportunity to play the role.*

---

*Cyrano was eventually played on screen by the Puerto Rico–born actor Jose Ferrer, whose portrayal turned him into a movie star overnight.

24

Sir Larry

EIGHT months after his opening-night performance of Lear, Olivier turned forty. Harcourt Williams, a leading member of the Old Vic, described him at that age as "a curious mix of pride and humility, authority and tentativeness, garrulousness and taciturnity, seriousness and comicality. Larry was a bundle of all the human contradictions you could think of. At a Board of Governors meeting he would be as somber as a funeral director. Five minutes later, backstage, he would be telling everyone the latest ribald jokes. But oh, how he hated being forty. His face was changing, he swore, filling out, becoming jowlier and more thick of chin. 'It's funny,' he'd say, 'when I was twenty I looked younger than I was. Now, at forty, I look older than I am. God, I'll only be able to play old parts now!'

"But he was a terrific chap. Completely natural. He and Ralph were working hard on the idea of getting a National Theatre started, and they started getting chummy with politicians, bankers, that lot. Yet Larry never showed any desire to become like them, all stiff and stuffy. And yet he would complain to me that, well, he didn't feel like an actor anymore. With all the adulation he'd gotten, he'd lost that actor's need for approval. You might even say that acting was beginning to bore him. He was leaning more and more toward directing and producing, because he no longer had the drive for attention. I remember that he was directing as well as acting in the film of *Hamlet* at the time, and he said, 'This would be fun really if I could only direct it and not play the part. I've come to the conclusion, old boy, that acting is a child's game and directing a man's.'

"I think that at forty Larry had lost the basic need that propels every actor. And yet he knew that he could not just give up acting—it was a duty he felt he owed to the public. So thereafter he approached it more as a duty than an enthusiasm. He saved his enthusiasm for directing and, eventually, administrating. In this way he was a very mature man at forty —indeed, more mature than his years might have called for. But he had done so much, achieved so much, that his attitude toward life was almost world-weary, as though it was impossible for him to get any more thrills out of his life or career. He was, if you will, gaining wisdom. He was becoming somewhat of a sage. And basically this turned his personality into one of—well, restrained sobriety. That's the most singular aspect of his character that I recall at that time: sobriety, and a tinge of sadness, resignation."[1]

•

The collapse of his *Cyrano* expectations in December of 1946 left Olivier feeling more wry than disappointed. Vivien, however, took the news badly, and soon there was a recurrence of her long-dormant mental trouble. The first episode occurred late in November while Olivier was in Paris on a brief Old Vic tour with *King Lear*. The next came a few weeks later, just before Christmas, and Vivien was forced to drop out of *The Skin of Our Teeth*. Some of her friends suggest that it was fueled by the fact that her daughter, Suzanne, then thirteen and back in England in Leigh Holman's custody, refused to visit Notley Abbey during the Christmas holidays. Others insist that it was insensitivity on Olivier's part that sparked it.

Shortly before he learned that they would not be doing *Cyrano*, Olivier was asked by Filippo del Giudice to follow up his much-heralded film of *Henry V* with a cinematic version of *Hamlet*, under the same conditions—that is, to produce, adapt, star and direct. Olivier had declined, using his commitment to *Cyrano* and its much greater salary considerations as an excuse. (Whereas Olivier expected to receive a hundred and fifty thousand dollars, and Vivien another hundred thousand for *Cyrano,* del Giudice, financed by the tight-fisted J. Arthur Rank, could only offer him ten thousand dollars for *Hamlet.*) However, when *Cyrano* fell through, Olivier went back to del Giudice and accepted his offer.

"Larry started working on *Hamlet* right away," recalls a friend of Vivien Leigh's. "Viv had been destroyed by the news that *Cyrano* wasn't going to come to pass—it was the second time in her career, I remember her saying, that she'd missed out on the movie. The fact that this time she would have been acting with Larry somehow made it worse. Anyway, when Larry shifted straightway from *Cyrano* to doing his film of *Hamlet,* Viv quite naturally expected him to include her as Ophelia. They had already done it together on stage, and for some reason she had the impression from Larry—or maybe she just assumed—that she would be playing Ophelia. I do believe that Larry's original intention was to use her. But he ran into a problem from the Rank people."[2]

The problem was that Olivier was about to turn forty. Vivien Leigh was almost thirty-four. The Hamlet of Shakespeare was in his twenties, while Ophelia was in her late teens. By dyeing his hair blond and using makeup, Olivier might still pass on screen for a younger man. But no amount of makeup could turn Vivien—now a mature woman—into a teenager. Afraid that an older woman playing Ophelia would hinder the film's success, the Rank organization insisted on a much younger actress for the part or else they wouldn't finance the film. After some argument, Olivier himself, fearful of losing the ten thousand dollars he had been offered in advance, acceded.

"When Larry broke the news to her she pretended to understand," says Vivien's friend. "But deep down she felt rejected and betrayed. And that started a new pattern of out-of-control emotional and mental fits. In fact I'd say it sent Viv over the edge once and for all. She'd seemed to have recovered from all that business, and then boom—it all started again and it was much worse than before. Where before she used to take her irrationality out on other people, friends or strangers, now she began taking it out on Larry. Larry was to blame in a way, although he had no idea that his very pragmatic decision to exclude her would have the effect it did. He was to blame but he wasn't to blame. Of course, when he realized what it was all about, he felt very guilty and went out of his way to make it up to Viv."[3]

One way he tried to make it up was to persuade Alexander Korda to cast Vivien in the lead role of a lavish film the producer was about to make of Tolstoy's *Anna Karenina.* And he persuaded Korda to give the important part of Count Karenin to Ralph Richardson so that Richardson, who was familiar with Vivien's problem, could monitor her behavior and save her from embarrassment during the picture's long, complex shooting schedule. Although neither Vivien nor Richardson was well suited to the roles, Korda allowed his affection for his friends to prevail over his hard business sense.

Filming on both *Anna Karenina* and *Hamlet* began in May 1947, just after Olivier's fortieth birthday—the former at Shepperton Studios and the latter at Denham. Vivien had a difficult time of it, and probably because of her role—Anna Karenina was a woman torn between conflicting needs—her mental state deteriorated through the summer. As Olivier became more deeply preoccupied with the myriad artistic and production details of *Hamlet,* however, he grew indifferent to Vivien's problems. According to a production aide, "Larry began staying overnight at Denham instead of going home. He was obsessed with getting *Hamlet* on film in the right way and had to block everything else in his life out. Yet he might have been better off going home, because whenever he stayed at the studio there would be countless middle-of-the-night phone calls from Vivien. 'She thinks I've abandoned her,' he said once after a particularly long and tortuous call."[4]

One of the few bright moments for Olivier during the difficult *Hamlet* filming came in June, when it was announced that he had been nominated for a knighthood in recognition of his service to England. What made the announcement especially pleasing was that just six months before, Ralph Richardson had been knighted. Although Olivier hadn't felt slighted—Richardson was several years older—he had felt disadvantaged in the face of Richardson's good-natured ribbing of both him and John Gielgud, who was two years older than Richardson. Now Olivier could join with Richardson in teasing Gielgud about their dual awards.

Olivier's investiture was another recognition of the importance of fine actors in England's cultural life and of the dignity the profession now carried with it. It was a sharp change from the days, not that distant, when actors were classed barely above felons. Thus Olivier, while making self-deprecating jokes about the award, also took it seriously. Not that he insisted on the opposite ("Gawd, keep calling me Larry, else you'll make me feel old before my time"). But he did make it a point to take a day off from *Hamlet* in early July to attend the investiture ceremonies at Buckingham Palace. There, dressed in morning clothes whose somber formality was in sharp contrast to his dyed-blond Hamlet hair, and looking exhausted from his labors on the movie, he received from King George VI the gentle sword-tap that marked him as, thereafter, Sir Laurence Olivier.

Later he and Richardson celebrated over a rather drunken dinner with Vivien, Kit Richardson and a host of other friends, Olivier boasting that although Richardson had been knighted six months earlier, he—Olivier—was the youngest actor in history to have earned a knighthood.

At that dinner was, among others, Cecil Beaton, who had designed the costumes for Korda's *Anna Karenina*. "Everyone had a rip-roaring good time except Vivien. I should say, everyone *tried* to have a rip-roaring good time. But Vivien was strangely quiet and broody throughout, and her mood put a damper on the festivities. I had been with her when the news of Larry's knighthood was announced. She'd reacted with utter indifference, although it meant that now she would be 'Lady Olivier.' And later, in the time leading up to the ceremony at the palace, she seemed to resent it more than anything else. She didn't even want to go to the ceremony. She only did so when Alex Korda closed production on *Karenina* for the day. But she wasn't enjoying any of it. She acted as though she was holding a grudge against Larry."[5]

The filming of *Hamlet* dragged through the summer and into the fall. Peter Cushing, a young actor Olivier had plucked out of obscurity to fill out the low-budget cast as Osric, said, "When the production started shooting in the spring, Larry was a kind, considerate, patient director. But as time went on he became more and more autocratic. At first it was 'Let's try it this way,' or 'What do you think about going from here to here instead of from there to there?' But toward the end it was 'Do it this way, do it that way, and don't argue, goddamnit!' We all started calling him 'Willie' behind his back, after the stories we'd heard about William Wyler. But I must say, the dictatorial method he settled on got great results. Whoever said *Hamlet* couldn't be done on film was made to eat his words by Larry."[6]

One of the reasons the filming dragged on for so long was the shapely Jean Simmons, the eighteen-year-old actress Olivier had chosen to play Ophelia in Vivien's stead. Although she had made some films, she was entirely innocent of any experience in acting Shakespeare and had to be coached intensively by Olivier. Some say that Olivier became enamored of Miss Simmons and fell into a brief affair with her. Others say that, yes, he was beguiled by her ripe sensuality but that her youthful innocence and sexual naiveté acted as a bar to seduction. Still others insist that his attachment to her, intense as it was over the several months of filming, was purely professional.

Whatever the case, Vivien Leigh suspected the worst, which only added to the high-pressure anxieties that were apparently behind her mental dysfunction. " 'Goddamn Larry is fucking his Ophelia,' Vivien said to me once when I dropped by to see her at Shepperton," recalls a close friend of both Oliviers. "I said, 'Viv, don't be silly, he's doing no such thing, it's all your imagination.' And she said, 'No, I'm sure of it, I'm losing him to a bloody child. Well, I shouldn't be surprised. I was barely out of my teens when Larry started fucking me.' I kept saying it couldn't be. Jean Simmons, after all, was going with another actor at the time—Stewart Granger, I think. I kept telling Viv she was imagining things. After I said it three or four times, she lashed out at me in a fury and accused me of calling her insane. She wouldn't speak to me for months afterward."[7]

According to others who knew her, Vivien Leigh finally became aware, at about the time she was making *Anna Karenina,* that something was profoundly wrong with her. "Yet she refused to acknowledge it, and any suggestion of it from others usually elicited a fearsome diatribe," says one. "I think her whole resistance to it was caused by her great fear that Larry would find out that she had a flaw, or that she'd be taken away from Larry. Of course, that was another symptom of her irrationality. She believed that Larry didn't know and that the most important thing was to keep it from him."

When *Anna Karenina* was released early in 1948, the critics remarked on a strangely lifeless, almost indifferent performance by Vivien Leigh and disliked the film as a whole. Such was not the case when Olivier's *Hamlet* reached the movie theatres a few months later. Although he had taken many liberties with the original text in adapting Shakespeare's celebrated play to the screen, Olivier was widely praised for both his portrayal of Hamlet and his imaginative conception and direction of the picture. The American film critic James Agee reflected much of the reaction when he wrote, in *Time* magazine, "In its subtlety, variety, vividness and control, Olivier's performance is one of the most beautiful ever put on film." Said an English critic, "Mr. Olivier has shown us with this *Hamlet* that there is nothing he cannot do, and do with stunning brilliance, in the world of theatre and motion pictures. Produce, direct, star—the actor is a one-man industry of excellence in the performing arts. He should not just have been knighted, he should be canonized as a national treasure."

Olivier, unfortunately, was not around to enjoy *Hamlet*'s enthusiastic reception. When the film first opened in London in May of 1948 he was in Australia, leading a six-month Old Vic tour of that vast British Commonwealth nation. The tour had been a year in the planning and was subsidized by the government as a way of expressing Britain's gratitude to Australia and New Zealand for their contributions to the war effort. Any profits the company made were to go to the Old Vic treasury in London.

Olivier's first job after completing *Hamlet* late in 1947 had been to organize the artistic side of the tour. Said an actor who went with the company to Australia, "Larry took on the Australian trip as his own separate fiefdom within the Old Vic. He hand-picked the actors who were to go, dictated which plays were to be performed, and so on. It was the first time I had seen him quite so autocratic. He ruffled a few feathers, and in fact his handling of the whole matter had negative repercussions for him later on. The main problem was that he planned the tour as his and Vivien's personal traveling theatre. Everyone else was cast in some sort of supporting role for his personal ambition. This didn't sit well with a lot of people."[8]

What the actor referred to was the fact that for the repertoire of three plays Olivier had chosen for the tour, all were co-starring vehicles for himself and Vivien Leigh. Olivier suspected that Vivien's exclusion from *Hamlet* had triggered the recurrence of her mental and emotional tribulations. Since he had come to feel responsible for her exclusion, and since he had come to believe also that only by working with him would Vivien return to the normalcy she had exhibited the year before, he conferred with Ralph Richardson and John Burrell and received their agreement to bring her into the Old Vic for the purpose of the tour. He then selected as the tour's three plays *Richard III*, starring himself (which was expected) and Vivien (not so expected) as Lady Anne; Vivien's commercial hit *The Skin of Our Teeth*, with himself co-starring as Mr. Antrobus; and an entirely new production for the Old Vic, Richard Brinsley Sheridan's comedy *The School for Scandal*, also starring Vivien and himself.

At first the plan produced raised eyebrows, then growing resentment among a number of members of the Old Vic. As one said, "Many of us thought that Larry was using the company for purposes that were completely antithetical to the Vic's charter, which was: 'The play's the thing, not who plays in it.' We were outraged that he seemed to be giving Vivien what appeared to be a nepotistic sinecure when there were several other actresses in the company who had labored faithfully for years in semiobscurity and should have been given a chance to play leads."⁹

The internal dissension had been muzzled by Richardson and Burrell while Olivier rehearsed Vivien and the other performers he had chosen to go to Australia. But after the troupe left for the South Pacific in February 1948, the dissidents who remained in London to finish out the Old Vic's season there formed into an organized clique that eventually went over Richardson's and Burrell's heads and let its views be known to the Old Vic's governing board. They would not be mollified by Richardson's claim that Olivier had chosen himself and Vivien to be the star focus of the Australian tour only to ensure the tour's financial success and thereby enrich the Old Vic's always hard-pressed treasury.

The tour itself was a financial and cultural success. To Australians, both Olivier and Vivien Leigh were living legends—Vivien especially because of her fame as Scarlett O'Hara—and the citizens of each city the troupe visited crowded the theatres to see their performances. The tour apparently had a salubrious effect on Vivien, as well. In a journal he kept of their six months in Australia, Olivier made repeated references to his wife's condition and spirits. The references indicated that she was once again free of her problem.

It was, ironically, Olivier who suffered a health problem while in Australia. At the age of forty-one, like an aging athlete, twenty years of stage acrobatics had begun to catch up with him. During the filming of *Henry V* four years before, he had severely strained his right knee when he fell from a horse during the Agincourt battle scene. He had reinjured the knee during the long sword fight with Laertes in the movie of *Hamlet.* Now, in another dueling scene, this one on stage in Sydney in *Richard III,* the knee gave way altogether. Olivier performed a few more times on crutches, but the swelling and pain only became worse. Finally, in New Zealand, he consulted a doctor, who recommended an immediate operation to remove the destroyed cartilage and tie up a ruptured ligament. When the doctor informed him of the likely alternative—a permanent limp—Olivier consented. He left the company, submitted to surgery, and had to spend several weeks in a cast, recuperating.

His recovery was complicated by the fact that in September, shortly after his operation and shortly before the company was scheduled to end its tour, Olivier received a letter from Lord Esher, chairman of the Old Vic governing board in London. Esher reminded him that his five-year contract with the Old Vic would be coming to an end the following June. Frostily acknowledging everything Olivier had done, along with Richardson and Burrell, to revive the Old Vic, Esher advised him that the Board of Governors had voted not to renew his contract beyond the coming season.

Previous chroniclers of Olivier's career have portrayed him as stunned and heartbroken upon receiving this news. Such was not the case, for he had already heard from Richardson, who was also being dismissed, about it. Richardson had told him that the dissident faction which had formed the winter before in reaction to Olivier's inclusion of Vivien Leigh in the Australian tour had gained influence in the councils of the Old Vic in Olivier's absence. It was this group, the Old Vic's "young Turks," that had gone to the governing body during the summer and lobbied for a change in the artistic management of the theatre. Complaining that Olivier and Richardson had been using the Old Vic to advance their own star careers at the expense of the younger performers, they had succeeded in persuading the Board of Governors to reorganize the theatre's artistic management.

Olivier understood; indeed, he was secretly relieved, since he had long been considering giving up his position at the Old Vic at the end of his contract and had worried about how to step out gracefully. His main purpose in having taken over the joint management of the company toward the end of the war—his and Richardson's ambition to transform it, with the government's financial backing, into a national theatre—was no closer to realization in 1948 than it had been when he signed on. Since all signs pointed to the likelihood that a national theatre was an empty dream, Olivier had decided that he must do something else to make money. The year before he had produced his friend Garson Kanin's American hit play *Born Yesterday* in the West End and had made some money on it. He was now thinking of giving up acting and becoming a full-time producer-director in the West End. He had also corresponded with Alexander Korda about co-producing further films in the wake of his *Hamlet,* which was destined to win five Academy Awards, including an Oscar for Olivier as best actor of 1948.

Olivier could not even resent the way in which he was informed of his forthcoming dismissal by Lord Esher. Aside from having earned the Old Vic a tidy profit on the tour, Olivier had achieved his goal of restoring Vivien to good mental health. And according to a young Australian actor hired by Olivier to play a walk-on role in *Richard III,* the Olivier-Leigh marriage seemed on an even keel once again. "I'd heard reports that there had been deep problems between them during the previous few years, but there was no sign of this all the time they were in Australia. In fact it was just the opposite—they often acted like newly marrieds with each other." A few years later, the actor made his way to London and appeared in several plays with both Olivier and Vivien. "The difference between them when they were in Australia and when I saw them again in London was shocking."[10]

25

Streetcar to Oblivion

"**L**ARRY'S first mistake was getting involved with *Streetcar Named Desire,*" said producer Saul Colin, talking about the events that led to the final collapse of the Olivier-Leigh marriage. "His second was letting Vivien get involved."[1]

•   —

Still on crutches, Olivier led the Old Vic troupe back to England in September of 1948 to find a Board of Governors grateful for the financial success of the tour and embarrassed at having acted hastily in voting not to renew his contract. Several members of the board approached him and offered to start proceedings to reverse the decision. No, said Olivier—he agreed, it was time for new blood at the theatre's helm and besides, he had already made other plans. Further, he would only consent to finish the last season on his contract, once his leg was healed, if the board allowed him to repeat his Australian stagings and then produce and direct a new production, with Vivien in the lead role, of Sophocles' tragedy *Antigone*.

"The board was only too happy to oblige," said Harcourt Williams. "Although the board members were mostly distinguished business figures and didn't usually concern themselves with the backstage problems of the company, I think they were by then aware that Larry had reasons for wanting to keep Vivien busy and working close to him. Ralph Richardson made this clear to them, and as a final gesture to Larry for his service to the Vic, they made no objection. And well they shouldn't have, for London theatre-goers were still mad about the Oliviers, and the organization profited handsomely by Larry's last season with Vivien."[2]

Antigone, in many ways the female counterpart of *Oedipus* in its tragic grandeur and emotional impact, "somehow got inside Viv and wouldn't let her go," according to an actress friend. "She hectored Larry into choosing the play and directing her in it because she was dying to do something of her own that would be comparable to his Oedipus. When they got back from Australia, their marriage was on good ground, but she still had a good deal of anxiety about keeping pace with Larry as an actress. Thus *Antigone*. Since Larry wanted to keep her happy, he went along with the idea. In the end, of course, it had the opposite effect. Vivien, with her always fragile mental balance and her tendency to blur the distinctions between fantasy and reality, allowed the emotions of her performance to get the better of her. She was constitutionally unable to draw away from the character once the performance was over—the way Larry, the way most actors, could. Antigone just got inside her and began to eat away at her."[3]

Vivien began again to suffer mental lapses in the spring of 1949 as she alternated at the Old Vic among Lady Anne in *Richard III*, Lady Teazle in *The School for Scandal* and Antigone. A two-month summer rest with Olivier at Notley Abbey after the season ended did nothing to improve her mental stress—according to several other friends it was the worst they had ever seen her, and Olivier was in a new state of depression over the development.

Matters went from bad to worse in September as he and Vivien began to rehearse the first West End production of Tennessee Williams's phenomenally successful American drama *A Streetcar Named Desire*. The Williams play had opened in New York almost two years earlier and had been acquired for the West End by producer Hugh Beaumont. Beaumont had delayed putting it into production, however, because he felt that its themes of homosexuality, brutality and insanity in New Orleans were still too revolutionary for London audiences, and because he had been unable to find a suitable star actress to play the twisted heroine, Blanche du Bois. After seeing Vivien in her opening night at the Old Vic in February 1949, though, he decided to proceed. And when he sent her a script, she was as eager to play Blanche as Beaumont was to have her. Her only condition was that Olivier direct the London version. Olivier agreed, although he was not entirely comfortable with the play and had misgivings about Vivien portraying a woman teetering on the edge of insanity. He took the assignment nevertheless because the play, after all, was a long-running hit in America and a handy vehicle by which to reintroduce himself as a director to the West End.

By the time *Streetcar* opened on October 11, Vivien Leigh was Blanche du Bois in more ways than just as an actress. During rehearsals she had taken on many of Blanche's delusionary colorations as her own, and soon the distinction between the stage character and the real-life woman began to blur. Vivien was generally praised for her performance, but her friends began to worry that the longer she played the part, the more it would damage her already shaky emotional equilibrium.

Olivier, on the other hand, had given up worrying. He now accepted the inevitability of his wife's condition and despaired of ever learning what, in particular, triggered her bouts of hysteria and depression.

And the reason he had given up worrying about the outbreaks themselves was because he was now confronted by a greater worry. One night after a performance as Blanche, she had failed to come home, but had gone out on a whim for a late supper with members of the cast of another play. Apparently in the grip of one of her amnesial depressions, she had sent everyone else on their way and remained alone with a young actor from the cast with whom she'd spent the evening flirting. She suddenly went beyond flirting and became very amorous with the actor, finally demanding that he take her home with him for a night of lovemaking. The young man had no hesitation in complying with her wish, since she seemed perfectly normal to him and gave him no impression that her motive was anything else but a compelling attraction to him. He walked her to his flat in Soho, but as he began to take the initiative she suddenly and just as unaccountably became resistant, talking unintelligibly. Thinking she had merely had too much to drink, he forced himself on her, stripping Vivien of her clothes and then having sexual intercourse with her while she lay in a stupor. When he was finished, she dressed and disappeared. She walked aimlessly through the empty streets of cold, predawn London until a patrolling police car came across her trailing her expensive fur coat through the stagnant puddles of a street near Covent Garden. Finally able to determine who she was, the policemen delivered her to Durham Cottage as dawn began to light up the sky over Chelsea. Olivier thanked the officers politely and got Vivien into bed.

Whether Olivier noticed the physical signs of Vivien's hour in Soho is unknown. But the young actor was not hesitant in spreading the word among his theatre friends that he had spent a night with the fabled Vivien Leigh, and Olivier soon picked up the rumors. When he questioned Vivien about it a few days later, she claimed no memory of the event. Indeed, she grew wrathful at his suggestion that it had occurred.

"Larry was stoical about it," recalls an old friend. "No, I don't think he believed the story that was going round, at least in the beginning. People were furious with the boy who started it—in fact, he was canned from his show a few weeks later and he didn't work for a long time. Nobody believed it! We all thought it was the fantasy ravings of this actor. But then, later, when Vivien began doing it with other people, running off on these one-night stands—well, maybe it was true. That didn't excuse the actor for babbling about it, though. He deserved what he got. Vivien was sick."[4]

Why did Vivien's mental instability suddenly take a sexual turn? Most of her friends today agree that there was a dual reason. First, she had been harboring a deep resentment and desire for revenge stemming from her suspicions about Olivier and Jean Simmons during the making of *Hamlet.* "There was no question about that," says one. "Viv had never forgotten that. Even though there may have been nothing to Larry and Jean's relationship, Viv remained convinced there had been. She was not consciously capable of revenge, but her mental breakdowns became a form of revenge in themselves. And the conscious remembrance of her suspicions about Larry having been unfaithful became grafted onto her —I suppose you would call it her subconscious. So gradually, as she continued to go through her mental breakdowns, she associated her own sexual infidelity as the best way to hurt Larry.

"And then there was the fact that she was playing Blanche du Bois at the time. Blanche was a character wrapped in a complex, distorted sexuality, and she gets raped by her contemptuous brother-in-law. I remember that when we discussed Viv's performance, she always insisted that Blanche enjoyed being raped by Kowalski. I believe that her sudden promiscuousness when she was under the influence of her mental blackouts had a lot to do with her ideas about Blanche, with the idea of wanting to be raped. I know that sounds terribly cheap-psychoanalysis, but just the same I believe it's very close to the truth."[5]

During her eight months in *A Streetcar Named Desire,* Vivien had several such encounters. The one that infuriated her friends most when they learned about it was with the up-and-coming actor Peter Finch.

The thirty-three-year-old Finch, London-born, grew up in Australia and had been working as an actor in Sydney when Olivier, during his Old Vic tour the year before, saw him in a low-budget production of Molière's *Le Malade Imaginaire.* Impressed by his ability and by the fact that Finch had formed his own acting company to bring theatre to Australia's outlying districts, Olivier offered him a place with the Old Vic if and when he decided to return to London. Finch took up the offer, but by the time he arrived in London five months later, having left his wife and daughter behind, Olivier was about to end his association with the Old Vic and was unable to fulfill his promise.

He felt responsible for Finch nevertheless, and in the bargain he liked the eccentric, unpredictable Australian. "Larry was getting into a period of his life," says a friend, "where he believed he had a responsibility to help younger talent find opportunities. A large part of that came from the criticisms he had received at the Vic about having ignored younger talent in favor of Vivien. No doubt Peter Finch would have labored in obscurity in Australia all his life had it not been for Larry suddenly being stung by the criticism. Peter was only eight or nine years younger than Larry, but I suppose because he was unknown he seemed even younger. Anyway, he became Larry's personal project. Larry felt that by helping Peter obtain some prominence, he would show his Old Vic critics that they were wrong."[6]

At the time Finch arrived in London in January 1949, Olivier was busy planning his return to full-scale West End management with a play called *Daphne Aureola,* which was to star Edith Evans and open in March. Unable to get Finch into the Old Vic, Olivier instead gave him the male lead in *Daphne Aureola.* The play was a modest hit and ran at the Wyndham Theatre for almost a year, overlapping with *A Streetcar Named Desire.* Peter Finch had gone from Australian obscurity to West End fame overnight. But that was not all.

In November, after *A Streetcar Named Desire* opened, Olivier decided to expand his Laurence Olivier Productions Ltd.—the name he gave to his management company—in order to present more plays. He enlisted

Alexander Korda as the primary investor in Laurence Olivier Productions, secured a long-term lease on the old St. James's Theatre and announced that his first production there would be *Venus Observed* by Christopher Fry, with himself directing and starring. He spent December and the first half of January, 1950, deep in preparations for *Venus Observed.*

In the meantime Vivien, still playing Blanche du Bois at the Aldwych Theatre, was growing more and more resentful of Olivier's separate professional life. *Venus Observed* had its successful opening on January 18, 1950, at the St. James's and ran until July. Vivien stayed with *A Streetcar Named Desire* until June. *Daphne Aureola* with Peter Finch closed in January, but Finch remained in London to pursue other acting opportunities.

A member of the *Streetcar* cast relates, "Pete had become a great pal of Larry's. One of the reasons Larry liked him so was because Pete didn't play the sycophant. I mean, Pete knew that Larry was responsible for his sudden success, but he didn't go around licking Larry's feet in gratitude. In a way he was much more independent and brash than Larry, and Larry admired that in him. And what Pete admired about Larry was his style and authority. Anyway, Pete became part of Larry's inner circle. He was almost like a younger brother—Larry trusted him because he was always so direct in his dealings with everyone.

"Well, Vivien became jealous of their relationship, and she got it into her head that she had to destroy it. How was she going to do this? She decided to work her sexual charms on Pete and then let Larry know that his friend had betrayed him. Pete had become quite a blade around London. Larry knew that he was in and out of a dozen beds, and that he had no scruples about who he slept with. So she was sure Larry would believe her rather than Pete."[7]

A friend of Vivien's claims, "It was much more complicated than that. Viv may have been jealous of the camaraderie between Larry and Finch, but she didn't set out consciously to destroy their friendship— Viv simply didn't have that kind of malice in her. What happened was that when she went into one of her mental states, she was no longer able to distinguish between Larry and Peter Finch. Because Finch was around so much in those days, because he and Larry were so devoted to each other, in her disarranged mind Finch became like a surrogate Larry. And she tried to seduce him, just as she might have Larry if he had been around. And the horrible thing was that Finch allowed her to go on with it, instead of telling Larry what was happening. For that he cannot be forgiven. I suppose he thought it was some special charm on his part, not Viv's sickness, that enabled him to 'conquer' her, if you will. He assumed that Viv was mad about him and would keep the facts from Larry, and so he went on blithely being pals with Larry and boasting to his close drinking pals of how he and Vivien were having an affair.

"Poor Larry, in the meantime, remained in the dark about the whole thing. Even if Viv had wanted deliberately to hurt Larry by having him find out from her, she couldn't. For the three or four times she was with Finch—she never remembered them afterward. Or if she did have some hazy memory, she was too ashamed to say anything."[8]

In July of 1950, Vivien Leigh went to Hollywood to make the movie version of *A Streetcar Named Desire* with Marlon Brando. Afraid to leave her on her own for the three months it would take director Elia Kazan to film the production, Olivier accepted an offer to play the male lead in the Hollywood film version of Theodore Dreiser's novel *Sister Carrie.* The offer had come thanks to David O. Selznick, who had just married actress Jennifer Jones. Miss Jones had been signed to play the title role. Although Selznick had nothing to do with the production, he was guiding his new wife's career and prevailed upon director William Wyler and Paramount Pictures to cast Olivier as the story's male protagonist, George Hurstwood.

Hollywood was unaware of the troubles of Vivien Leigh and Laurence Olivier. Except for a few friends such as David Niven and Danny Kaye, so far as anyone knew the Oliviers' storybook romance of the late thirties was still in full flower. To keep the myth alive, Kaye and his wife threw a huge but exclusive welcoming party for them at the Beverly Hills Hotel shortly after Olivier arrived in August to start on *Sister Carrie.* The fact that he was "Sir Laurence" and she "Lady Olivier" impressed the party-goers considerably more than that he had won two Oscars and Vivien one.

Although she would win a second Academy Award for her performance in the movie of *Streetcar,* the filming of the picture did nothing to improve Vivien's state of mind. Nor did *Carrie* excite Olivier, and when the two were finished with their respective tasks in late November they sailed together by slow freighter back to England.

"It was Larry's idea," said Spencer Tracy, with whom Olivier had become good friends. Tracy, married but long separated and having a secret affair with Katharine Hepburn, was an alcoholic who sympathized with Vivien Leigh's problems. "It's the drinking," he told Olivier when he learned about Vivien. "It often happens to me too. I go off on these benders and can't remember a thing afterward. There's nothing wrong with her mind, it's just the booze. Get her off the booze and you'll see a tremendous change."[9]

Was Vivien an alcoholic? Yes, say most of those who knew her. Not a Spencer Tracy-type of alcoholic who would drink himself into oblivion. But a woman dependent on alcohol nevertheless. "A day did not go by when Viv didn't have five or six drinks, usually starting with lunch," says a close friend. "It was either champagne or gin martinis, and they were part of her regular daily diet—much more important to her than food. She didn't drink herself into stupors though, just to get high and stay high. She needed to be high because it gave her courage. She said it enabled her to work better.

"Of course, Larry was no teetotaler. He was always good for three or four whiskeys, some wine, what have you. I wouldn't say he was an alcoholic but he was a robust social drinker. I don't know if he drank because Vivien drank or she drank because he did. The point is that he could handle it and she couldn't."[10]

"I told him to get her off the booze," Spencer Tracy said later. "And to get her off it, he would have to get off it. So he decided they would go back to England by freighter. Three weeks at sea with no booze. He wanted to see if a life with no booze would make any difference with Vivien."

Apparently it did. As another friend remarked to me about seeing her just after her arrival in London before Christmas, "Viv came back looking just terrific, better than I'd seen her in ages. She'd gained weight and lost that sallow, haunted look she had before she went. She was bright and cheerful. She said it had been a marvelously peaceful voyage and that everything between her and Larry was super again. They had resolved to give up drinking for good and had experienced a rebirth of their marriage."[11]

Olivier had another purpose in returning to England by slow boat. Before leaving for Hollywood, he had committed himself and Vivien to participating in the Festival of Britain, a year-long government-sponsored fete to promote postwar tourism to England. Since the festival was designed to show the world all of Britain's native institutions at their best, almost everyone in the theatre became involved. Olivier had decided that as the country's best-known theatrical pair, he and Vivien must do something together that would dazzle the millions of tourists who were expected during the festival year. After searching around for an appropriate idea, an appropriate vehicle, he settled on two. He and

Vivien would star together in repertory in Shakespeare's *Antony and Cleopatra* and Shaw's *Caesar and Cleopatra,* alternating the two plays at the St. James's Theatre under the banner of Laurence Olivier Productions Ltd.

The freighter voyage back to England, then, also served to provide Olivier and Vivien with the time to work on the two plays—the one gracefully traditional in style, the other bitingly modern.

Caesar and Cleopatra opened at the St. James's on May 10, 1951. The Shaw play, and the following night's presentation of the Shakespeare version, brought a new outpouring of public adulation to the Oliviers for their daring and virtuosity. The critics, though, were less than adulatory, most deriding the scheme as—however admirable—a publicity stunt. One in particular, Kenneth Tynan, made a controversial name for himself by blasting Vivien's ineptitude as the twin Cleopatras and by taking Olivier to task for "downplaying" his roles in order to focus the audiences' attention on his wife.

The public refused to heed the critics and kept the St. James's box office busy for six months, after which Olivier transported the productions to New York for another four months at Broadway's Ziegfeld Theatre. The New York critics were captivated by the Oliviers' double-barreled performances, and the Ziegfeld box office was further stimulated by the fact that Vivien's Oscar-winning portrayal of Blanche du Bois had recently hit the screens. Having last appeared on Broadway together in their disastrous *Romeo and Juliet* in 1940, the acclaim they received in New York was sweet vindication indeed. The pity was that Olivier could not enjoy it: Vivien was drinking again, and she had once more embarked on a pattern of periodically deranged mental behavior.

An American actor who had been hired to play a supernumerary in the Shakespeare *Cleopatra* at the Ziegfeld recalls, "There was a lot of coolness backstage between Olivier and Vivien Leigh toward the end of the run. There was an English actor in the production, Edmond Purdom, and it was clear to just about everyone in the cast that something was going on between him and Vivien. Vivien was the one who pursued it, not Purdom—in fact I'd say he was embarrassed by it. Olivier seemed aware of what was going on and was very nice about it to Purdom, but he was cool and abrupt with Vivien."[12]

It is often observed by commentators on the theatrical arts that fine actors do not come into the full expanse of their powers until they reach their mid-forties; and yet because of the star system, particularly in movies, and of Western culture's obsession with youth, most such actors are washed up by the time they are in their forties. When Olivier closed the New York *Cleopatra*s in April of 1952 and returned to London, he was about to turn forty-five. Because he was to do so little of substance in the next two years, he might well have thought of himself as washed up.

Says an Olivier friend, "There's some truth to that. When Larry hit his mid-forties he was dead tired of acting, bored with it. And he was also afraid. It was like a midlife crisis many actors are forced to go through who have been successful when young. He looked at himself in the glass and saw himself aging, and realized that there were a lot of parts he could no longer play. He had to wait to go through this period of physical adjustment until he was properly old, properly grey and wrinkled, so that he could play old parts, character parts.

"But there was more to his inactivity than that. He was deeply involved in keeping his producing operation at the St. James's going. Most of all he was laboring under a tremendous weight with Vivien. She just kept getting worse, in stages. Finally he realized that there would be no end to the troubles she caused him. He felt trapped, and he fought a violent struggle within himself between his instinct to be free and his innate decency and sense of responsibility to Vivien. His work became a way of escaping from his problems. Which is why it lost that incandescent quality. It wasn't his age, primarily, it was his depression. He lost pride in himself because he no longer knew what to do about Vivien. Oh, he kept up a good actor's front, but he was bottomlessly disappointed in himself, in Vivien, in life. One was reminded of his old prescription about loving the characters he played just as he loved himself. Well, he had trouble loving himself at that time. It was no wonder that he could have no love for his characters. And it showed, not only in those performances he did but in the characters he chose to perform."[13]

The first character Olivier chose to portray after playing Caesar and Antony was MacHeath in a movie version of John Gay's eighteenth-century musical play *The Beggar's Opera*. Producing the dated costume film as well as starring in it, he early on decided to adorn MacHeath with all the facile tricks of the actor's trade in order to better engage audience interest. The result was an unintentional comedy of overacting that failed to sully his reputation among the public only because so few people went to see the movie.

While Olivier was filming *The Beggar's Opera* during the summer of 1952, Vivien was once again confined to Notley Abbey, this time under semipsychiatric care. A lung infection shortly after her return from New York necessitated treatment with drugs. In June, the drugs had combined with her alcohol intake to unleash a prolonged episode of hysteria and near-catatonia. Olivier and her doctor finally summoned a psychiatrist.

After Vivien recovered, the psychiatrist talked with her for several days without revealing the nature of his medical specialty. By then Vivien was well aware that something was radically wrong with her, but she refused to acknowledge it still. When she learned by chance that the doctor was a psychiatrist, she went into a panic and ordered him away.

But by then Olivier was adamant. The physician had diagnosed her as suffering from acute manic-depressive disease—the first time Olivier had heard a medical name applied to Vivien's condition. The doctor also assured him that several months' rest, without drinking, should restore her personality to normal. The disease itself would probably not disappear, but if Vivien could adjust to living without alcohol, it might remain largely dormant.

Olivier was grateful at least to discover that Vivien's problem was a known disease and that there were ways of controlling it. Over the next few months he convinced her to accept the reality of it and to work on restoring herself to normalcy. She appeared to cooperate, passing her days at Notley Abbey entertaining friends and puttering in the gardens. But her cooperation was not all it seemed to be.

"Whenever Larry was around, Viv didn't drink," a man who saw much of her at the time said. "But during the day, when he wasn't there, she took a nip now and then. She was deathly afraid of Larry finding out, so she took to drinking vodka, which left no breath odor. She didn't drink much, just enough to keep herself with a slight buzz on, and her condition actually improved."[14]

26

The Knight and the Garter

"**L**ARRY was beginning to wonder
if it wasn't he who was driving Vivien insane," Angela Baddeley once said.
"He talked about it once, and he blamed himself. Viv had a negative
reaction to everything he thought he was doing right for her, and then
when he tried to do the opposite, thinking that might be what was right,
she reacted negatively to that too. He was in a terrible bind about what
to do and what not to do. He was no longer in love with her, he said. He
still had great affection for her, and he still felt thoroughly loyal, but how
could he go on loving this woman who had turned his life, their life
together, into a third-rate drama? And yet he blamed himself. He tortured
himself with guilt. He never showed it to anyone, but one night down at
Stratford he got drunk and showed it to me. He was in tears."[1]

•

By the New Year of 1953, Vivien's condition had stabilized and she
seemed well enough to go back to work. When she was offered the

248

starring role in a Warner Brothers movie called *Elephant Walk,* she was anxious to do it despite the fact that it called for two months of location shooting in the tropical heat of Ceylon and then two more months in a studio in Hollywood. A friend said, "She was eager to get away from Larry for a while to show him that she was no longer dependent on him. Yet once she got away, she blamed him for letting her go. She even accused him of forcing her to go, which was not the case at all. Larry had great misgivings about her doing the film."

Olivier's misgivings were so great that he persuaded the movie's producer, Irving Asher, to put Peter Finch into the co-starring role opposite Vivien. He wanted someone he trusted to be on the scene to look after her. Finch, delighted that his first movie was to be a co-starring role in a big-budget Hollywood production, solemnly promised Olivier that he would act as his surrogate in Ceylon. Olivier still had no idea that his friend had already played the role.

Vivien left for Ceylon late in January 1953, accompanied by Finch. He would later say to me, in defending himself against accusations that he had betrayed his benefactor Olivier, "Listen, Larry should never have let Viv go in the first place. He did it because he needed the money and Viv was getting a hundred and fifty thousand dollars. Is it my fault Viv picked on me to cling to? I was just trying to act in Larry's best interests. I told him that. Would he rather have her fall into the clutches of some grip or assistant cameraman? I did what I did to save Larry from embarrassment. Viv too."[2]

At the end of February, Olivier received an urgent call from producer Asher in Ceylon: Vivien had cracked up, what should he do? Olivier caught the first available plane and arrived in Ceylon to find Vivien perfectly normal: the crisis had passed. Although troubled to learn that she had been sharing her hotel suite with Finch, he accepted Finch's explanation that he had merely moved in to protect Vivien from hurting herself, and that nothing amorous had gone on between them. "Shit," Finch said to Olivier, "she calls me 'Larry' half the time."

Olivier returned to London after five days in Ceylon. A week later the *Elephant Walk* company flew to Los Angeles to continue production at the Warner Brothers studio. In April, while Olivier was on a working holiday in Ischia, planning a new stage production as part of the coming summer's coronation celebrations,* he received another emergency call,

---

*King George VI had died the year before; his successor and older daughter, Elizabeth, was due to be crowned queen.

this one from his friend Danny Kaye in Los Angeles. Vivien had suffered a violent breakdown, Kaye told him. She had been put to bed, heavily sedated, on a psychiatrist's orders. The doctor wanted to put her into a psychiatric hospital, but he needed Olivier's permission since Vivien was totally irrational. Olivier refused permission. He asked Kaye to "hold the fort" until he could get there.

It took him three days to travel to Los Angeles. When he arrived, accompanied by his friend and agent Cecil Tennant, he was stunned to find Vivien drugged and barely conscious. Rather than allow her to go into a hospital in Los Angeles, he decided to get her back to England where doctors with whom she was familiar could look after her. Danny Kaye and David Niven made the travel arrangements, Kaye flying to New York in advance to arrange a place to keep Vivien on the stopover between flights.

With Vivien still heavily sedated and lying on a nurse-attended rolling stretcher, Niven saw the Olivier party off from Burbank Airport. Kaye met them at New York with a nurse and limousine and took them to the Long Island home of a friend, where they stayed overnight. The next afternoon he delivered them to Idlewild Airport to board their flight to London. By then much of Vivien's sedation had worn off and she fought furiously, irrationally, for twenty minutes before the nurse could inject her again and maneuver her onto the plane. Exhausted by her exertions and aided by the drugs, she slept for the entire ten hours it took the plane to cross the Atlantic while Olivier brooded to Cecil Tennant on the whims of fate.

Upon their arrival in London, Olivier and Tennant whisked Vivien to a psychiatric hospital in Surrey, where she was placed in isolation with no visitors allowed. By then the newspapers had gotten wind of the affair, and when Olivier finally got back to Notley Abbey he found a throng of reporters and photographers waiting for him. Assured that he would not be able to see Vivien for at least two weeks, he ordered Cecil Tennant to turn the car around and head for the London airport. That night, in a state of utter exhaustion and despair, he was on a plane back to Ischia. Not a small ingredient of his anguish was his knowledge, learned from Irving Asher in Los Angeles, that Peter Finch may have been behind Vivien's breakdown. Finch, Olivier had been told, had been living with Vivien in more ways than one.

Vivien's recovery was remarkably rapid, considering the violent depths to which she had apparently plunged. But then perhaps it wasn't so remarkable. According to one who knew her, "When Viv had that attack in Hollywood, it was just another one of her brief eruptions. But the people she was with had never seen it before and they panicked, calling doctors and getting her injected with God knows what drugs. That's what made things so bad. Viv was coming out of it, but then she realized that she was all doped up and that sent her into a frenzy. She wanted to tell them, 'I'm all right, I'm all right,' but no one would listen —not even Larry could help. So then she really went off the deep end. But once she was in hospital in England, the doctors quickly realized that she was all right and they took her off the drugs. Sure, she needed some rest, but her mind was more or less back to normal. She was terrified by the experience—not by her breakdown, but by the way she'd been treated. She was ready to acknowledge her problem by then, but she was sure the big brouhaha in Hollywood wouldn't have happened if Larry'd been with her. He would have dealt with her breakdown as he always did—by keeping her confined for the day or two it took her to get over it. She pleaded with Larry never to let her be away from him for such a long period again. It was Larry's absence, she claimed, that had caused everything."[3]

By summer's end of 1953, Vivien was back at Notley and itching to return to work. But not to *Elephant Walk*—she had been replaced by Elizabeth Taylor. Her April breakdown was fobbed off to the skeptical press as a combination of an infection she had contracted in Ceylon and exhaustion. When Vivien began to appear in public again in London looking healthy and happy, if somewhat bloated, no further questions were asked.

During the period following the two *Cleopatras*, Olivier had continued to present plays at the St. James's under the banner of Laurence Olivier Productions Ltd. Although he'd had a few successes, by and large his venture was losing money. He had hoped to recoup some of his losses through Vivien's $150,000 salary for *Elephant Walk*, but that prospect was now foiled. He had also planned to put on a new play to coincide with the summer's coronation festivities, when London would be packed with tourists. The play was a quickly slapped together light comedy by Terence Rattigan called *The Sleeping Prince,* a "fairy-tale" story about an encounter between a Central European prince and an American showgirl during the London coronation of King George V in 1911. Olivier was sure that it would have great appeal to the masses, fulfill his commitment to contribute to the coronation and earn Laurence Olivier Productions some money in the bargain.

Vivien's breakdown had forced him to postpone the production, but upon her recovery he was able to proceed. With himself directing the play and starring as the Prince opposite Vivien as Mary Morgan, the showgirl, *The Sleeping Prince* had its West End premiere on November 5, 1953. The date was Vivien's fortieth birthday, a fact that she was depressingly reminded of the next day when several reviewers criticized her as being too old to play the sexy young American. Olivier's performance was received no more enthusiastically by the critics, some of whom wondered if he had decided thenceforth to rest on his reputation, and the play as a whole was dismissed as unworthy of his talents. Nonetheless, it was a great hit with a public eager to see Olivier and Leigh in anything. It ran for eight months and easily could have run for a year or more. By June of 1954, however, Vivien had suffered several mental relapses and seemed once again on the verge of a major breakdown. Moreover, Olivier had signed a contract with Alexander Korda's London Films to produce, direct and star in a film version of his celebrated *Richard III*—a movie to be done along the lines of his previous *Henry V* and *Hamlet*. Since *The Sleeping Prince* could not survive without himself and Vivien as the stars, he closed the play in July and went straight to work at Shepperton Studios on *Richard III*.

Vivien's manic-depressive episodes had started again after she learned that Olivier intended not to use her as Lady Anne in *Richard III*. He got her doctors to explain that after the rigors of appearing nightly in *The Sleeping Prince* she needed a long rest. But as Angela Baddeley later said, "Vivien was convinced it was because Larry thought she was too old. This put her on a new rampage, and she lit into him about his own age. 'You're forty-seven!' she would scream at him. 'What makes you think you can play Richard at forty-seven? Please, Larry, don't do it, you'll be the laughingstock.' Once she was sure Larry wouldn't use her, she tried to get him not to do the picture. She needed him to herself for the summer, she complained. Larry was betraying her by putting his career first. The fact that Larry was being paid a good deal of money by Korda didn't occur to her."[4]

What complicated the situation was Olivier's casting of the twenty-three-year-old Claire Bloom as Lady Anne. Bloom was an experienced Shakespearean actress who had first played Ophelia at seventeen, had starred in the celebrated movie *Limelight* with Charlie Chaplin and was at that time a leading performer with the Old Vic. She was also a jolly, ambitious young woman. Vivien, aware of this, convinced herself that Olivier had given Claire Bloom the role of Lady Anne because he was sleeping with her, and her anger turned into jealous rage.[5]

Olivier threw himself into the filming of *Richard III* in the fall of 1954 with his customary obsessiveness. Directing a cast that included John Gielgud and Ralph Richardson in the principal supporting roles, he strove to outshine them both and succeeded. The critics called his portrayal of the Machiavellian Richard his greatest film performance yet, surpassing even those of Henry V and Hamlet.

But it was not only his acting that came in for widespread acclaim. Film experts celebrated his direction of the picture and wondered once again whether he might not be more valuable to the world as a movie director than an actor. James Agee wrote in *Time:* "When Olivier has directed himself on stage, the results usually have been less than satisfactory. And yet when he has directed himself on film, not to mention an entire production, he has never failed to produce a masterpiece. Is this because he has only directed himself in Shakespeare on the screen? It would be hard to credit; we have seen several instances in which he directed himself in Shakespeare on stage and flopped. . . . It is a pity that Olivier came out of a theatrical tradition that thumbed its nose at motion pictures. Otherwise he might have chosen the screen instead of the stage as the central focus of his career. . . . It would certainly be interesting to see him direct a modern feature."

It took Olivier only four months to complete *Richard III,* a considerably more rapid pace than his *Henry V* and *Hamlet* and one which several observers attributed to the confidence he had gained in himself as a film director. Although the observation might have been true, the fact that his Laurence Olivier Productions was co-producing with Korda's London Films also figured in the speed of the picture's production. Olivier, in for a large share of the profits, had learned to pare costs and brook no expensive wastes of time.

And then there was Vivien. Fuming and growing once more delusionary at Notley Abbey, she made his life a hell of vindictive phone calls and irrational accusing letters while he worked full-time at Shepperton. Olivier finally went to Korda and begged him to give Vivien a starring role in another movie the Hungarian was planning to make, hoping that work would divert her attention from him. The film was *The Deep Blue Sea* by Terence Rattigan, and Korda was skeptical both about Vivien's suitability for the lead part of Hester Collyer and about her ability to handle a tough shooting schedule without causing problems.

"Alex was fully aware of Vivien's mental problems," says a man who was a friend of both. "Vivien had been down to the south of France the summer before for a stay on Alex's yacht, and he had been saddened to see her floating in and out of reality. He gave her the part in *Deep Blue Sea,* but with great reluctance and only because he wanted to make Larry's life easier."[6]

The Deep Blue Sea, filmed early in 1955, turned out to be a financial failure for Korda, largely because of Vivien Leigh's lifeless portrayal of the vibrant, sensuous Hester Collyer. But Vivien got through the filming without difficulty and it appeared at the end of the production that she was back on an even keel again. Heartened by this, Olivier decided to accept an offer for both of them to perform in a year-long, three-play festival at the Shakespeare Memorial Theatre at Stratford.

The main reason for Olivier's decision was his desire, after filming *Richard III,* to restore himself to the throne of England's greatest Shakespearean actor. The three plays he and Vivien were asked to do were *Twelfth Night, Macbeth* and Shakespeare's rarely performed tragedy *Titus Andronicus.* Although all three were new to Vivien, Olivier had done the first two earlier in his career and was thoroughly familiar with them. It was *Titus Andronicus* that really engaged his interest. He had read it often during the previous few years and was fascinated by its bravura, Grand Guignol breadth. "I gave up the better part of a year just to play that part for a few weeks," he said later.

The Stratford season opened in April with Olivier playing Malvolio and Vivien in the lead female role of Viola in *Twelfth Night,* directed by John Gielgud. "The basic antagonism between Larry and Johnny Gielgud came out during rehearsals," said Angela Baddeley, who was in the cast. "I must say, I think Larry was a bad boy about it. He was very waspish and overbearing with Johnny, and Johnny became intimidated by him and lost his authority. Almost everyone in the cast sided with Larry, laughing at his wisecracks about Johnny's direction. I felt very sorry for Johnny."[7]

Gielgud himself describes the experience in his book, *An Actor and His Time:* "In 1955 I directed *Twelfth Night* at Stratford with Vivien Leigh as Viola and Laurence Olivier as Malvolio. Somehow the production did not work, I do not know why. . . . I know that the actors were not very happy with my production. . . . I thought Vivien Leigh was enchanting —though the critics did not care for her very much—but she was torn between what I was trying to make her do and what Olivier thought she should do, while Olivier was set on playing Malvolio in his own particular, rather extravagant way. He was extremely moving at the end, but he played the earlier scenes like a Jewish hairdresser, with a lisp and an extraordinary accent, and he insisted on falling backwards off a bench in the garden scene, though I begged him not to do it."[8]

Next was *Macbeth,* which opened at Stratford on June 7, 1955, and starred Olivier in the title role and Vivien as Lady Macbeth. Trader Faulkner, an Australian actor who played the key role of Malcolm, was quoted as saying that he thought "Larry had agreed to do *Macbeth* only to give Vivien a chance at Lady Macbeth. Larry seemed rather bored throughout, and that made Vivien highly nervous because she had gotten poor notices for her Viola and felt totally out of her element as Lady Macbeth. There was a great tension between them."[9]

Another member of the cast suggested the reason. "Peter Finch began coming around during *Macbeth.* Evidently he and Larry had reached some understanding and Larry tolerated his presence. Actually, I think he thought of it as a kind of godsend. Vivien started spending more and more time with Finch, and that seemed to take the pressure off Larry. There were times he even seemed happy to have Finch there. He would leave Vivien with him and go off drinking."[10]

And, said a friend, "Larry very quickly realized that Peter Finch represented something important to Viv. She was much more relaxed when Finch was around her than when he wasn't. Finch was like a second Larry for her, but a Larry she felt she didn't have to measure up to. In fact she could treat Finch with a slight condescension, which made her feel superior to him and gave her a sense of power and authority she never had with Larry. Finch took it all because he was in love with her. He accepted the position he was in—a kind of pawn between Viv and Larry. Larry was no longer friendly with him, nor did he play the outraged cuckold. He apparently accepted and then simply ignored the whole thing. He knew he had to live with Vivien. So evidently he said, if that's what she needs to keep her calm, I'll go along with it. Of course, Viv was still not beyond using Finch to taunt Larry. She wasn't in love with Finch; she just loved the idea of him always being there when she wanted him."[11]

Olivier has said that the only reason he agreed to play Macbeth at Stratford was to prepare himself for *Titus Andronicus.* If *Macbeth* was a drama of horror and madness, *Titus Andronicus* was manifestly more so. When he opened in the play on August 16, the critics were swept away by the awesome scope of his portrayal. It was a portrayal that critic Bernard Levin described as "not so much on the heroic scale as on a new scale entirely, the greatness of which has smashed all our measuring rods and pressure gauges to smithereens." Kenneth Tynan, then the

Observer's chief critic, called it "a performance which ushers us into the presence of one who is, pound for pound, the greatest actor alive."

Olivier came away from Stratford at the end of 1955 secure in the knowledge that he had reclaimed his Shakespearean throne with his stage interpretation of Titus and his screen portrayal of Richard III, which had been released a few months earlier. Believing that he had little more to prove, he turned to the challenge the movie critics had posed: to direct a modern, Hollywood-type feature film. He had talked to Korda about it, and the Hungarian had agreed to find an appropriate property for him and work out a production-distribution deal with a major Hollywood studio. But whatever plans Korda had been making collapsed when, in mid-January of 1956, he died of a massive heart attack.

Shortly thereafter, Olivier received a cable from a photographer in New York named Milton Green. Green, known in America as Marilyn Monroe's official photographer and close friend, had seen *The Sleeping Prince* in London in 1954 and wanted to buy the screen rights for a major Hollywood production starring Monroe as the showgirl. He had Monroe's approval and the approval of Lee and Paula Strasberg, her acting mentors, provided that he could find an acceptable leading man to play the Prince. Greene could think of no one more acceptable than Olivier, who had originated the role on the stage. And what a publicity bonanza: Monroe and Olivier in the same picture! The world's most famous movie star and the world's most celebrated theatrical performer! The Blonde Bombshell and the Prince of Players! Or as a publicity agent would later jokingly put it, "the Knight and the Garter!"

Olivier cabled back his acceptance of Green's offer provided that he be engaged as the picture's producer and director as well, and that the film be made in England. If Green thought the terms stiff, he soon found out that he was wrong. He went to Warner Brothers to see if they would be interested in financing the production in exchange for distribution rights. The studio agreed to Olivier's terms and happily so. Marilyn Monroe was a notorious time-waster and had caused expensive budget overruns on most of her previous movies. Warners was sure that with Olivier producing and directing, she would not be permitted to get away with her usual temperamental antics.

Olivier flew to New York in February to meet Monroe, who was living there with her husband, playwright Arthur Miller, while studying in the private classes of Lee Strasberg, the well-known advocate of the Method school of acting and the master of the Actors' Studio. The announcement of the Monroe-Olivier alliance was made at a tumultuous press conference at the Plaza Hotel. Producer Saul Colin, a close friend of Strasberg's, was at the press conference and described Olivier as astonished by the hysteria that attended every public appearance Marilyn Monroe made. Colin quoted Olivier as saying to him, while traveling later in a limousine to visit the Actors' Studio, "Saul, I wonder if I've made a mistake?"[12]

Olivier returned to London shortly thereafter to prepare for the production, which would not begin until July, and to sell his house in Chelsea. Alexander Korda's death had left Laurence Olivier Productions with some large and pressing debts. Rather than let the company fall into bankruptcy, Olivier had decided to sell Durham Cottage to help meet his obligations. To replace the Chelsea house as his and Vivien's London residence, he rented the small Belgravia town house of his friend Sir William Walton—the composer of the music for his three Shakespeare films.

In April, Vivien opened in the West End in Noel Coward's latest play, *South Sea Bubble.* A few weeks later she informed Olivier that she was pregnant. A great shroud of mystery has lain over this event ever since. Even close friends were never sure whether Vivien was actually pregnant. Nevertheless, it was announced that Vivien had suffered a miscarriage in August, while Olivier was in the midst of filming *The Sleeping Prince.* With the reputed miscarriage came a further descent into madness.

The Sleeping Prince, later retitled *The Prince and the Showgirl* to underline Marilyn Monroe's presence in the movie, took four frustrating months for Olivier to film. Not even he could control Monroe's quixotic personality. "For the first time since practically the beginning of his career," says a man who worked on the production, "Larry was up against a woman who had absolutely no awe of him, and he found this more disconcerting than anything else. I mean, he was a man used to actresses who would always try to please him, who would always defer to his opinions and suggestions, whether he was directing them or just acting with them under someone else's direction. But Marilyn Monroe gave not a shit about him—who he was or what he represented. She was just too dumb and uncultured and obsessed with herself. She took advice from only one person, and that was Paula Strasberg, her so-called acting coach, who was always about the set. Larry tried to be polite to Monroe at first—friendly, encouraging and supportive. But that didn't work— Monroe was going to do things her way no matter what. Then he tried to be stern and authoritative. Same result. So finally he said, 'Shit, let's just get on with it and get it over.' He was fed up with neurotic women."[13]

When *The Prince and the Showgirl* was released the following year, it was a resounding flop. Despite the relatively good notices for Olivier's portrayal of the Prince and for his direction, audiences recognized it for what it was—a weak-storied vehicle for two world-renowned stars produced more for its publicity value than for the purpose of sincere entertainment, not to mention art. Did Olivier later disavow it, or hold a grudge against Marilyn Monroe for ruining his debut as a director of modern films, as he often did with work of his that he didn't like? On the contrary, he has often expressed fondness for the movie, and even more fondness for having had the chance to work with Marilyn Monroe.

"When Larry talks like that," says a friend of today, "he's not really paying homage to the picture or to Marilyn. What he is acknowledging, without saying so, is the effect the chance to make the picture had on what was to follow in his career. You see, making the picture and working with Monroe put him in contact with Arthur Miller. It was his association with Miller that had the important impact on him."[14]

27

Joan Plowright

KENNETH TYNAN: "It was Marilyn Monroe, strangely enough, who enabled Larry to resolve in his own mind what he should do about Vivien. Larry once told me that for the three or four years prior to his working on *The Prince and the Showgirl* he was in a miserable quandary about Vivien. Each time she'd have a breakdown he'd say, 'Aha, that's it, this time I'm leaving.' But then she'd bounce back and he'd say, 'Wait a minute, perhaps I was too hasty.' And it went on and on like that, with each passing year producing a greater emotional paralysis in Larry, and a greater inability to act upon his own needs. He wanted to get out, but he knew that if he did he'd be consumed by guilt for abandoning this helpless creature.

"But then he met Monroe. More to the point, he met Arthur Miller. Now here was America's most celebrated playwright, a serious man of great theatrical achievement, married to America's most famous actress. Larry became—well, not chums with Miller, but they got on. The thing was, Larry identified with Miller, if you will. He saw the troubles Miller was going through in his marriage to Monroe, who was not far from being a madwoman with all her psychoneurotic idiosyncracies—whereas Miller was a stable, sober character much like Larry. And here was Larry, married to the equivalent of Monroe in fame and even more unstable than her. It was like seeing a mirror image of himself. And when he saw the damaging effect Marilyn was having on Miller, he suddenly saw something of himself in Miller.

"He and Miller talked about it—about the trials of being married to huge stars who, in one way or another, were round the bend. Miller was very defensive, he went on and on trying to justify his sufferance of Marilyn. But Larry soon came to realize that it was just rationalizing. He could see Miller being consumed by the relationship with Marilyn. Miller himself was confused, paralyzed, and he couldn't work, he couldn't do the things he needed to do, he couldn't concentrate.

"Larry pitied Miller in a way. But then he realized that he was in the same boat. Miller was justifying and rationalizing much as Larry had done five years before. Now it was five years later and Larry was still doing it. He thought: 'My God, do other people pity me the way I pity Arthur?' And that did it. He resolved once and for all to get hold of his life and change it. He realized, he said, that he was about to be fifty, and that he didn't want to live the rest of his life in that personal purgatory he found himself in."[1]

•

Arthur Miller was important to Olivier in another way as well. In the spring of 1956 a turbulent new wave had crashed upon the tranquil shore of the London theatrical world with the opening of a play written by a young actor named John Osborne. Called *Look Back in Anger,* the raw, angry drama was representative of a revolutionary tide that had welled up among England's working classes a few years earlier—a current of bitter younger-generation reaction to the country's postwar reversion to the old class values and attitudes that had dominated Britain for decades before the war. *Look Back in Anger,* less a play than a radical political treatise, typified the bitter undercurrents lurking in Britain's young generation.

Olivier had gone to see the play at the Royal Court Theatre in May of 1956 while preparing the filming of *The Prince and the Showgirl.* He had disliked it intensely, both for political and for dramaturgical reasons, and was doubly disappointed that his former Old Vic acting colleague, George Devine, had put it on. Devine had started an acting school at the

Old Vic a few years earlier and from that had formed a satellite acting company called the Young Vic. As a result of his contacts with rising young actors and writers, he had tried to persuade the Old Vic's board of governors in 1955 to let him use the Young Vic as a testing ground for the new currents in playwriting. Rebuffed, he had left the Old Vic organization and founded the English Stage Company early in 1956. Financed by Lord Harewood, a cousin of the queen, he secured a lease on the small, venerable Royal Court Theatre and presented *Look Back in Anger* as one of his early productions.

Arthur Miller predated England's "angry young men," as the new generation of British playwrights came to be called, by a good fifteen years. He had been writing bitter social dramas in America since the beginning of the war. His *All My Sons* and *Death of a Salesman*, produced in New York soon after the war, had established him as chief spokes-man of a new theatrical sensibility that was only just then, in 1956, beginning to find expression in London.

After Miller arrived in London with Marilyn Monroe for the filming of *The Prince and the Showgirl*, Olivier took him to see *Look Back in Anger*. Later, in analyzing the controversial play, Miller completely changed Olivier's negative attitude toward it. "Indeed," Kenneth Tynan told me, "he persuaded Larry that Osborne's play represented an impor-tant wave of the future. And he made Larry feel remorseful not only for not having recognized that fact, but for devoting his talents to such a meaningless piece of trivia as *The Prince and the Showgirl* when there was so much that was more vital going on at the Royal Court and elsewhere. It was that influence from Miller, plus his perceptions of Miller being married to Monroe, that got Larry to thinking about what he was doing and what he should be doing. He concluded that in all areas of his life he was stagnating. He was starting to feel his age, and he realized that he'd better do something to change the way he was feeling."[2]

As a result, at a lunch with George Devine after finishing *The Prince and the Showgirl* in November, Olivier asked him if John Osborne had another play in the works. As it happened Osborne did, and Devine described it. Called *The Entertainer*, it was the story of an aging, third-rate English music-hall comedian unable to face reality as his meager life crumbles about him. The central character, Archie Rice, Devine was quick to emphasize, was a metaphor for England itself.

"Sounds a bit like Willy Loman in *Death of a Salesman*," Olivier said.

"Larry," answered Devine, "it's *our* Willy Loman. And it's perfect for you. If you were to do it, it would be the event of the year."

261

"Really?" said Olivier. "Let's have a look at the script, then."[3]

Olivier had a high-salary offer pending from Hollywood for him and Vivien Leigh to co-star in the film version of Terence Rattigan's latest hit play, *Separate Tables,* when he received a copy of John Osborne's *Entertainer* script. Because Vivien, recently diagnosed by one psychiatrist as suffering from nascent schizophrenia, was undergoing electroshock treatments, Olivier had little enthusiasm for appearing in another movie with her, no matter how attractive the money. His reluctance changed to resolve when he read Osborne's script.

Archie Rice was a marvelous part. He was every cheap, hapless, whisky-soaked vaudevillian Olivier had seen during his early days of touring the seaside resorts of England. Forget the metaphor—he was flesh-and-blood real, possibly even the kind of pathetic self-delusive performer Olivier might have turned out to be had he had no talent. He phoned Devine immediately and said, "I'll do it. Pay me whatever you want. When do we start?"

Devine and Osborne were enthralled. With Olivier as Archie Rice, a long-running hit was all but guaranteed. But they had a further idea: why not Vivien Leigh as Phoebe, Archie Rice's frumpy shrill-voiced wife? Olivier vetoed the suggestion, but not before Devine had talked to Vivien separately about it. Already exhibiting the puffy-faced signs of her alcohol addiction, Vivien agreed to play the role "if it was all right with Larry," according to Devine.

When Vivien discovered that Olivier didn't want her, she went off on another binge of madness at Notley, smashing lamps, china and valuable porcelain figurines into bits and shards. "That's the way Vivien was becoming," said Angela Baddeley. "She was extraordinarily fond of all the fine furnishings and decorations she and Larry had surrounded themselves with at Notley, and very meticulous about their preservation. Yet in the depths of one of her spells, she wouldn't think twice of destroying some treasured object."[4]

Although the play was picked apart by the critics when it opened early in the spring of 1957, Olivier's virtuoso portrayal of Archie Rice in *The Entertainer* saved it. John Barber in the *Daily Telegraph* wrote: "Olivier is tremendous. . . . [He] has it all. The puffed cheeks and uneasily refined accent. The gurgling, leering funny stories. And the too-hearty laugh that conceals the pang of shame. For there is more to this man than you think. 'Old Archie,' he boasts, 'is dead behind the eyes.' Then he hears his soldier son has been killed. And the man's agony shows naked. Before your eyes, you see how a body crumbles as the heart cracks within."

Despite Olivier's exemplary notices, the play had to struggle for audience recognition because of the critics' skepticism about its value as drama. Since Olivier had committed himself to a late-spring tour of Europe with *Titus Andronicus* as part of Britain's contribution to that year's International Theatre Festival, Devine closed *The Entertainer* after five weeks with plans to reopen it in the fall. In May, Olivier left with the original Stratford cast of *Titus Andronicus,* including Vivien, for Paris —the first stop of the six-week, six-country tour.

Olivier was feted on his fiftieth birthday in Paris by the *Titus* troupe. According to actress Maxine Audley, who played Queen Tamora in the play, it was a harrowing occasion for him because of Vivien's disruptive behavior. "Viv could always get through a performance without causing any trouble. It was as though some button was pushed inside her when she had to go on stage that turned her into an actress. But before and after, one didn't know what to expect of her."[5]

Matters went from bad to worse as the tour progressed through Europe. Vivien was known largely in the Eastern European countries as Scarlett O'Hara, and she was mobbed by hysterical admirers in every city the company visited. Not surprisingly, the mob hysteria heightened her own, and by the time the company arrived in Warsaw, doctors had to be summoned to attend to her. Maxine Audley said that Olivier took pains to remain aloof from Vivien.

The company returned to London at the beginning of July and opened for a limited run of *Titus Andronicus* at the Stoll Theatre for those who had not been able to see the play at Stratford two years before. Olivier had moved himself and Vivien out of Sir William Walton's house and into a rented flat at 54 Eaton Square. He seldom stayed there, however, preferring rooms at the Connaught Hotel in Mayfair. His decision to separate himself more or less permanently from Vivien came after she noisily invaded a session of Parliament one afternoon in July to protest against the planned demolition of the St. James's Theatre. Her breach of protocol was noted with barely disguised amusement by the newspapers the next day. Olivier was not amused.

Olivier's growing estrangement from Vivien brought about a curious change in his relationship with Tarquin, by then almost twenty-one but still ill at ease with his father. During the previous ten years, Vivien had evinced much more affection for Tarquin than she had for her own child, Suzanne. Tarquin felt closer to Vivien than to his father. Now Olivier made an effort to correct the situation. He invited the young man to join him on an August tour of Scotland, where Olivier wanted to scout locations for a new film idea he had—a motion-picture version of *Macbeth* in the style of his previous Shakespeare screen successes. During their two weeks together traveling about Scotland, they had long, increasingly intimate talks about each other, about Vivien's condition and about the ironies of life. Olivier later would say about the experience that he was thrilled finally to have "discovered" his son.

Macbeth had been germinating in Olivier's mind for several months, and his tour of Scotland was designed to aid him in working out a production budget he could present to the studios. In the end, nothing came of it. Despite his prior successes with Shakespeare on film, he could interest none of the American or British companies in a financing deal. With Alexander Korda dead and Filippo del Giudice out of the film business, it appeared that his days of committing the Shakespeare classics to the screen were over.

In the fall, Olivier prepared to reopen in *The Entertainer* for an eight-week run before taking the play to New York. A few days of rehearsals were required to accommodate several new cast members. Among them was a twenty-eight-year-old actress who had been engaged to replace Dorothy Tutin, the performer who had played Olivier's daughter in the original production. The actress's name was Joan Plowright.

It was a name that seemed to suit her, a hardy, down-to-earth name that fit well with her plain features, her strong body and her stolid, sincere nature. Married to actor Roger Gage, she had had only a few minor roles in London before she auditioned for the part of Archie Rice's daughter Jean. She was sure she had failed to get the part, since John Osborne didn't care for her looks and George Devine was even less enthusiastic about her. But Tony Richardson liked what he later called her "muffin-faced plainness" and called Olivier in for a look. When he saw her, there was no more discussion: she had the part.

The reason Olivier gave for his choice of Joan Plowright was that he believed she would improve the play with her unflashy, straightforward style of acting. Plowright said later that she was feeling a bit fearful when she actually met Olivier at her first rehearsal, but that all he had to say to her was a hasty, indifferent "Good morning, nice to have you with us."

There seemed to be more to Olivier's choice of Plowright, however, than just her acting style. Joan, for all her plainness, was dark-complexioned and, aided by her rich mop of unruly hair and the Bohemian-style clothes she wore, projected the sensuous look of a gypsy. As Olivier would later remark to Kenneth Tynan, "She reminded me of my mother."[6]

She reminded other people of their mother too—indeed, among her circle of friends in London she was thought of as something of an "earth mother," a young woman who was never happier than when tending to the problems of others. With her husky, commanding voice, her strong North Country accent, her almost matronly bearing and her placid, mature manner, she had gathered a wide band of devoted friends among the younger theatrical generation. "But it was her eyes that really got to you," says one of them. "Great, huge, dark liquid eyes that seemed to contain all the wisdom of the world and made you trust her as you would your own mother. The only difference between Joanie and your own mother was that in her eyes there was no judgment or criticism, just love and approval."[7]

It was that aura of love and approval that apparently attracted Olivier as soon as he began to rehearse with Joan Plowright. Joan, still somewhat in awe of him, was relaxed when doing scenes but nervous and awkward off the set. Olivier was no different. "It was odd," recalled a cast member. "Larry, this man of supreme self-confidence and charm around actors, seemed discomfited and shy around Joanie. Yet one could tell there was something going on there. At 'notes' meetings after rehearsals, one would catch Larry gazing pensively at Joanie while everyone else was listening to Tony Richardson."[8]

Olivier finally broke the ice by inviting Joan Plowright to join him for a meal between a matinee and evening performance after *The Entertainer* reopened. Said the cast member, "Joanie of course had heard all about Larry and Vivien Leigh—all the romantic business of years before and all the ugly rumors that were going on about then. Evidently she asked him about them and Larry burst forth with a great, impassioned tale of woe and anguish about Vivien, about his loneliness and feelings of futility and so on. Joanie came back dumbstruck with pity for Larry and told a few of us what agony he was going through. She spoke with such compassion that it was easy to discern that she was in love with him."[9]

Her feelings remained unexpressed, mainly because Olivier refrained from expressing his own emotions about her. He had reason to remain quiet. In the first place, he wasn't sure of the nature of his feelings: was he attracted to Joan Plowright because she was so consoling of him, or because she herself seemed to need consoling? Second, she was married—although, he had learned, not happily so. Third, he was almost twice her age—old enough, really, to be her father.

Was that it? Was his attraction to this young woman who played his daughter in the play some weird extension of the feelings he, as Archie Rice, had formed toward Archie's daughter? As part of his characterization, he had invested Archie with an undertone of lust for his daughter Jean. During the time he actually *was* Archie for three hours every night, he began to experience an actual sexual desire for Jean. Had this transformed itself into a real-life lust for Joan Plowright?

It was by raising the question in a conversation with Joan, after *The Entertainer* moved to New York early in 1958, that Olivier finally revealed his mixed feelings. From that moment, Laurence Olivier and Joan Plowright became lovers.

New York was the perfect place for them to develop their relationship. *The Entertainer* ran through the spring of 1958. It was Joan's first visit to the city, and she was shown around in proper style by Olivier. They were far away from the prying British press and from their respective domestic troubles in London. They needed to take only minimal precautions to keep their affair hidden from the New York newspapers. By the time they returned to England in the summer, they had made a pact to marry as soon as they could obtain divorces.

Joan wondered how her husband would react.

"Not to worry," Olivier said. "I will go and see him, talk to him. I have experience at this sort of thing, you know."[10]

Olivier did not go to see Joan Plowright's husband upon his return to London. There he found Vivien performing in a hit play, *Duel of Angels,* and seeming much better. He was confronted again by a crisis of loyalty. He explained his dilemma to Joan. Because she was still not altogether ready to face her husband, she urged Olivier to move back in with Vivien at the flat in Eaton Square. The last thing she wanted to do was wreck any chance Olivier might have of reviving his marriage. Despite the love he had professed for her, she knew that he still clung to a residual hope that Vivien would someday magically recover and once again be the woman he thought he had married. "See what happens," Joan said. She was content to exist for a while on the memory of their affair in New York.

Olivier moved back to Eaton Square. But he remained only long enough to learn once and for all that it was his presence in Vivien's life, more than anything else, that seemed to provoke her mental storms. All the accounts he had received from friends indicated that she had gone through the three months of his absence without a single untoward episode, lamenting their separation to friends but not once suffering a breakdown. Even her doctors were encouraged, and Olivier thought that now, maybe now, it's finally over.

It wasn't. Shortly after his return, Olivier agreed to spend the summer acting in a film version of George Bernard Shaw's *The Devil's Disciple* with Burt Lancaster and Kirk Douglas. These American stars, like many others, had formed their own independent producing companies following the breakup by the American government of the Hollywood studio monopoly over production and distribution. In fact it had been Burt Lancaster, through his Hecht-Hill-Lancaster producing organization, who had tried to get Olivier and Leigh to appear with him the year before in the screen version of *Separate Tables*. Olivier, not wanting to work with Vivien, had declined. But he had said at the time, "Find a good property that I can appear in without Viv, and I'll do it with you."

Lancaster had found the property—*The Devil's Disciple*—and when he asked Olivier to play General Johnny Burgoyne, Olivier agreed. Not only was the two-hundred-thousand-dollar salary attractive, but the picture was to be filmed in England. What's more, because he had been having difficulty in selling the idea of a film of *Macbeth* to Hollywood, perhaps he could interest Lancaster to join in. When Olivier had first proposed the project the year before, he'd left the actors he intended to use for Lady Macbeth and Macduff unnamed. Now that Vivien seemed better, the film would benefit financially by having her as Lady Macbeth. And Burt Lancaster could play Macduff.

But while Olivier was making *The Devil's Disciple,* Vivien suffered a violent relapse. Some say it was because she had learned about Olivier's relationship with Joan Plowright. (Vivien had been to see *The Entertainer* during its second run at the Royal Court and had been heard to say about Plowright: "Who's the ugly girl?") Others claim it was due to the fact that someone connected with the Hecht-Hill-Lancaster organization had told Vivien that Olivier had turned down *Separate Tables* because he hadn't wanted to appear with her in the film. Still others insist that it was caused by nothing more than Vivien's psychic inability to tolerate the things in her life that were most important to her: "This demonic need to destroy her most precious possessions kept growing and growing," says one. "And Larry was the most precious."[11]

Whatever the reason, Vivien's outburst was the end of any hope

Olivier had that she would ever return to normal. In describing it not long ago to *The New York Times,* he said, "I was afraid of killing her. . . . She was slapping me across the face with wet flannels, striking me, until I went into my room and closed the door. She kept beating on the door, beating and beating until I couldn't take it anymore. I came out and grabbed her and threw her across the room. She hit her head on the edge of the bed and it cut her just one inch below the temple. One inch higher and that would have done it. . . . I knew then it had ended. If I went on, sooner or later it would go too far. I knew I had to get out."[12]

Get out he did, and it was not long before he resumed his affair with Joan Plowright. Their brief separation had deepened their need for each other. Lust took a back seat and love became the dominant motif as their relationship, still more or less secret, blossomed. "What else can I say?" Olivier remarked a few years later. "Joanie just made me deliciously happy. It was not the happiness one associates with youthful infatuation and the satisfaction of sexual hunger. I was well beyond that, thank God. It was, and still is, the warm glow and heat of a good fire after being out in the cold for too long."[13]

To expedite the affair and provide it with a cover, Olivier chose Joan to play opposite him in the fall in a British television production of Ibsen's somber drama *John Gabriel Borkman.* Critical opinion of his first venture into television acting was, though mixed, generally on the negative side. It was as if Olivier's presence and talent were much too magisterial for the tiny screen. The notices were forgotten a few months later, though, when *The Devil's Disciple* was released on the large screen. "It is a film to see," said the London *Evening Standard,* "just because Laurence Olivier gives the performance of his life. And because, in his superb self-confidence, he dared to take the third lead. Knowing that he would steal the film from Burt Lancaster and Kirk Douglas, the two male leads. And he does. Those two able actors look like stupid oafs."

Just after finishing the Ibsen play for television, Olivier received word of his brother Richard's death from leukemia. "Dickie" Olivier had been living with his family in a tenant cottage on the Notley Abbey property for the previous few years, managing an adjoining dairy farm and looking after the grounds at the Abbey. With his gradual estrangement from Vivien, Olivier had lost interest in the Abbey. Now, with his brother gone and no one to keep the grounds in order, he decided to put it up for sale.

Joan Plowright and he were to have another separation in the spring of 1959, this a longer one designed both to prevent their affair from coming to light and to give him an opportunity to continue his efforts to make a deal for his projected film version of *Macbeth* (Olivier had begun to mention Joan as his prospective Lady Macbeth). The summer before, while filming *The Devil's Disciple,* Kirk Douglas had offered Olivier two hundred fifty thousand dollars to appear with him in Douglas's first independent production—a costume spectacle of ancient times called *Spartacus,* to be filmed in Hollywood. Olivier had accepted the offer not just for the money, but because he wanted to make personal contact with many of the new studio heads and production executives in Hollywood who were succeeding the old-time moguls as the wielders of power and financing.

Olivier had to remain in Hollywood for almost six months on the *Spartacus* shooting, but he was still unable to make a deal for *Macbeth.* The new regime in Hollywood, he discovered, was interested not in quality films but in expensive, simple-minded, mass-market extravaganzas or else low-budget trash. It was enough to make him wish for the return to power of such former nemeses as Louis B. Mayer, Samuel Goldwyn and David Selznick; for all their often obnoxious personal eccentricities, they had at least striven for first-class entertainment. The very wish made Olivier feel, for the first time in his life, old and outdated. He was fifty-two. So far as Hollywood was concerned, he'd learned, he was now considered a character actor, a supporting player, and no longer a star who could carry a picture—any kind of picture. Contemporary movie audiences in America did not go to see films for their character actors.

With his hopes for *Macbeth* dashed, and as if to show his contempt for the new Hollywood posture toward him, Olivier returned to Stratford in July of 1959 and gave what many were to call his greatest portrayal ever, this in Shakespeare's *Coriolanus.* His 1938 interpretation of Coriolanus, with all its stunning vocal effects and breathtaking stage acrobatics, had been the first to elevate him into the pantheon of Shakespearian actors. Repeating it twenty-one years later, he was able to use his age and experience to give it even more riveting power and authority without sacrificing an iota of spectacle. Few who saw his performances have forgotten his terrifying death scene, when he fell headfirst from a towering platform only to be caught by the ankles by two strong soldiers and left to dangle in midair.

According to Kenneth Tynan, there was more to Olivier's super-bravura performance than just a working-out of his anger over the movie industry's rejection of *Macbeth.* "Larry did that Coriolanus specially for Joan Plowright. He was deeply involved with her by then, but still on the Q.T. It was his secret paean to her, his celebration of his love for her, his saying to her, 'Look how young you make me feel!' "[14]

The two were able to be together almost continuously during the late summer and fall of 1959, for while Olivier was performing in *Coriolanus* by night, he and Joan were repeating their roles of Archie Rice and his daughter in the film version of *The Entertainer* by day. The filming included four weeks on location in the northwest seaside resort of Morecambe, and there, after Joan had split up with her husband, the two began to live together openly.

Olivier's exposure to the new wave in the British theatre, and particularly to Joan Plowright, brought about a change in his attitudes far more sweeping than that Arthur Miller had helped to provoke. Joan, still not yet thirty, was an articulate advocate of the new stage forms and was particularly enchanted by the rising Theatre of the Absurd movement exemplified by such English writers as Arnold Wesker and Harold Pinter, the Irish playwright Samuel Beckett, and Eugene Ionesco in France. And when George Devine acquired the English stage rights to Ionesco's latest Paris hit *Rhinoceros,* he begged Olivier to play the lead role of M. Berenger.

It was a revolutionary part for an actor of Olivier's stature, but he agreed to do it—provided Joan perform in it with him. "I needed Joanie's much more intelligent perspective about this sort of play," he later said, "otherwise I could never have done it, because it was totally against my idea of theatre. Experimental drama had never been my forte."

Rhinoceros was an instant hit, audiences mobbing the little Royal Court to see the king of the stage play a role that seemed completely, bizarrely out of character; mobbing the theatre also to see Olivier and Plowright together, for rumors of their love affair were now rampant. Many women were fascinated, and not a few shocked, to learn that the still captivatingly handsome Olivier had chosen, as one put it, "such a frumpy slice of cake" as his paramour. When the movie version of *The Entertainer* was released later in 1960, it did not suffer at all financially for the stories of the Olivier-Plowright romance. Indeed, said the woman in charge of publicity for the picture, "Half the women in England are going to see it just to get a close-up look at Joan Plowright."

Rhinoceros ran to full houses through the spring of 1960 and into the summer, prompting George Devine to move it to the larger Strand Theatre. Joan Plowright was moving too, from the play to a summer revival of Arnold Wesker's *Roots* back at the Royal Court. She had been stung by insinuations in the press that she had only gotten where she had by virtue of being Laurence Olivier's "new protégée." She told Olivier that she could not stand that sort of leering commentary and thought it better that they not appear together again. "Next they'll have me as some evil predator trying to succeed Vivien as the queen of the theatre," she said.

It was then that Olivier proposed that they proceed with their plans to marry. He wrote to Vivien, who was in New York repeating her starring role in *Duel of Angels,* requesting a divorce. Then he went to see Roger Gage and, with great apologies, asked him to file for divorce against Joan.

In New York, Vivien was already deep in an affair with Jack Merrivale, the actor whom Olivier had employed for their 1940 American tour of *Romeo and Juliet* and who was appearing with her in *Duel of Angels.* Undergoing shock treatments once again, she wrote back to Olivier agreeing to his request and promising to file for divorce as soon as she returned to England. In the meantime, Olivier moved into Joan Plowright's flat in Kensington after she refused to inhabit the Oliviers' place in Eaton Square.

In August, Joan was offered another opportunity to go to New York, this time to play the lead in *A Taste of Honey.* Through the theatrical grapevine came news that the American movie actor Anthony Quinn had been engaged to play the flashy role of King Henry II in Jean Anouilh's period drama *Becket* on Broadway. It was one of those "the-stage-is-my-true-milieu" adventures that American screen celebrities occasionally indulge in. Olivier cabled the producers: READ ABOUT QUINN IN BECKET. WOULD BE INTERESTED TO PLAY B. IF NOT ALREADY CAST. LAURENCE OLIVIER.

The part of Becket, the smaller of the two leads in the play, had already been cast with an actor much less well known than Anthony Quinn. But the cable quickly changed that. Olivier and Quinn in the same play—it was a producer's bonanza. Although Quinn possessed deep reluctance—he had, after all, expected the play to be a vehicle for his first starring Broadway appearance—he consented.

Olivier opened with Quinn in *Becket* at Broadway's St. James Theatre in the late fall of 1960. The critics could do little but wonder at the incongruity of the casting, one remarking that Olivier's low-keyed portrayal of the title character must have been deliberate so as not to steal Quinn's thunder, such as it was. But largely on the strength of the drama's star names, it ran for six profitable months—both stars worked for modest salaries.

Olivier cared little for the change in the critics' opinions. For with him in New York at the nearby Lyceum Theatre, and in the suite they shared at the Algonquin Hotel, was Joan Plowright, starring in *A Taste of Honey.*

On December 2, 1960, Vivien Leigh Olivier—Lady Olivier—was granted a divorce from her husband on the grounds of his adultery with Joan Plowright. In order to satisfy a legal technicality, she conceded that she too had committed adultery with unnamed men in previous years and months—in Ceylon, in London, in New York, elsewhere. But Olivier's affair with Joan Plowright was the cause of the divorce action, and since the two lovers had signed legal papers admitting to their sexual relationship, the court granted the divorce to Vivien. An hour before, it had approved Roger Gage's petition for divorce from Joan, also on the grounds of adultery. The judge decreed that the twin divorces would become final three months later.

Three months and a few days later, Joan Plowright became the new Lady Olivier in Wilton, Connecticut. It was St. Patrick's Day of 1961. Richard Burton—then appearing in New York in *Camelot*—and his wife, Sybil, drove up to Wilton for the ceremony before a local justice of the peace. That night Olivier and his new wife were back on their respective stages, Burton on his. Burton would say later: "If someone had told me back in Wales, fifteen years before, that I would one day be serving as best man for Larry Olivier, Sir Laurence, I'd have summoned him a bloody ambulance."[15]

28

Lord Olivier

"**L**ARRY'S marriage to Joan Plowright brought about a radical change in his life," a close friend of both said. "Joanie was an earth creature as compared to Vivien, the goddess of fire and air. It was probably a kind of organic shock for Larry to be living with such a woman of stability and good sense after almost twenty years with the unpredictable Vivien. And it corresponded with the changes Larry was going through as he entered his mid-fifties. He had lots of regrets about his personal life—his failed first marriage, a son he'd never been able really to get close to, the lack of any sense of family with Vivien and so on. Joanie was very much family-oriented, and she came along in Larry's life just when he was mourning the lack of any cohesive sense of family in his own life.

"So he and Joanie created a family, and more than anything else that became Larry's greatest pride and joy. It gave him something to live for that was more important than acting. Through his work, his life had been suffused with both a strong grounding in history and a powerful sense of the present. Now he was endowed with a responsibility for the future. And the future became his abiding concern. When he married Joanie, he was tired of all the public acclaim and adoration he had received—he had become so accustomed to it that it meant nothing to him. But basically he had never lost his actor's need to impress. Who was there left to impress? Well, his new children. Suddenly he had a reason to strive for new heights of achievement.

"And so he did. Larry might have retired and faded into some comfortable, genteel obscurity after he married Joanie. But then his children came along, and they gave him a new burst of ambition. He's often said that he only continues working to provide for his children. But that's only half of it. He keeps working because his children are the only public whose approval he craves. He wants them to remember him not as some old fellow who was once an actor, but as a vital old boy who, when he went down, went down acting, and acting gloriously. He knows who he is, but he wants his children never to forget who he was."[1]

•

Olivier and Joan Plowright returned to London from New York in June 1961. Just before their marriage, he had been offered the opportunity to start a regional theatre in the small, ancient cathedral city of Chichester. Since the idea of a national theatre that he, Ralph Richardson and others had been lobbying for during previous years seemed to be forever trapped in a limbo of governmental indecision, he accepted the Chichester job. It provided him with carte blanche in every aspect of the creation of the new theatre, from overseeing the construction to selecting plays and hiring performers.

Chichester was fairly close to Brighton. Olivier and Joan both remembered the pleasure they'd experienced at Morecambe when filming *The Entertainer* together, and they decided to settle in Brighton, first because of its convenience to both Chichester and London and second because, as Olivier later put it, "I found living by the sea wonderfully more invigorating than inland—I slept better, I felt better."[2] After buying a comfortable old Regency house facing the sea, Joan settled in to await the birth of their first child while Olivier embarked on a busy schedule of work in London and Chichester.

Olivier's success at Chichester, where he put on several well-received plays in 1961 and 1962—including Chekhov's *Uncle Vanya* in which he co-starred with Michael Redgrave—proved to be the impetus for the government's decision to go ahead at last with a national theatre.

In 1962 legislation was finally approved to launch the long-planned National which would include the Old Vic. An expensive modern building complex was commissioned for the south bank of the Thames, just across Waterloo Bridge near the site of the original Old Vic. While that was being built, the Old Vic Theatre, recently rebuilt, served as headquarters for the new National Theatre. There was little debate on the question of who would organize and direct the enterprise. Olivier was offered the post of director.

Working from a Quonset-hut office on the building site, he set out in the spring of 1963 to organize a complete producing and acting company that would be ready to take the stage in the fall under the banner of the National Theatre. He alienated more than a few people by selecting his talent mostly from the ranks of such newer organizations as George Devine's English Stage Company rather than from the veteran Shakespearean repertories, and many of his critics blamed his dependence on Joan Plowright for this. In response, Olivier said that the National, as he envisioned it, was a theatre of the future and as such demanded the services of those who could serve it well into the future. "I am not interested in using the National to institutionalize the comfortable but often money-losing ways of the past in this country. If this is going to work, we will need new ideas, blood, new approaches. Anyone who thinks our goal is to keep repeating the classics is wrong. We will do our share of classics, but the National is for everyone in England. It is especially for new writers as well as old, for new actors as well as old, for new directors as well as old."[3] To underline his philosophy, Olivier chose as his two chief assistant directors the young William Gaskill and John Dexter from the Royal Court, and he hired the still youthful critic Kenneth Tynan as literary director.

Olivier inaugurated the first National Theatre season in October 1963 with a production of *Hamlet,* directed by himself and starring Peter O'Toole, who had just spent two grueling years filming the title role in *Lawrence of Arabia.* In a later interview in the *Transatlantic Review,* O'Toole said that having played Hamlet at the Old Vic four years before, he had no desire to play the role again and was looking instead for another movie to star in. But, he explained, "Have you ever tried to argue with Olivier? He's the most charming, persuasive bastard ever to draw a breath. I said 'No,' but then I said 'Yes.' Then I said I wanted to play it in a very cut version—'I'll only do two and a half hours,' I told Larry. A week later I was doing the uncut version which takes five hours. Then I wanted to play it with a beard because I said why should I be the only man in Elsinore with a razor blade. Three weeks later I'm standing on the stage clean-shaven in a Peter Pan suit with my hair dyed white. Such is the power of Olivier."[4]

Olivier followed *Hamlet* with his Chichester production of *Uncle Vanya* and a staging of Shaw's *Saint Joan,* starring Joan Plowright. All in all, his first year as head of the new National brought him more criticism than praise, setting a pattern that would dog him throughout his tenure there. First, he was attacked for bad judgment in using the eccentric and lackadaisical O'Toole in *Hamlet.* Although his *Uncle Vanya* was well received, a few critics wondered about his motives in putting on *Saint Joan.* Did he intend to use the National Theatre as a showcase for his new wife? Joan Plowright, though an earnest and competent actress, was certainly not a star. "First they attacked Larry for using an incompetent star in *Hamlet,* " said a defender, "then they raked him over the coals for using a competent non-star in *Saint Joan.* He knew, then, that as head of the National he would forever be in a no-win situation. He was fair game for anyone with an ax to grind."[5]

Olivier redeemed himself somewhat the following spring with a performance of *Othello* that revived his might and majesty as an actor. Yet it also sharpened criticisms of his role as the National's director. The consensus was: "This man is still too great an actor to be spending most of his time running a theatre. He was born to act. Now, by acting only occasionally, he cheats both himself and the world."

Olivier pressed on, responding that it was both his responsibility and dream that the National Theatre succeed. What he didn't tell them was that at the age of fifty-seven, he had not only lost his primal need to act but had found his energy increasingly sapped by the demands of major stage roles.

Yet in 1964 he added to the demands on his energy by accepting a part in an Otto Preminger mystery movie, *Bunny Lake Is Missing,* and then committing himself to the arduous task of filming *Othello.* With *Bunny Lake Is Missing,* Olivier began a practice of appearing in high-paying movie character parts to augment the modest salary he was receiving as head of the National Theatre. He had produced a son and daughter by Joan Plowright—Richard Kerr Olivier, then three, and Tamsin, two. He needed the money he earned from these films to guarantee their education, he later said.

His appearance in *Bunny Lake Is Missing* revealed an entirely new side of Olivier—one that guaranteed him the comfortable financial future he sought. He played a phlegmatic police detective—a supporting role—

with such understated truth and ironic wit that he practically stole the film from its principal actors. Not only that, but his presence gave the otherwise ordinary picture a depth and weight it would not have had with another performer in the role. Film producers began to perceive Olivier in a new light: he was an attractive character actor whose technique and intelligence, added to his reputation, might tend to pressure movie critics into treating the pictures he appeared in, if only in cameo roles, with greater respect and seriousness. They were right, and they were willing to pay handsomely to get Olivier even for only a few days' work before the cameras.

In 1965, while again playing Othello, working in another play *(Love for Love)* and dealing with the daily administrative problems of the National Theatre, Olivier took two hundred thousand dollars to appear in another big-budget Hollywood movie, *Khartoum*, with Charlton Heston. In this middle-eastern desert drama in which he portrayed an Arab tribal chieftain, Olivier did little more than play a mysterious modern-day Othello, dark skin and all. Yet again, although he seemed merely to walk through the part, he stole the picture easily from the teeth-clenching, posturing Heston.

In 1966 Olivier neither directed nor appeared in anything, but instead devoted all his time to the administrative side of his job. In the summer of that year his and Joan Plowright's third child, Julie Kate Olivier, was born. For the first time in his life he kept what amounted to banker's hours, commuting back and forth each day by train between Brighton and Waterloo Station. He would tell journalist Harold Hobson, "I know nothing more beautiful than to set off from home in the morning . . . and to look back and see your young held to a window and being made to wave to you. It's sentimental and it's corny, but it's better than poetry, better than genius, better than money."[6]

A late-blooming family man, Olivier kept to the same routine more or less for the next four years, doing relatively little performing at the National and spending most of his time, between fewer movie appearances, on the slow and frustrating behind-the-scenes business of getting the theatre complex built. His task was complicated by a public flap in 1967 over Kenneth Tynan's decision to present a controversial play by the German playwright Rolf Hochhuth, which cast Winston Churchill in an unfavorable light for his role in authorizing the massive fire-bombing of German population centers during the war (the play was called, in English, *Soldiers*). As a result of the controversy, Olivier was pushed to the verge of resignation as the director of the National. But he refused to resign, and instead rescued his position by his riveting performance as Captain Edgar in a production of Strindberg's *Dance of Death.*

In mid-1967, however, he was struck by cancer, which was later complicated by a bout of pneumonia that stemmed from the treatments he was undergoing for the cancer, and then by appendicitis. The cancer was in his prostate gland, but after several months of radiation therapy he was pronounced provisionally cured.*

Olivier refused to be bowed by the knowledge that he had cancer. Although the radiation treatments severely sapped his energy and created a sudden appearance of old age, he declined to reduce his work load. He continued to appear whenever he could in *Othello* and *Dance of Death,* both still regular attractions in the National Theatre's repertory schedule. When he appeared, the houses were full. When an understudy was announced, the plays performed to a half-filled theatre. What's more, he undertook to direct a production of Chekhov's *Three Sisters* at the National to mark Joan Plowright's return to the stage after the long hiatus occasioned by the births of their three children.

Olivier followed *Three Sisters,* which was generally well received, by embarking with the company on an exhausting tour of Canada in the fall of 1967. During the tour he had to give up performing *Othello.* Even before he learned that he was suffering from cancer, each performance had left him feeling afterward "as if I had been run over by a bus." Now, in the wake of his cancer treatment, he could no longer bear the strain of the role. "With all the preparation, it became like a sort of pontifical midnight Mass," he said two years later. "It became so sacred it was awful. Putting on makeup, playing and taking off makeup was a seven-hour job, a dreadful punishment. You knew the audience had been waiting all night long out in the street, and your sense of responsibility was heightened to an extent it should never be. It became an obsession. When I did get cancer and they said, 'No more *Othello* for you,' I was secretly relieved."[7]

Nevertheless, Olivier continued to play in *Dance of Death* and took a small role in the Georges Feydeau farce *A Flea in Her Ear,* for which he won high praise in Canada. Returning to England late in 1967, he was

---

*In July 1967, while Olivier was undergoing radiation therapy in a London hospital, Vivien Leigh died at her home outside London, apparently from asphyxiation brought on by a return in acute form of her earlier tuberculosis. Olivier checked himself out of the hospital against doctors' orders to help with preparations for Vivien's funeral.

immediately off for Rome where he took another high-paying movie role in the M-G-M production of Morris West's best-selling novel *The Shoes of the Fisherman,* co-starring Anthony Quinn, Oskar Werner, David Janssen and Vittorio DeSica.

A relative of the picture's producer, George Englund, was on the scene for much of the filming. "Olivier was just fantastic," he told me. "We were all staying at the Excelsior Hotel, and at night Olivier and Tony Quinn and Oskar Werner and George and several others would gather in one or another's suite. Olivier was obviously not feeling well, but he'd begin talking about acting and everyone would be mesmerized. He would do performances—ten or fifteen minutes of roles he had played years before. He never even had to hesitate to remember a line. And he'd do them in different styles—fast, slow, soft, loud and so on —just to show how a character could be changed by the different shadings he put on him. It was remarkable.

"He was also a brilliant mimic. He would do Hamlet or Lear the way a Tony Quinn or DeSica might have done them had they ever played the characters. When he did Lear in the Tony Quinn style, it was a whole new version of Lear—totally Tony Quinn. Quinn was astonished. Yet when he tried to copy Larry, it fell totally flat.

"The most astonishing thing I remember, though, was when he and Oskar Werner got into a kind of good-natured duel—each reciting *Hamlet.* Oskar had done *Hamlet* many times in German and was probably considered the foremost German-speaking Shakespearian actor. Well, Larry did a speech from *Hamlet* in English, then Oskar did the same speech in German. Everybody agreed that Oskar measured up to Larry, even though we didn't understand everything he said. But then came the astonishing part. Larry stood up and recited the speech again—but this time in perfect German, the very words Oskar had used. And you know what? He was better than Oskar."[8]

Nineteen sixty-nine was a relatively reclusive year in the life of Olivier. He did little stage work, devoting most of his time to his young children, to the still-troubled administration of the National, and to further remunerative appearances in movies, most of them insignificant. But he re-entered the public spotlight in 1970 in a virtual maelstrom of activity. During his siege with cancer, the press had all but consigned him to the scrap heap, if not the grave. He became intent on proving the press wrong. Early in 1970, he was nominated by the Prime Minister for elevation from his knighthood to what is known in England as a life peerage, which would thereafter entitle him to sit in the House of Lords and be called Lord Olivier. It was the highest honor an Englishman who was not a member of the hereditary aristocracy could receive, and he was only the second actor in history to be given such an award. Although he could not have turned it down without causing a scandal, he accepted the title only on the condition that "all England understands that I do so not for the aggrandizement of me, but on behalf of, and in recognition of, the entire acting profession."

Then, after directing a film version of Chekhov's *The Three Sisters,* he returned to the stage at the National as Shylock in a popular but controversial production of Shakespeare's *The Merchant of Venice,* directed by the brilliant young doctor-turned-theatrical figure, Jonathan Miller. Olivier "was back in harness," as one observer noted.

Olivier's appearance as Shylock was one that he approached with great reluctance at first. He did not feel up to another major stage role, and the unsympathetic and always controversial Shylock doubly frightened him. It took Kenneth Tynan to persuade him that Shylock represented an opportunity to display yet another aspect of his artistry.

Once he had agreed to play the role, Olivier plunged into it with what Jonathan Miller has said was almost too much enthusiasm. During rehearsals Miller, a Jew by birth, had to fight with Olivier to keep him from turning Shylock into a stereotypical Jewish caricature. Eventually Olivier toned down his characterization, but just barely enough for the critics. Most felt that Shylock was one of Olivier's least-worthy Shakespearian portrayals, despite its flashes of acting brilliance. The public disagreed, though, and the production became an instant hit. Later, Olivier would concede that he never felt comfortable with the Shylock he had created.

Despite the success of *The Merchant of Venice,* the National Theatre was still in trouble. Indeed, it seemed like an expensive ship adrift without power or rudder. There was pressure on Kenneth Tynan to leave as a result of the Hochhuth controversy. Gone were assistant directors William Gaskill and John Dexter, who had quit after arguments over the future direction of the enterprise. And many of the young actors Olivier had brought in during the National's first two years were lost to the movies. Still unbuilt was the theatre's permanent home—the seven-and-a-half-million-pound Waterloo Road complex that had been approved long before by the government but was still wrapped up in bureaucratic and architectural snarls.

In the fall of 1970, Olivier had to drop out of *The Merchant of Venice* when he developed an acute thrombosis in his right leg, the result of the stresses the leg had been put to in previous years. As he was seen hobbling around with a cane during the months that followed, the newspapers hinted that his acting career was at an end. Then, in the spring of 1971, two large-scale productions announced earlier—*Coriolanus* with Paul Scofield (considered by many as Olivier's successor as the king of the British stage) and *Guys and Dolls* with Olivier as Nathan Detroit—had to be scrapped. In May, the press launched a wholesale critical attack on the government-subsidized National, condemning it as a failure and suggesting that despite the acting brilliance of its director, it might do better without him. Some articles even demanded his resignation.

The attacks hurt Olivier, but he would not yield to them. "Once our theatre is built, everything will be all right," he said. "It's this having to work under antiquated conditions that is causing us so much trouble. So long as the Board of Directors want me, I intend to stay here until I can see the theatre a physical reality."⁹

To underline his resolve, Olivier persuaded the National's board to take leases on the West End's Cambridge and New theatres and planned to present the 1971–72 season there instead of across the river. "At least we'll make it more pleasant and convenient for people to come to our productions," he told a journalist. And to try to ensure the success of the move, he decided to take the lead role of James Tyrone in Eugene O'Neill's difficult American tragedy, *Long Day's Journey into Night,* which was scheduled to open at the New Theatre in the fall of 1971.

"Larry did it because he thought he was saving the National," said Kenneth Tynan. "He was—what?—sixty-four and not in very good physical shape. He'd been through two bad illnesses and they showed more than he liked to admit. His cancer therapy had turned him almost overnight into an old man. He'd lost a lot of hair, and what he hadn't lost had turned almost white. The pain from his leg problems had given him a permanent pallor. The Tyrone part was a dreadnought of exhaustion. Yet he did it, and he did it magnificently. No, it was not Olivier at his best. But all things considered, it was a miraculous performance."¹⁰

It was also his last major performance on a stage, "my true swan song," as he was later to say. But it had the desired effect. *Long Day's Journey into Night* marked a reversal of the National's falling fortunes, and when Olivier finally, grudgingly, gave up its directorship in 1973 to Peter Hall, twenty-five years younger, it was well and healthily poised to move into its new facilities on the south bank of the Thames.

The public story of Laurence Olivier since 1973 is one mostly of a series of film performances, a few of them memorable, in such movies as *Sleuth, Marathon Man, The Betsy, The Boys from Brazil, A Little Romance, A Bridge Too Far, The Seven Percent Solution, The Jazz Singer,* and *Inchon,* in which he portrays General Douglas MacArthur in Korea.

The private story is one of disease and progressive physical debility. After leaving the National Theatre, and recovered from his cancer, Olivier contracted a serious ailment called dermatomyositis—an inflammatory disease that wastes away the body's muscles. "That was it, I thought," he told a journalist in 1979. "It left me so weak that I could no longer stand up. Once I got out of bed and collapsed, bashing my eyes on the corner of the bed. Joanie was terrified and I thought I was done for. And I almost was. . . . It creeps up on you, taking a little bit each day. And the horrible things it does to your skin."[11]

Olivier was close to death until massive doses of cortisone drugs brought him back from the brink. Although not cured, the disease has been kept under control with his continued use of drugs. Today, Olivier, though not an invalid, is severely restricted physically in what he can do. At seventy-four, with his eyesight and hearing failing, and suffering from further ailments common to aging, he looks considerably older than many men of his years. And yet his mind remains sharp, his humor biting. "I am now in my anecdotage," he says in response to questions about what he intends to do with the rest of his life. "All I am good for anymore is to be an old fellow who can tell, I hope, an interesting story or two to his children."

Having flirted with death, though, he finds it very much on his mind, particularly the manner in which he would like to die. Having lived an extremely public life, but always on his own terms, he would like to die on his own terms as well. Which means alone, "the way animals go off alone to die. To go like one of the furry creatures into the forest, crawling underneath the bramble bush," he told *The New York Times* in 1979. "It's rather more noble than wishing your family all around, somebody feeling your pulse . . . a lot of people fussing about. I find the little animal has more nobility somehow. Don't you?"[12]

And how would he like to be remembered after he's gone? Hailed universally as the greatest actor of his age? As the man who gave new meaning to the art of tragedy? As a legend in his own time?

None of those. Olivier has always gotten more pleasure from making people chuckle than making them cringe. The performers he admires most are comedians and comic actors. Even to his most tragic characters he has sought to bring a sense of humor, if not humor itself, which perhaps has been the key to his success. If he had it to do all over again, he might well become a comedian.

"God help me if I'm turned into some kind of institution, some monument. Let them say, if they have to say anything: 'Here lies Laurence Olivier. He was funny.'"

SOURCES AND
REFERENCES

1. Something in a Name

[1] Sir Ralph Richardson to author, telephone interview, 1979.
[2] London *Daily Telegraph,* May 14, 1939.
[3] *Dick Cavett Show,* PBS, 1980.
[4] London *Daily Telegraph,* May 14, 1955.

2. Agnes Olivier

[1] Kenneth Tynan to author, 1979.
[2] London *Daily Telegraph Magazine,* February 22, 1973.
[3] Davina Rhodes to author, 1980.
[4] Olivier to Kenneth Tynan, BBC interview, June 23, 1967.
[5] London *Daily Telegraph,* May 14, 1937.
[6] Olivier as quoted by Kenneth Tynan to author, 1979.

3. An End to Childhood

[1] *Sunday Times* (London), November 16, 1953.
[2] *Ibid.*
[3] John Cottrell, *Laurence Olivier* (Englewood Cliffs, N.J.: Prentice-Hall, 1975; London: Weidenfeld and Nicolson, 1975).
[4] Manchester *Guardian,* April 3, 1947.
[5] Source to author, 1979. Source requests anonymity.
[6] London *Sunday Express,* March 26, 1964.
[7] Birmingham *Post,* July 17, 1958.
[8] Manchester *Guardian,* April 3, 1947.
[9] *Ibid.*
[10] Cottrell, *op. cit.*
[11] Source to author, 1979.
[12] Reconstructed from accounts of various sources.
[13] *Saturday Review of Literature,* September 13, 1946.

Sources and References

4. A Life in Limbo

[1] Kenneth Tynan to author, 1979.
[2] Reconstructed from accounts of various sources.
[3] Reconstructed by Kenneth Tynan based on his 1967 BBC interview preparations with Olivier.
[4] Reconstructed from various published accounts of the scene, including Olivier's.

5. Rite of Passage

[1] Source to author, 1978. Source requests anonymity.
[2] Source to author, 1976.
[3] Alan Webb to author, 1971.
[4] Reconstructed from accounts of various sources.
[5] Source to author, 1980.
[6] Source to author, 1980.

6. The Birth of a Career

[1] Birmingham *Post,* November 3, 1956.
[2] *Ibid.*
[3] *Ibid.*
[4] Source to author, 1979. Source requests anonymity.
[5] Reconstructed from accounts of various sources.
[6] Source to author, 1973.
[7] Sir Ralph Richardson to author, 1979.
[8] *The Observer* (London), March 12, 1962.
[9] Source to author, 1973.
[10] London *Daily Mail,* April 21, 1961.
[11] Birmingham *Post,* November 3, 1956.
[12] Denys Blakelok, *Round the Next Corner* (London: Gollancz, 1967).
[13] London *Evening News,* August 30, 1946.
[14] John Cottrell, *Laurence Olivier* (Englewood Cliffs, N.J.: Prentice-Hall, 1975; London: Weidenfeld and Nicolson, 1975).

7. Leading Man at Twenty-one

[1] Birmingham *Post,* November 3, 1956.
[2] Sir Ralph Richardson to author, 1979.
[3] Reconstructed from accounts of various sources.
[4] London *Evening Standard,* June 7, 1970.
[5] Sir Cedric Hardwicke to author, 1971.
[6] London *Evening News,* August 30, 1946.
[7] *Dick Cavett Show,* ABC network, 1973.
[8] Source to author, 1979. Source requests anonymity.

Sources and References

[9] London *Daily Express*, May 26, 1961.
[10] London *Daily Herald*, May 24, 1966.
[11] Reconstructed from accounts of various sources.
[12] Source to author, 1973.
[13] Manchester *Guardian*, June 14, 1949.
[14] New York *Herald Tribune*, June 17, 1956.

8. Jill Esmond Olivier

[1] Cathleen Nesbitt to author, 1974.
[2] Source to author, 1979. Source requests anonymity.
[3] London *Daily Mail*, 1929.
[4] Manchester *Guardian*, September 4, 1947.
[5] London *Daily Mirror*, December 12, 1950.
[6] Source to author, 1979.
[7] London *Evening Standard*, February 12, 1961.
[8] *Variety*, August 8, 1956.
[9] Reconstructed from accounts of various sources.
[10] Felix Barker, *The Oliviers* (London: Hamish Hamilton, 1953).
[11] Source to author, 1973.
[12] Source to author, 1979.

9. Private Lives

[1] Source to author, 1980. Source requests anonymity.
[2] Source to author, 1979.
[3] Reconstructed from accounts of various sources.
[4] Sir Noel Coward to author, 1971.
[5] Olivier to Kenneth Tynan, BBC interview, June 23, 1967.
[6] *The Observer Review* (London), 1952.
[7] Noel Coward, *Present Indicative* (New York: Doubleday, 1937).
[8] Manchester *Evening Chronicle*, September 13, 1930.
[9] Source to author, 1971.
[10] Source to author, 1979.
[11] Reconstructed from accounts of various sources.

10. Hollywood

[1] Source to author, 1980. Source requests anonymity.
[2] Saul Colin to author, 1967.
[3] Reconstructed from accounts of various sources.
[4] Source to author, 1979.
[5] Saul Colin to author, 1967.
[6] Reconstructed from accounts of several sources.
[7] Olivier as quoted by Kenneth Tynan to author, 1979.
[8] Los Angeles *Examiner*, June 16, 1931.

[9] Reconstructed from accounts of various sources.

[10] New York *World Telegram,* June 17, 1939.

[11] *Dick Cavett Show,* PBS, 1980.

[12] Source to author, 1980.

[13] Quoted from *Photoplay,* June 1938.

[14] Reconstructed from accounts of various sources.

[15] *Los Angeles Times,* November 3, 1932.

[16] *Hollywood Reporter,* February 17, 1952.

[17] Reconstructed from accounts of various sources.

11.   Garbo

[1] Maynard Morris to author, 1961.

[2] Source to author, 1979. Source requests anonymity.

[3] Source to author, 1973.

[4] Jack Hawkins to author, 1970.

[5] Reconstructed from accounts of various sources.

[6] *The Picturegoer,* November 1936.

[7] Olivier as quoted by Kenneth Tynan to author, 1979.

[8] London *Evening News,* May 17, 1933.

[9] *Motion Picture Herald,* 1952.

[10] *Ibid.*

[11] Norman Zierold, *Garbo* (New York: Stein and Day, 1969; London: W. H. Allen, 1970).

12.   Coming of Age

[1] London *Sunday Express,* September 2, 1949.

[2] Jed Harris to author, 1980.

[3] Reconstructed from published accounts of James Dale and other sources.

[4] Jed Harris to author, 1980.

[5] *The New York Times,* September 12, 1940.

[6] Harold Clurman to author, 1979.

[7] Source to author, 1973. Source requests anonymity.

[8] *Sunday Times* (London), November 18, 1963.

[9] Noel Coward to author, 1971.

[10] London *Daily Express,* December 12, 1950.

[11] Jack Wilson as quoted by Saul Colin to author, 1967.

[12] London *Daily Express,* October 19, 1950.

[13] London *Weekend Telegraph,* August 12, 1969.

13.   Gielgud

[1] Jack Hawkins to author, 1970.

[2] Olivier as quoted by Kenneth Tynan to author, 1979.

[3] Source to author, 1979. Source requests anonymity.

[4] Source to author, 1980.

[5] Source to author, 1980.

[6] Denys Blakelok, *Round the Next Corner* (London: Gollancz, 1967).

[7] Source to author, 1973.

[8] Source to author, 1979.

[9] Reconstructed from various published reminiscences of Anthony Asquith.

[10] Reconstructed from accounts of various sources.

[11] Source to author, 1980.

[12] *David Frost Show,* Westinghouse Broadcasting, 1970.

[13] John Cottrell, *Laurence Olivier* (Englewood Cliffs, N.J.: Prentice-Hall, 1975; London: Weidenfeld and Nicolson, 1975).

[14] London *Daily Telegraph,* October 7, 1935.

[15] London *Sunday Express,* July 12, 1935.

[16] Source to author, 1980.

14. Vivien Leigh

[1] Source to author, 1979. Source requests anonymity.

[2] Source to author, 1979.

[3] Source to author, 1980.

[4] Source to author, 1980.

[5] London *Evening News,* May 13, 1947.

[6] London *Daily Express,* August 6, 1952.

[7] Source to author, 1979.

[8] Source to author, 1973.

[9] Source to author, 1979.

[10] Eve Phillips to author, 1974, 1977.

[11] Reconstructed from accounts of various sources.

[12] Eve Phillips to author, 1974, 1977.

[13] Source to author, 1980.

[14] Source to author, 1979.

15. A Hamlet in Life

[1] Source to author, 1975. Source requests anonymity.

[2] Source to author, 1975.

[3] London *Sunday Telegraph,* June 19, 1955.

[4] Reconstructed from accounts of various sources.

[5] Source to author, 1980.

[6] Source to author, 1975.

[7] Source to author, 1980.

[8] Raymond Massey as quoted by Kenneth Tynan to author, 1979.

[9] Eve Phillips to author, 1977.

[10] James Wong Howe to author, 1976.

[11] Tyrone Guthrie to author, 1972.

[12] Source to author, 1979.

[13] From published excerpts of Oswald Frewen's diaries and other sources.

Sources and References

16. Hamlet on Stage

[1] Jack Hawkins to author, 1970.
[2] Logan Gourlay, ed., *Olivier* (London: Weidenfeld and Nicolson, 1973).
[3] Tyrone Guthrie, *A Life in the Theatre* (London: Hamish Hamilton, 1972).
[4] Kenneth Tynan to author, 1979.
[5] Jack Hawkins to author, 1970.
[6] *Dick Cavett Show,* PBS, 1980.
[7] Source to author, 1980. Source requests anonymity.
[8] Reconstructed from 1972 interview with Tyrone Guthrie and other sources.
[9] Reconstructed from accounts of various sources.
[10] Source to author, 1979.
[11] Source to author, 1979.
[12] Source to author, 1980.
[13] Source to author, 1980.

17. The Dream Couple

[1] Margaret Leighton to author, 1971.
[2] Reconstructed from accounts of various sources, including excerpts of Oswald Frewen's diaries.
[3] Source to author, 1980. Source requests anonymity.
[4] Reconstructed from accounts of various sources.
[5] Eve Phillips to author, 1977.
[6] *Films and Filming,* April 1955.
[7] Source to author, 1979.
[8] London *Daily Express,* March 20, 1968.
[9] Source to author, 1980.
[10] Jack Hawkins to author, 1970.
[11] London *Sunday Telegraph,* March 10, 1951.
[12] Source to author, 1977.
[13] Source to author, 1980.
[14] Source to author, 1979.

18. Hollywood Redux

[1] Ruth Gordon, *An Open Book* (New York: Doubleday, 1980).
[2] Angela Baddeley to author, 1975.
[3] Source to author, 1979. Source requests anonymity.
[4] John Cottrell, *Laurence Olivier* (Englewood Cliffs, N.J.: Prentice-Hall, 1975; London: Weidenfeld and Nicolson, 1975).
[5] David Niven, *The Moon's a Balloon* (New York: Putnam's, 1972; London: Hamish Hamilton, 1971).
[6] *The Observer Review* (London), February 2, 1969.
[7] *Transatlantic Review,* 1961.
[8] Jerry Dale to author, 1980, 1981.
[9] Reconstructed from accounts of various sources.
[10] Reconstructed from accounts of various sources.

[11] Jerry Dale to author, 1980.

[12] Reconstructed from accounts of various sources.

[13] Rudy Behlmer, ed., *Memo from David O. Selznick* (New York: Viking, 1972; London: Macmillan, 1973).

19.   Keeping the Secret

[1] Anne Edwards, *Vivien Leigh* (New York: Simon & Schuster, 1977; London: W. H. Allen, 1977).

[2] Jerry Dale to author, 1980.

[3] Jerry Dale to author, 1981.

[4] New York *World Telegram,* June 17, 1939.

[5] Source to author, 1979. Source requests anonymity.

20.   The Star-cross'd Lovers

[1] Jerry Dale to author, 1980.

[2] Reconstructed from David Niven, *The Moon's a Balloon* (New York, Putnam's, 1972; London: Hamish Hamilton, 1971), and other unpublished sources.

[3] *Sunday Times* (London) *Weekly Review,* November 3, 1963.

[4] Olivia de Havilland to author, 1974.

[5] Jerry Dale to author, 1980.

[6] Sewell Stokes, *Without Veils: The Intimate Biography of Gladys Cooper* (London: Peter Davis, 1953).

[7] Jerry Dale to author, 1980.

[8] Source to author, 1979. Source requests anonymity.

[9] Jerry Dale to author, 1980.

[10] *Photoplay,* June 1949.

[11] Jerry Dale to author, 1980.

[12] Jerry Dale to author, 1980.

[13] Jerry Dale to author, 1980.

[14] Edmond O'Brien to author, 1978.

[15] Cornel Wilde to author, 1978.

[16] London *Daily Mirror,* August 9, 1969.

[17] Reconstructed from accounts of several published sources, including Anne Edwards, *Vivien Leigh* (New York: Simon & Schuster, 1977; London: W. H. Allen, 1977).

21.   Mr. and Mrs. Laurence Olivier

[1] Source to author, 1980. Source requests anonymity.

[2] Reconstructed from accounts of various sources.

[3] Reconstructed from accounts of various sources.

[4] Reconstructed from accounts of various sources.

[5] Letter from Rob Walker to author, 1980.

[6] London *Sunday Express,* March 13, 1961.

Sources and References

[7] Jerry Dale to author, 1980.
[8] Source to author, 1979.
[9] Reconstructed from accounts of various sources.

22. Olivier's War

[1] Joseph McGrindle, ed., *Behind the Scenes: Theatre and Film Reviews from the Transatlantic Review* (London: Sir Isaac Pitman & Sons, 1971).
[2] London *Daily Mail,* October 19, 1959.
[3] Kenneth Tynan to author, 1979.
[4] Source to author, 1979. Source requests anonymity.
[5] Source to author, 1980.
[6] Sir Ralph Richardson to author, 1979.
[7] Sir John Gielgud to author, 1979.
[8] London *Evening Standard,* May 23, 1967.
[9] *Ibid.*
[10] *Ibid.*
[11] Olivier to Kenneth Tynan, BBC interview, June 23, 1967.
[12] *Dick Cavett Show,* PBS, 1980.
[13] Cecil Beaton to author, 1974.
[14] Source to author, 1979.
[15] Source to author, 1980.
[16] Sir Ralph Richardson to author, 1979.
[17] Olivier to Kenneth Tynan, BBC interview, June 23, 1967.

23. Pursued by the Furies

[1] Source to author, 1979. Source requests anonymity.
[2] Source to author, 1979.
[3] Jack Hawkins to author, 1970.
[4] John Mason Brown, *Dramatis Personae* (New York: Viking, 1963; London: Hamish Hamilton, 1963).
[5] Kenneth Tynan to author, 1979.
[6] *Dick Cavett Show,* PBS, 1980.
[7] London *Evening Standard,* May 23, 1967.
[8] Jack Hawkins to author, 1970.
[9] Jerry Dale to author, 1980.
[10] Jerry Dale to author, 1980.
[11] Source to author, 1980.
[12] Logan Gourlay, ed., *Olivier* (London: Weidenfeld and Nicolson, 1973).
[13] Olivier to Kenneth Tynan, BBC interview, June 23, 1967.

24. Sir Larry

[1] Audrey Williamson, *Theatre of Two Decades* (London: Rockliff, 1951).
[2] Source to author, 1979. Source requests anonymity.

Sources and References

[3] Source to author, 1979.
[4] Source to author, 1979.
[5] Cecil Beaton to author, 1974.
[6] Peter Cushing to author, 1977.
[7] Source to author, 1980.
[8] Source to author, 1979.
[9] Source to author, 1980.
[10] Source to author, 1979.

25. Streetcar to Oblivion

[1] Saul Colin to author, 1967.
[2] Manchester *Guardian,* October 5, 1959.
[3] Source to author, 1979. Source requests anonymity.
[4] Source to author, 1979.
[5] Source to author, 1978.
[6] Source to author, 1979.
[7] Source to author, 1979.
[8] Source to author, 1980.
[9] Reconstructed from accounts of various sources.
[10] Source to author, 1980.
[11] Source to author, 1980.
[12] Source to author, 1979.
[13] Source to author, 1980.
[14] Source to author, 1979.

26. The Knight and the Garter

[1] Angela Baddeley to author, 1975.
[2] Peter Finch to author, 1977.
[3] Source to author, 1979. Source requests anonymity.
[4] Angela Baddeley to author, 1975.
[5] Source to author, 1980.
[6] Source to author, 1979.
[7] Angela Baddeley to author, 1975.
[8] John Gielgud, *An Actor and His Time* (New York: Clarkson N. Potter, 1980; London: Sidgwick & Jackson, 1979).
[9] London *Daily Telegraph,* February 13, 1968.
[10] Source to author, 1979.
[11] Source to author, 1980.
[12] Saul Colin to author, 1967. Additionally, the author was present at several discussions during the period among Lee and Paula Strasberg, Colin, Monroe, Green and others involved in the initial *Sleeping Prince* preparations.
[13] Source to author, 1980.
[14] Source to author, 1980.

Sources and References

27. Joan Plowright

[1] Kenneth Tynan to author, 1979.
[2] Kenneth Tynan to author, 1979.
[3] Reconstructed from published accounts of George Devine and other sources.
[4] Angela Baddeley to author, 1975.
[5] Maxine Audley to author, 1979.
[6] Olivier as quoted by Kenneth Tynan to author, 1979.
[7] Source to author, 1978. Source requests anonymity.
[8] Source to author, 1979.
[9] Source to author, 1979.
[10] Reconstructed from accounts of various sources.
[11] Source to author, 1979.
[12] *The New York Times Magazine,* March 25, 1979.
[13] Olivier as quoted by Kenneth Tynan to author, 1979.
[14] Kenneth Tynan to author, 1979.
[15] *Dick Cavett Show,* PBS, 1980.

28. Lord Olivier

[1] Source to author, 1979. Source requests anonymity.
[2] *Dick Cavett Show,* ABC network, 1973.
[3] London *Daily Mail,* March 3, 1963.
[4] John Cottrell, *Laurence Olivier* (Englewood Cliffs, N.J.: Prentice-Hall, 1975; London: Weidenfeld and Nicolson, 1975).
[5] Source to author, 1980.
[6] Cottrell, *op. cit.*
[7] London *Sunday Telegraph,* July 20, 1969.
[8] Stephen Englund to author, 1980.
[9] London *Evening Standard,* May 17, 1971.
[10] Kenneth Tynan to author, 1979.
[11] *The New York Times Magazine,* March 25, 1979.
[12] *Ibid.*

Index

294

Index

Index

Index

Index

Index

Index

302

49000